Following the Tambourine Man

Writing American Women
Carol Kolmerten, *Series Editor*

Other titles in Writing American Women

FOLLOWING *the* TAMBOURINE MAN *A Birthmother's Memoir*

JANET MASON ELLERBY

Syracuse University Press

For a listing of books published and distributed by Syracuse University Press, visit our Web site at SyracuseUniversityPress.syr.edu.

Credits for song excerpts:
Chapter 16: "Little Green." Words and music by Joni Mitchell. © 1967 (renewed) Crazy Crow Music. All rights administered by SONY/ATV Music Publishing, 8 Music Square West, Nashville, TN 37203. All rights reserved. Used by permission.
Chapter 17: "Mr. Tambourine Man." Copyright © 1964 by Warner Bros. Inc. Copyright renewed 1992 by Special Rider Music. All rights reserved. International copyright secured. Reprinted by permission.
Chapter 17: "Love Minus Zero/No Limit." Copyright © 1965 by Warner Bros. Inc. Copyright renewed 1993 by Special Rider Music. All rights reserved. International copyright secured. Reprinted by permission.
Chapter 17: "It's All Over Now Baby Blue." Copyright © 1965 by Warner Bros. Inc. Copyright renewed 1993 by Special Rider Music. All rights reserved. International copyright secured. Reprinted by permission.
Chapter 31: "Stay in Touch." Words and music by Joni Mitchell. © 1998 Crazy Crow Music (ASCAP). All rights administered by SONY/ATV Music Publishing, 8 Music Square West, Nashville, TN 37203. All rights reserved. Used by permission.

ISBN-13: 978-0-8156-0889-9   ISBN-10: 0-8156-0889-6

Library of Congress Cataloging-in-Publication Data

Ellerby, Janet Mason.
Following the tambourine man : a birthmother's memoir / Janet Mason Ellerby. — 1st ed.
p. cm. — (Writing American women)
ISBN-13: 978-0-8156-0889-9 (cloth : alk. paper)
ISBN-10: 0-8156-0889-6 (cloth : alk. paper)
1. Ellerby, Janet Mason. 2. Birthmothers—United States—Biography.
3. Adoption—United States—Psychological aspects. I. Title.
HV874.82.E55A3 2007
362.82'98092—dc22 [B]   2007013148

Manufactured in the United States of America

For Kezia, Helen, Todd, and Merideth

. . .

In Memory of Anne Ellerby Andreasen
1942–2005

JANET MASON ELLERBY has a doctorate from the University of Washington. She is a professor of English at the University of North Carolina at Wilmington and the author of *Intimate Reading: The Contemporary Women's Memoir* (Syracuse University Press, 2001).

Contents

Illustrations

Acknowledgments

Thanks are due to the University of North Carolina at Wilmington for granting me the necessary uninterrupted time to write this book.

Special thanks to Christine and Forest Williamson for lending us Velveeta, their home on Martha's Vineyard, and for providing me with an awe-inspiring vantage point from which to write.

For their perceptive, helpful ideas, and unflagging encouragement: Glenn Wright and Carol Kolmerten at Syracuse University Press.

For her insightful and careful reading and informed advice on how to deal with some of the book's more problematic issues: Stacey Holman Jones at the University of South Florida.

For my devoted friends who read the manuscript in all its permutations and kept telling me I did have something significant to say: Moira MacDonald and Clyde Comstock.

Particular thanks for unlocking the door that had been sealed for too long: Debbie Horne. For opening that door and holding my hand as we walked through it together: my daughters, Helen Setzer and Kezia De Puy. For welcoming me into her life and letting me draw on her story in order to tell my own: my daughter, Merideth Fiorucci. For being the very best of sons: Todd De Puy. For always bringing *all* their children, grandchildren, and great-grandchildren home without a second thought: my loving parents, Tom and Helen Ellerby. For encouraging me to write this book as they faced their own challenges: Ray and Anne Andreasen. For answering Debbie's e-mail and my prayers: Cathy C. in Mississippi.

To dear friends, my steadfast cheering section: Karen Courington, Betsy Ervin, Karen Comstock, and Julie Chappell.

Thanks also to Michael Fiorucci, Rob Setzer, Maria Fernanda Bravo, Katie and John Andrew, Pam and Chris Frye, Christine Hardee, Rita Clifford, Mary Ellen and Bob Allen, Chris Gould, Kathy Rugoff and Jeff Eng.

And, above all, always and forever, to John, my best reader, editor, friend, and fellow adventurer, who showed me how it is that grace happens.

Portions of this book were first explored in *Intimate Reading: The Contemporary Women's Memoir*, Syracuse University Press (2001), and "Untangling the Trauma Knot: Autoethnography and Annie Ernaux's *Shame*," *MOSAIC* (September 2005).

THE *Loss*

1 The Black Dress

Akron, Ohio, 1965

I GIVE BIRTH TO SORROW on a frigid Tuesday in March at dawn. I have been in labor throughout the night at the Florence Crittenton Home for Unwed Mothers. I have put on my favorite dress for the ride to the hospital—a worn, thin, black cotton summer dress with tiny orange and white sprigs of wildflowers in a neat pattern across it. Diana, an older girl I looked up to, had worn this dress throughout her stay at Florence Crittenton, and I have coveted it even though my parents have spent a lot of money on an array of new maternity smocks that hang in my closet. Diana found it in the large box of castoffs that girls leave behind when they themselves are released from Florence Crittenton. And when it was time for her to leave, she passed it on to me with a hard, sardonic chuckle that I didn't know how to interpret.

When I finally get to the hospital room, a nurse helps me slip the light dress off. She unfastens my bra for me. Perched on the side of the hospital bed, we pause as a contraction grips my body. I push myself through grueling minutes of straining effort as she chants in my ear, "Don't push. Don't push." The wave subsides and my body loosens. She kneels down and pulls off each wooly knee sock, then steadies me as I stand and step out of my stretched-out underpants. It is comforting to feel her hands undressing me. Like a child again, I am not shy about standing naked in front of her. She whispers softly, "You're okay. You're fine," as she slips a starchy, white hospital gown up my arms so that it covers the front of my body but leaves my back and bottom exposed. I don't care about this. She firmly ties two strings behind my neck to keep the gown from sliding down. She keeps up the gentle murmur of reassuring words. She helps me climb onto the hospital bed and covers me with a clean white sheet and a white cotton blanket. Then, she goes to the other empty bed in the room, takes the blanket from it and puts it over me as well. She thinks this extra warmth might help me to stop shivering, but I have begun to cry, not because of another pain but from the exquisite relief that her gentleness gives me. I watch her put the lovely black dress, my shoes, my bra, my socks and my underpants in a plastic bag, everything except the gold wedding band on my left ring finger that my aunt has given me to wear.

When the doctor comes into the room, I can tell that he is surprised by how young I am. He looks young too. Since I am still crying, the nurse speaks for me. She tells him my name is Jan, that this is my first baby, and that my water broke at approximately two A.M. It's now sometime after five A.M. and still quite dark outside, though I can see snowflakes rushing by the uncurtained window. He seems to decide then to be kind rather than impatient as he asks the nurse to hold my hand while he examines me. I don't want him to pull the covers down, so he carefully untucks the sheet and blankets from the bottom of the hospital bed and softly lifts them over my legs. When he checks to see how dilated my cervix is, I am having another contraction. It doesn't matter to me that his fingers are inside me. I have to give myself over completely to the pain that grips me, turning my stomach into a huge, wooden-like ball that my body must expel. When he takes his hand away, he asks me why I waited so long to get to the hospital. I don't try to answer him because I don't know.

I cannot hear what the nurse and the doctor say next, but almost immediately another nurse comes to the room with a gurney, and they all help me to move onto it from the hospital bed. I am very awkward and have a hard time helping them because my body only wants to shiver and push. They let me keep the blanket the nurse took from the extra bed, but now I feel exposed. They push me quickly down a nightmarish, dim corridor to another larger room. The walls are bright white, the lights are harsh, and it is refrigerator-cold. Again I have to be moved, this time from the gurney to the table where I will give birth. The sense of safety I had found in the first room has dissipated into a strange ascending terror. I am past all reassurance. Now I am only body, a body that is demanding and controlling, instinctively grunting, pushing, panting, straining. I am also powerless, wholly dependent on the strangers that surround me. I do not want to get on the table, so the young doctor must speak sternly so that I will help them shift my body. Then he has to speak sternly to me again so that I will turn onto my side and curl up. He explains that he has to give me a shot in my spine so that my baby can be born, and I will not be in so much pain. But I am having such an overwhelming contraction that getting into this position is almost impossible. Still, I want to do as he says, so I manage to comply, tipping my orbed, rigid stomach to the side, drawing up my legs, but unable to stop pushing. I do not feel the shot or even see the needle, but almost instantaneously all feeling subsides below my waist. I watch them lift my dead legs up and tie them up on stirrups that are much bigger that any I had had to use before. There hasn't been time to shave my pubic hair, so I hear them talking about dousing me with antiseptic, but I do not feel that. I am still very cold and shivering, so the kind nurse covers me with the blanket from my shoulders down over my enormous belly. Everyone in the room gathers beyond the barrier my raised legs have created. Later I will learn that the doctor performed an episiotomy, but I do not know this at the time. I hear them excitedly exclaiming: "She's crowning . . . Here we go . . . Careful . . . Here's another contraction . . . Here it comes . . . Here it is . . . Careful . . . Okay, Jan, your baby's head is out . . . Now it's shoulders . . . Oh . . . Oh, how pretty . . . You have a beautiful baby girl . . . Look at her . . . Here she is!" The young doctor, who I don't know, and who was not supposed to deliver my baby, and who doesn't know she isn't mine, and who has decided to be kind to me, holds up my daughter for me to see. Sorrow starts to cry with me.

It is March 20, 1965—the date two new lives begin. Sorrow is born and I am desperately, ineluctably reborn.

Martha's Vineyard, Massachusetts, 2004

This is the second time I am writing about bearing Sorrow. I thought by writing a book about telling secrets and revealing my own secret about Sorrow's birth and adoption, I would be released from my ongoing sorrow and shame, and in many ways, revelation was redemptive. I now live more forthrightly in the world. I resist the urge to dissemble and edit. I take more risks with honesty. And, telling my secret gave me the most precious gift—my first daughter, returned to my life. But that book—*Intimate Reading*—is really about women who decide to stop telling secrets. What I still need to write about is the story of losing Sorrow. I feel relieved now that I have started writing. People I know are surprised. They want to tell me that I should be over that night by now, to "let go of it," "let it be," "lay it down." For after all, wasn't there a miracle? Wasn't what had been lost now found? Isn't that more than enough? Isn't that closure? No.

In some ways Sorrow's birth was not extraordinary. Many girls give away their babies and then safely stuff their memories in the cotton wadding of cultural justification that reminds them over and over that they did "the right thing" for their baby. The generous thing, I tell myself, but to no avail, for I am corrected when I speak of Sorrow as my gift to give. To say I "gave her up" is taboo in the language of adoption. Instead I am instructed to say that she was "placed," that "an adoption plan" was made. I try to adjust losing Sorrow to these soothing, rational niches—"gift" or "place" or "plan"—but my memory always resists that taxonomy. The truth is that she was taken.

There are those who can recover from loss, who can refocus a life, give up an unhealthy fidelity to sorrow. They start out on a different path, one that moves optimistically forward, that rarely switches back to relive that day when everything changed. And then there are those who cannot leave the day behind. Even as our lives move on in hopeful and fulfilling directions, we are caught in the tide of an eternal return, a steady rhythm of ebb and flow that both eases and hinders our journey forward. Sorrow's birth is rooted inside me, a dazzling white room of pain and confusion where two girls cry out for each other. The scene lives in me, full of intensity, irreconcilably, stubbornly enduring.

Although experts tell us that memory is always flawed and that what I recall might be as much fiction as reality, I seem to be able to summon the minutest of details of my three months at Florence Crittenton, of the night of Sorrow's birth, and of the days that followed. I could draw you the floor plan of Florence Crittenton. I could conjure up its quiet atmosphere of teenage girls moving humbly through its rooms—never the raucous bravado one might expect of thirty "fallen" girls living together in a vast and ancient house. I had my own tiny transistor radio that fit into a neat black leather pouch. I played it quietly when I was alone in my room, or I would put the little earphone that came with it into my right ear so as not to disturb the strange placidity that enveloped the house. The only disruption was an earsplitting bell that clanged in the morning at 6:30 sharp to jolt us awake.

The home's one television was in the TV room on the second floor, and it could be on from 10 to 12 in the morning, after our breakfast and chores were completed, from 1 to 4 in the afternoons, those sacred hours for soap operas, and from 7 to 10 in the evenings. Breakfast was served at 7:30, lunch at noon, and dinner at 5:30 always, no matter what. For those of us who attended high school in the basement, classes ran from 9 to 11:45: first English, then social studies, both taught by Mrs. McCorkle, then science and math, taught by Mrs. Jamison. In the afternoon, from 1:00 to 2:00, I had my very own French tutorial from Madame LaPierre, a long-retired classics professor from Kenyon. We had to be in bed with lights out at 10:15, in time for the housekeeper's bed check.

I lived on the second floor in a small, narrow room with Tina. I was lucky to get this room since most of the girls were assigned to larger rooms with three or four beds and little privacy. I can remember exactly the way my bed was situated in a corner of the room. I liked the way it was pushed against the wall. As I lay in bed with the wall on my right, on my left, right next to a tiny bedside table was a barred window with a frayed, dirt-stained shade that either flapped up hysterically or drooped lifelessly. With the right wrist action, I could keep the shade up and open the window. One day I put six red apples that my aunt had brought me on the sill between the glass and the bars to try to keep them fresh, but they froze, and when I brought one in to eat, it went from rock hard bright to brown, mushy and inedible. I left the others out there in a neat red line, hoping birds might find them, and I could watch them chip away at the alternately frozen and spongy fruit, but it was winter in Akron, Ohio, and no birds found their way to my icy sill. My bed had a tattered, beige bedspread, soiled and musky. I could have washed the spread in one of the antiquated wringer washers in the basement, but instead I would lie on it and inhale the compendium of odors that took me back to my grandmother's body when she used to hold my face against her large breasts.

I am quite sure of the weather. Snow remained on the ground for almost the entirety of my stay, so to go outdoors always required boots, coat, gloves, and hat. Indoors the radiators banged insistently and their heat bore down on me oppressively and relentlessly. I would open my window and take huge gulps of crisp air, but Tina was always cold and wouldn't let me to keep it open for long.

After I left Florence Crittenton, there was a chasm between me and everything I had been before. I would pretend to be the same; I would joke around; I half-heartedly wrote my old friends and shyly made new ones where I went to live next, but I was someone new and different from every other sixteen-year-old girl I encountered. Everything doubled. I had one life that I lived on the surface that I constructed with care, and I had a secret life and a secret self that I painstakingly hid. On the outside, I had become a much better student because I could concentrate now with a ferocity that had escaped me before. I learned that a kind of scholarly, focused absorption would kept the secret self at bay, so I worked hard, memorizing irregular French verbs, the Gettysburg Address, the anatomy of the flower—the corolla, composed of petals, the calyx, composed of sepals, the stamens, and the pistil. I immersed myself in long novels, especially *Tess of the D'Urbervilles,* which I secretly read and reread, earnestly and relentlessly. I tried to dog-ear page after page of my copy so that if someone picked it up, it wouldn't open automatically to page 61, the page that gave me away, the one I always returned to so that Hardy's words for Tess became a kind of mantra that consoled and pardoned me too as I whispered them to myself: "She looked upon her self as a figure of Guilt intruding into the haunts of Innocence. But all the while she was making a distinction where there was no difference. Feeling herself in antagonism she was quite in accord. She had been made to break an accepted social law, but no law known to the environment in which she fancied herself such an anomaly."

Nonetheless, what had happened was something to be judged. My boyfriend Alec and I had sex; I would say we made love, but I was too intimidated, naïve, and ashamed to find love in that dark encounter. It was not date rape or nonconsensual sex. I was not impassioned, but I was willing. When I picture myself on that avocado green couch in Alec's living room, I see one of those pliable dolls, stretching into the position required for the moment, speechless astonishment on my frozen doll face. Although I loved Alec intensely then and for years after, that night is drained of love. It lives on, a starkly black-and-white hour of acquiescence. Because of Alec's unremitting pressure, because of my fear of his inevitable renunciation, because I was far more desperate than any sixteen-year-old should be, that night I agreed to all the steps. No one should be judged. I yielded willingly. My needs for Alec far outweighed the emotional pluck I would have needed to muster once again a joyless defense.

For years I waited for the scene to correct itself. I believed he would return and keep the childish promises he had made. We would finally begin the life we were meant to live together, happily ever after. I could not imagine any other ending. Whenever I would return to my hometown, I would immediately be on alert for his possible presence. His parents' home was only a block from my church. I would go to the Sunday morning service nervously but eagerly, preparing myself for what I believed would be our inevitable reunion. This time, I would tell myself, we would pass on the gleaming sidewalk, or better yet, he would see me from his parents' front window as I walked penitently through the shimmery, dewy, morning. Before ever having read Proust, I created a Proustian moment for him. He would watch me going by and the gentle sway of my hair would send a gush of emotion surging back through forgotten channels of yearning. Tender, innocent love would be reborn. He would remember that it was I who was crucial to his life story.

Throughout the church service, I would picture him waiting patiently for me outside. As I walked back to my car, I would study his parents' low house, the trimmed front yard, the louvered side door by the garage where he would emerge. This was the same door we had come out of into that night after furtively performing our awkward sexual initiation in the darkened, stuffy living room. But the front of his parents' house would stare blankly at me as I passed; its unperceiving windows were cruel; over and over they ignored my passing; again and again the watched door did not swing open. Still, I couldn't let go of the image of us finally making love on crisp, white sheets, the sun pouring unabashedly in on us from the large window onto our white bed and gleaming bodies. To live that particular moment seemed the only way to correct my life.

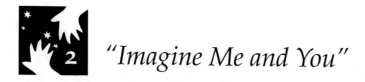

"Imagine Me and You"

San Marino, California, 1966

SHORTLY AFTER I TURNED EIGHTEEN, Alec did come back to me, appearing at my parents' door on a warm, early summer morning. I had just graduated from San Marino High School, and I was home alone. This sounds like it could be the meeting I had been preparing for, the one that would transform the heartbreaking past into the golden future. But he surprised me. The setting was wrong; I was wrong. I had on a pair of ridiculous red and white striped pedal pushers that used to fit but now pulled tightly around my hips and thighs. This was to my great disadvantage. Candy, the girlfriend with whom he had replaced me, was a thin girl. Everyone wanted to be thin, even then. Twiggy was the model of fashion. My girlfriends were already saying things like "You can't be too thin" and were trying out diets like the one where you could only drink Tab and eat cottage cheese.

That morning my hair wasn't dirty but it wasn't clean either; it lay lank and dull. My skin felt greasy and pasty. I had my period. Alec and I talked, but I knew he found me listless and uninspiring. Conversation flagged. We began to kiss. Compliantly I followed his lead to my bedroom and with all our clothes still on, we got into my unmade bed—the curtains were drawn, the window closed, the air musty, the room messy. As he pulled off my T-shirt, he remarked on my new "love handles." I had never heard this term but I was far too uncomfortable to ask, "What are they?" "What do you mean?" That he could so nonchalantly use this term was for me obvious evidence of the sexual savvy he had gained during his two years at university. In comparison, I felt conspicuously artless. My early experience of carrying a baby full term and giving birth to her far from home had erased any sense of appealing girlishness I might once have flaunted. It had turned my body into something dreadfully, monstrously adult. Although I now knew what it could miraculously produce—a perfect baby—I had not an ounce of savoir faire, not a glimmer of sexual know-how. Burgeoning with emotional need for Alec, I was laid flat by a heavy, malodorous shame.

As Alec stroked my breasts and squeezed my "love handles," I closed my eyes, trying to transform this unnerving moment into something magical. I was much too shy to tell him I was menstruating. I could hardly say anything, dumbstruck by his presence, his reality, and his confidence. When he discovered I had my period, he got up from the bed, and walked out of the house. That was the last time we ever touched.

How could my star-crossed love for him, my stubborn steadfastness, persevere given such humiliation? The narrative I was living, a narrative fed me by the fairy tales of my childhood and the fiction and music of my adolescence, stories of first love that would ultimately and ineluctably triumph, could not bend to accommodate this latest mortifying scene. The scene had to be put right, replayed, but it could not be recast. It was Alec, my one and only hero, who had to correct the past. However, not only did he refuse the part I had written for him, he was oblivious that he was still even in my persistently naïve story.

San Marino, 1967

A song that played on the radio during that spring of my first year away at college was "Happy Together" (1967). The Turtles sang the song cheerily, and it was full of lots of "S" words. I would sing along with the Turtles, whispering sibilantly all the "S's": "Imagine me and you, as two / No matter how they toss the dice, it had to be." My best friend, Connie, liked the way I would sing the "S's." I had told her all about Alec. I would say, "I can't get over him," as if he were a large obstacle in the path of my maturity that I couldn't get around. But I never dared to even hint to her that we had had sex, and, of course, never, never that I had secretly had "his" baby and given her away. I knew Connie would reject me if she knew that part of my love story. She had her own personal nickname for me—"Ell." I loved it that she called me "Ell," that she had picked me as her friend and even named me with her special endearment. I told her that when I sang along with the Turtles, I was always singing about Alec, that "no matter how they toss[ed] the dice, it had to be."

On the first day of Connie's visit to San Marino for our college spring break, I drove her by Alec's house. His father was cutting the lawn and seemed glad to see me when I pulled up to the curb and stopped the car. He called Alec to come outside to talk to us. I caught my breath when Alec grudgingly emerged. As I introduced him to Connie, I was so proud of her. She made pleasant, relaxed remarks as I, once again shy and silent, watched; her sweetness seemed delectable; her brown friendly eyes were sparkling, her chestnut hair shiny and bouncy. She saucily remarked that she had heard a lot about him. Surely when he saw that I had made such a beautiful friend, he would appreciate my value again. But he was annoyed and curt, quickly turning around and going back through that same side door from which I kept imagining he would one day eagerly emerge, at last ready to rewrite our story, which had now turned so sour. On this day, even his father was embarrassed by his rudeness and apologized for him. No need. I forgave Alec everything. Of course, I thought, it was annoying for him to be interrupted by a cloying old girlfriend, showing off her jaunty friend from Oregon.

In some strange way, his rejection became the rejection I expected from all others. My self-confidence was abysmal. On this day, I feared Connie would see me for the pudgy dullard I felt I really was, that she would stop calling me "Ell." All the way back to my parents' house, we sang "No matter how the toss the dice, it has to be / The only one for me is you and you for me / So happy together . . . How is the weather?" Unaware of so much, Connie allowed me to maintain my imaginary future, and I continued to excuse Alec's many rejections, to hoard my damning secret, to hide my ruined body. With no other recourse imaginable, I clung tenaciously to the love story I believed would someday be mine—Alec and me, the sunny room, enraptured love, our destiny together.

Martha's Vineyard, 2004

The transforming scene would never be played. Reversal is not part of this dénouement. The last time I spoke with him, twelve years later, twenty-six years ago, he abruptly ended our short, awkward conversation with the excuse that he had to help a friend move.

Now it occurs to me that he had his own counternarrative, constructed from the scripts available to California surfing "bums" and, maybe, all good-looking eighteen-year-old boys in the United States in the late sixties. He probably told his college buddies, in a swaggering sort of way, something about me. Maybe they laughed at the indelible connection that I so earnestly believed should be honored. I may have even been part of a mean joke they shared, as they griped about those first girlfriends— the ones who offered up their virginity, the ones who felt too much, who would not give up, who would not self-effacingly retreat into their macho lists of sexual conquests.

That same summer of our last embrace, that day he refused my body and walked out of my room, I saw him one other time, shortly before we were both to depart again for our respective universities. He stopped by on a smoggy, dried out September afternoon. My mother was home and none to glad to see him, so we went out for a hot, aimless drive. There was no fresh breeze to be found, and although I was sure I was meant to be sitting right by his side, I could not hit upon a way to amuse or charm him. As he languidly pulled into my parents' driveway, set to say his indifferent good-bye, I was frantic to exert some lasting claim on him.

As we sat there in the sweltering front seat of his car, partially but futilely shaded by the dusty olive trees whose fruit left indelible purple blotches on whatever was parked beneath, I took an impulsive plunge into the past. I told him I had given birth to Sorrow—that we had made a daughter, that she was a year old, that she lived somewhere in Ohio. He listened quietly, paused reflectively, and then replied, "I don't believe you."

No, he did not believe me nor did he want to hear my story. He would have none of it. If what I claimed were true, he avowed, he would have known. My parents would have come to his parents. He would have been held responsible. "No one," he said, "could have kept a secret like that." I was only telling him this now, making this up just so that I could "get him back," he accused. There was some truth to that—I desperately wanted him back. But my telling backfired. I gained nothing but his distrust and contempt. Shaken that he could so cavalierly deny my truth, stunned that he refused to consider the story I had to tell, insulted by his pitiless though prescient observation that I only "wanted him back," I gave up and got out of his car, deflated, ashamed, powerless.

In the narrative that he and his friends shared, I must have figured crudely, nothing more than his first *cherry*. I was the implacable girl who was fanciful enough to think that because we were each other's first love, we were meant to be linked for life; the hanger-on that he was coming to disdain, desperate enough to claim that a child had come of our one and only sexual encounter. Love was never a part of his dorm-room talk.

Alec's vulgar version was beyond my imagination. It didn't fit any of the scripts I had to work with. But to understand his take now is helpful. He was callow and untouched. He had no secrets, no need to lead a double life. His gender and his privilege had protected him. He had been absent from the complicated narrative that I had lived through in Ohio without his knowledge or support. He had no means to conceive of its enormity. Instead, he could make my heartbreaking revelation into a small and petty ploy. Knowing why and how he could do this removes some of the humiliation and hurt, but it does not soothe my anger, even today.

3 *Fishnet Stockings*

San Marino, Spring 1964

ALMOST SIXTEEN and intensely in love with Alec, I lie awake late into the night, listening intently to my bedside radio, waiting to hear Paul sing "Till There Was You" (*With the Beatles,* 1963). The British Invasion has begun, and I have each of the Beatles' first albums: *Please, Please Me* (1963), *With the Beatles* (1963), *A Hard Day's Night* (1964). I listen to them over and over again, carefully writing out all the lyrics and then committing each song to memory. I buy the sheet music for Vince Guaraldi's "Cast Your Fate to the Wind" and learn to play it on the piano—because that's just what I want to do, forego all caution, embrace all possibilities. I want to be "Under the Boardwalk" (Drifters, 1964), to "Get Around" (Beach Boys, 1964), to "Twist and Shout" (Beatles, 1964), to be "Just Like Romeo and Juliet" (The Reflections, 1964). Mostly I want to just have "Fun, Fun, Fun" (1964) as the Beach Boys instruct me to do. The lyrics I pay attention to urge a playful hedonistic defiance. Even my reading feeds this fervor to break out. When we read *Huckleberry Finn* in sophomore English, I savor the last lines, anticipating my own launch into "the Territory," just like Huck before Aunt Sally can "sivilize" him. Escape—out of the house, into the night, the cars, the cigarettes, the alcohol. I want to grow my hair long, make my skirts short, to dance, to drink, to speed, to scream, to dare, dare, dare. Everything forbidden is enticing.

Three friends from grade school accompanied me into this hedonism, but they did not have steady boyfriends; hence, they were apparently under no pressure for petting and certainly none for sex. To me, these girls seemed gloriously mischievous. They were early harbingers of the "merry pranksters," although it was still several years until I would hear of Ken Kesey and realize our part in the emerging zeitgeist.

Our leader was Jackie. Looking back, I am still astounded by how audacious she was and how effortlessly any sense of guilt escaped her. She was the epitome of charming irresponsibility, though this same thoughtlessness could make her cruel, even Machiavellian. One afternoon for no reasons other than that she relished my tears and delighted in her own power, Jackie took a lipstick to my new white cardigan, chasing me and slashing big pink Xs across my back as I hurtled down the school corridor, begging her to stop. The sweater was so smeared with the thick pink grease that I stuffed it in a trash can rather than take it home and try to explain the mess to my mother. Easier to say the cardigan was lost than to try to explain the glee I saw in Jackie's eyes as she came after me, lipstick poised, bent on making me shriek in protest, weep in defenselessness.

On this particular afternoon in the early spring of 1964, Jackie led Tammy, Caroline, and me into the Shopping Basket on Huntington Drive. This was the market where my mother shopped every day for dinner, and it was quite possible we could have met her there. Jackie's plan? We were there to shoplift a bottle of liquor. In California, hard liquor can be purchased in the grocery store and just like in any "package" or state-run liquor store, several aisles display carefully lined up bottles of glistening liquors—every color and every brand one could want. Jackie's plan was to set up a decoy. She and Tammy would pretend to shoplift some candy to create a distraction, though they would finally pay for it. In the meantime, Caroline and I would lift a bottle of vodka. Jackie had sampled her parents' liquor cabinet, and vodka, she declared, had the least taste and would be the easiest to get down.

Had we been wearing the jeans and baggy sweaters that would soon comprise our complete wardrobes, this would not have been such a delicate feat, but at San Marino High School, we had a school uniform of sorts—gray skirts or gray jumpers. I suppose this dress code was an effort to keep our parents from having to give in to our pleas for new clothes and to impose an outward show of homogeny amongst us, but the regulation was a failure. Since the code only required a gray skirt or jumper, girls could go to extremes of extravagance when choosing sweater sets, blouses, blazers, shoes, and stockings. There was no fooling us. We knew early on the worth of a cashmere sweater set from Bullock's and the power it bequeathed as opposed to an ignominious pastel, "Peter Pan" blouse from the Broadway. The hierarchy of the wealthy was always obvious in our school clothes despite the gesture toward gray uniformity.

On the day we went to steal the vodka, I was wearing a hated baggy gray jumper, which on this day I finally appreciated. Because of it, I could not be asked to carry the bottle out of the store. Jackie was daring, but even she was sensible enough to realize that the jumper made it impossible for me stuff the bottle between my stomach and my underpants inconspicuously. I know she would have chosen me had I been dressed differently since I was the least favored in her clique. The danger of the heist would have fallen to me—the most expendable member. But that day it was Caroline who had on a gray skirt with an elastic waistband along with a pullover sweater that would nicely hide the bottle's protrusion—a harbinger of the secret baby I would be hiding in a few months under my own shapeless clothing. Caroline was not subtle in her shoplifting effort. I led her to the aisle and hovered around her as she fumbled with her skirt and sweater, sliding the bottle inside her panties—they were still the little girl kind, white cotton with pink strawberries—and then shoving her school books up against her stomach to hold the glass bottle firmly as we exited the store. We broke into a run—an exhilarating charge, shrieking down Huntington Drive toward Caroline and Tammy's neighborhood. How did four giggling girls pull this sloppy, foolhardy thievery off? It seems incredible, but it must have had to do with Jackie's intrepid recklessness. She was never one to get caught.

A few years later, I heard a rumor that Jackie had been arrested for indecent exposure in her college town. What could she have been doing to garner such an arrest? Was it merely midnight skinny-dipping, or innocent-enough topless sunbathing, or was she too following the tambourine man, dancing gleefully naked, "silhouetted by the sea, circled by the circus sand"? (Bob Dylan, 1964). It doesn't surprise me that she may have been so bold, but I am taken aback that she actually got caught. Nonetheless, the untamed spirit of her transgression befits the Jackie I knew.

Now we had a bottle of vodka in our possession. Jackie took it home to hide until Friday night. Her mother was the most lenient and so the least likely to snoop through her drawers. Although she may not have been one to pry, when we were home alone at Jackie's house, we did our own poking around. We carefully examined her mother's lingerie, even eventually locating her mysterious diaphragm, which we could not believe worked the way we thought it might. We read out loud to one another pertinent passages from Jackie's father's small collection of soft-porn paperbacks. Once, when Jackie had a slumber party, her mother allowed us to roam the streets late into the night, and we ended up walking miles to Alhambra to steal makeup from Woolworth's.

Friday night is finally upon us. Jean—a smart girl who sometimes joins us but risks little—has the use of her parents' car for the evening. She is the only person we know who has turned sixteen and gotten her driver's license. She pulls into my driveway and honks. I can see myself, running out the front door toward Jean's car, my scrubbed, shiny face, my hair temporarily in a neat pageboy, my pressed dotted Swiss green blouse, my knee-length black skirt. On the outside I look like such a healthy, guileless teenager—not unlike Betty on the sitcom reruns we watch of *Father Knows Best*, although I have great disdain for Betty's bangs and ponytail. But I am a clever actress. I have donned a costume for this necessary exit from my parents' purview that I will quickly replace with a very different look. A split between my selves has already begun: I play the pert sweetheart for my parents but the cheeky bad girl for my peers; the permissible and the impermissible; the acceptable and the naughty.

I have told my parents we are going to a double feature at the Academy Theater on Colorado Boulevard and then to Bob's Big Boy for hamburgers and lemon cokes. This they allow; my curfew is midnight. They have forbidden me to go with my girlfriends to my real destination: the Pasadena Civic Auditorium where dances are held every Friday night. Their reason seems fanatical to me. For such "functions," they say, an "escort," a word we would never use, must accompany me. Alec is grounded this weekend for talking back to his mother, but I wouldn't want him to "escort" me to the Civic anyway. Everyone goes there entangled in a crowd of friends. Boys go with boys, girls with girls. The groups eye one another across the dance floor, and occasionally a boy will break off from his huddle, saunter to the girls' clutch, and ask a girl to dance. After each dance, both quickly retreat into their respective huddles. An "escort" is unwanted, but there are desirable accoutrements: alcohol, a short skirt, lots of black eye makeup, white lipstick, and fishnet stockings. Jackie has assembled all the necessary ingredients for the night: the vodka, the car, the driver, and the four of us have sprung free. Tammy's parents and little sisters are out for the evening, so that's where we go first.

Our night begins with rolling up our skirts to make them into minis, donning our secretly stowed fishnet stockings, layering our eyes with black liner, mascara, green and blue shadow, and making our lips look bloodless with chalky, white lipstick. Even though this is Southern California and the Beach Boys are singing "Little Surfer Girl" (*Surfer Girl*, 1963), we don't want to look like Gidget. We want to look like Joan Baez and Mary Travers, the sultry beats of Greenwich Village, a place we are just beginning to hear about but immediately want to imitate. Haight Ashbury and its wilder extravagance are not yet on the horizon. The Beatles still look clean-cut with their bangs and their five-button suits. The flamboyant amalgam of what will become hippies will soon emerge, but I won't get my first pair of bell-bottoms for four more years. On this night we don't look like hippies or the beats, but we think we look seriously slutty—definitely girls on the prowl. Perhaps my parents had good reason for their taboos.

We drink the vodka, holding our noses as we force it down our throats, trying not to gag. Caroline can gulp it with surprising ease and drinks far more than the rest of us, though we all feel heady and giddy. For a little while we return to our girlhoods as we take to Tammy and her sisters' bikes and fly around the neighborhood, whooping at each other, thrilled with our freedom, conspicuously flushed even through all the layers of our sticky makeup. Jean, the driver, only sips her vodka; instead of joining us on the bikes, she watches us from the sidelines, amused but controlled.

That was the best part of the night, racing each other down the darkening streets. When we finally pile back into Jean's car and arrive at the door of the Civic Auditorium, all the fun vanishes. The man at the door won't let the stumbling, slurring Caroline into the auditorium. Tammy and Jackie disappear blithely through the doors and into the pounding music, and though I beg her, Jean refuses to take charge of Caroline and goes in too. I am left to stay outside and walk Caroline up and down the street until she looks sober enough to be admitted. I can hear the Righteous Brothers singing live—"You've lost that lovin' feeling / Baby that lovin' feeling"—from the deserted sidewalk. I can't abandon Caroline to the night and go in too, so without any idea of what else to do, I march her around and around the block and finally back up to the entrance, squeezing her arm, urging her to stop giggling, to stop leaning on me, and to look "normal." But again the intractable doorman declares, "You can't bring her in here." What to do? Caroline can hardly stand up. I can't ask my parents to come get me out of this. The only other teenager I know who can drive, besides Jean, is Alec. With Caroline now down on all fours on the sidewalk, throwing up in the gutter beside me, I frantically call Alec from the pay phone on the corner of Colorado Boulevard, terrified that at any moment a police car will drive by, spot the moaning girl, and haul us both off to the police station.

Alec does manage to persuade his parents to let him come and get us. "Bring some towels," I warn. I prop Caroline up next to me on the low wall that borders the sidewalk and wait for Alec to get there. I can still recall her bitter breath and the acrid smell of her soiled clothes. Together, Alec and I take her, now barely conscious, home. I haltingly concoct a conceivable story for her horrified mother when she meets us at the door:

"Caroline got suddenly, inexplicably ill," I manage. "She must have food poisoning!" I add.

But Caroline's father is a doctor. It takes him little time to figure out the real cause of her ailment.

I never got into the Civic that night, never saw the Righteous Brothers live. My parents learned of the escapade when Caroline's mother called mine the next day to relate all that Caroline had confessed to and, by the way, to thank me for not deserting her on the street in Pasadena. Her gratitude did nothing to diminish my mother's fury at my disobedience and deceitfulness.

Martha's Vineyard, 2004

Looking back, I am amazed how our driver, Jean, stayed so completely removed from the trouble the rest of us got into after that night, though the severity of the punishments that our parents meted out varied considerably. The egregious Jackie, our ringleader, faced negligible consequences—a stern reprimand but nothing more; Tammy was grounded for weeks; Caroline had to write a report on the dangers of alcohol poisoning for her father; and I was forbidden to go with Alec to his all-night graduation party. But I keep thinking of Jean.

Within the arbitrary parameters established for all of us, she had done nothing wrong. Her parents had trusted her with the car, permitted her to go to the dance, and smart girl that she was, she stayed within the boundaries they had drawn. She avoided that first divide, the first psychological rift to which I would now be committed. Behind my exterior, obedient facade that I maintained for adults was a very different girl lying in wait—a wild child, willing to experiment with alcohol, sex, defiance.

But was I? Had I not traded my obedience to my parents to slavishly follow Jackie's example? How desperately I wanted her approval. How dearly I wanted to be chosen as a member of her crowd. I suspect now that my newborn defiance had more to do with trying to please the new leader of the pack than with any independent feistiness of my own. After all, I did everything she told me to do—assisting in the shoplifting, sneaking out with the right clothes, applying the right makeup, gulping down the vodka, and finally forfeiting the night out to care for Caroline when no one else would.

We were five girls—all on the cusp of vast cultural change. Dylan had just released *The Times They Are A-Changin'* (February 1964). And they were. Already we were hearing the mantra of our generation: "Question authority!" Already we felt the allure of mind-altering substances. Already the sexual revolution was seeping into our consciousness, our hormones.

Each of us moved from that night into different, though not unpredictable, lives. Jean courted stability, went to UCLA, married a rich man. Tammy disappeared into Haight Ashbury and died young, a suicide. Caroline was arrested at a sit-in at the Bank of America in Santa Barbara; later she married, but I heard recently that her only child died tragically. Jackie, the great finagler, practices law.

It occurs to me now that parents everywhere must have realized they were losing control, that their "sons and [their] daughters [were] beyond [their] command" (Dylan, "Times They Are A-Changin'"). Lying in bed at night, waiting for me to come home, my own mother and father must have deliberated over how to rein me in. More supervision? Earlier curfews? No more Beatles? No more boyfriend? Their WWII generation must have already felt their sense of propriety slipping away. Eventually many of their children would career into a completely altered social reality. My disobedience must have felt like an ungrateful rejection. But there was so much enticement.

My mother was fifty; my father fifty-one. Their careers were demanding but rewarding. They had gotten my two sisters through adolescence in the fifties, and now here I was, even more problematic. What could they have done? How to intervene? How to stop the landslide of their principles? No one quite understood yet, but very soon, "a hard rain [was] . . . gonna fall" (*The Freewheelin' Bob Dylan*, 1963) and wash away most of the long-standing, dependable codes that we were just beginning to scorn and defy.

4 Richard Nixon and Me

San Marino, 1962

TWO YEARS BEFORE my night-out escapade with Caroline, there was a photo taken of me: a preposterous snapshot given my liberal politics today, one that always makes people who know me laugh incredulously when I bring it out. But, while I was still the girl my parents expected me to be, I was asked to be a Nixonette, and I merrily, unthinkingly donned my white dress and red, white, and blue banner. One of our Nixonette duties was to stand on the curb in front of the San Marino Republican Headquarters and welcome the candidate to town. Judging from the look of the women's hats, their eyeglasses, and their clothing, you'd think it was still the early fifties, not 1962.

Richard Nixon was running for governor of California, and my mother was involved with his local campaign. When he came to San Marino that day, we Nixonettes eagerly lined up so that he could be photographed with a flock of adoring girls. There we are, grinning broadly in the sunshine, clapping appreciatively though discreetly for him, our hands in white gloves. In my picture, he looks just like his caricatures: in a dark suit, white shirt, and tie, he grins maniacally. As his minions, we wear our white eighth-grade-graduation dresses with our Nixonette sashes across our new breasts and white straw boaters on our heads. Red, white, and blue pompoms and buckets filled with *Nixon for Governor* buttons are our accessories. We were asked to wear high heels, for what reason I cannot imagine, and my mother purchased my first pair just for the occasion.

Janet at fourteen with Richard Nixon, 1962.
Photographer unknown. Courtesy of the author.

This was the summer I grew to my full height of 5'9", and my graduation dress, only months old, is clearly too small. The waist is high; the sleeves are straining around my shoulders. At fourteen, I am already a big girl barely contained in a little girl's dress. My right foot is at an odd angle because I have let my ankle collapse outward so that the high heel is parallel to the ground.

I can see that I am completely uncomfortable with my height. I look so ungainly, so awkward, hence the absurdity of my posture. There it is— that full-size body, straining against distressed seams, the same body that will always give me pause, that I will forever try to trim down, reduce, restrain, contain. I'd like to say that I look reluctant, disinclined, out of place, or even better, contemptuous. But, in fact, I simply look goofy. Who did I dress up for? What was I clapping for? Why was I smiling?

My merriment had nothing to do with Richard Nixon. I had no idea what his platform was. I was still at the age where almost everything in my tightly circumscribed world went without question, so it was completely natural that my parents would be conservative Republicans; surely someday I would be as well. I hadn't begun to read anything outside the purview of my parents' auspices. My bookshelf boasted *Heidi, Misty of Chincoteague*, sets of *The Little House on the Prairie, Anne of Green Gables,* and *Nancy Drew.* My most audacious reading so far was *Cherry Ames, School Nurse.* I was immersed in a receivership of an ideology from which I could get no distance. Little about growing up had rubbed me the wrong way, yet. The most seditious thing I had done so far was to break windows in a huge, soon-to-be-demolished house a few blocks from our home. This once grand "estate" would be subdivided to make room for eight modest homes for this bedroom community of the discreetly prosperous.

Richard Nixon, a man I would come to despise, lost that election and retreated briefly from politics, though not without first making his bitter and ironic remark, "You won't have Nixon to kick around anymore." And my role as a Nixonette is almost the final curtain call for my innocent adolescence before the unstoppable turn my life would take, a sharp pivot away from the automatic, the known, and the expected. I would take that turn with the fresh eagerness of an adventurer. I am not nostalgic, simply amazed as I look at Richard Nixon and me. There was that time . . . and then . . . I changed.

San Marino, 1964

Another photograph two years later: I am with Alec at his all-night graduation party. Although my parents had forbidden me to attend this celebration after the fiasco with Caroline at the Civic Auditorium, Alec's parents pleaded with them to let me accompany Alec. After all, they argued, he should not be punished for my mischief and without me, he would not attend. My parents relented.

Janet at sixteen, Alec's graduation party, 1964.
Photographer unknown. Courtesy of the author.

I love this picture. Alec has turned away from the camera, but I'm looking straight ahead, openly, sweetly, trustingly. Rather than goofy, I look pretty. I have on a white dress again, but this one is new and it fits. We are seated, so you can't see the dress's skirt in the photo, but I remember how much I loved its yellow embroidery and piping. My body is neatly contained by the dress's bodice. Underneath I wear my sister's "merry widow"—the kind of corset that Madonna will make famous decades later. The corset makes my waist look tiny. The spaghetti straps make my arms look slender. My hair is in a tidy pageboy, with an innocent bow tied fastidiously at the top to hold the strands away from my face. This is the girl I was meant to be.

Certainly, I had been in some typical adolescent trouble. Getting caught sneaking out to the Civic Auditorium had been no small matter and Caroline's drunkenness had made the transgression much worse. And my parents had been deeply distressed by a couple of other escapades that spring:

1. Alec has come over to the house where I am babysitting, and as we are making out in the couple's bed, we are surprised by them when they return home early. For some weird reason, I confess to getting "caught" to my mother the next morning. She instantly spirals into an astounding fury, slams out of the house, and drives like a crazy person to apologize to the people I was babysitting for. I learn something from this: she is volatile and she is clearly not someone to confide in.

2. I am permitted to go to a school dance with Jackie, Caroline, Tammy, and Jean. Tammy is to come back to my house to spend the night, but we get separated at the dance. When it's time to leave, she doesn't show up at Jean's car for our ride home. We wait for awhile, but Jean will not break her curfew and finally insists on taking me home without Tammy. My father is waiting up for us, and when he finds Tammy is not with me, he is immediately, surprisingly alarmed. He calls her mother to tell her she is missing, and then, stationed in his chair by the front door, he sits up all night long waiting. By morning he is distraught, convinced that she is dead. Tammy's mother calls at 8:30 to let us know that Tammy has been found. She had slept at another friend's house and casually and typically neglected to call me or her mother to let us know her whereabouts.

I learn something from my father's close-to-hysterical response; he is vulnerable; he has to be protected from me and the trouble I can trigger. I will eventually understand why Tammy's failure to return echoed his own secret trauma, that it reenacted a horrific night of waiting twenty years earlier that ended with unimaginable tragedy. He had worked assiduously to never relive such a loss of control again, but I brought unpredictability back into his home. Still, as I look back at these infractions, they seem minor—almost clichés. Adolescent flouting of parental authority, if not banal, is surely unsurprising.

Partway through Alec's graduation party, an all-night event, I change out of my embroidered white dress into jeans. I have forgotten to pack my bra, so it's either wear the "merry widow" all night or go braless under my sweatshirt. I decide on the latter, which excites Alec tremendously for the rest of the night. We leave early and go to our favorite parking spot. He is desperate to have intercourse. We climb in the back seat; I think I'm willing, but we are clumsy and unskilled. He ejaculates before there is any penetration, but we're getting very close, dangerously entwined.

The photo at Alec's graduation was taken one month after my sixteenth birthday—a marker of sorts for girls then if not now—an innocent doorway through which I thought I should step into young womanhood. But the myth was already a little tarnished for me; I remember remarking caustically to Alec that I surely did not fit the rhyme "Sweet sixteen and never been kissed." I also remember how sulky I was on the day itself because I had to bake my own birthday cake. I had actually been baking my own birthday cakes for a long time; in fact, as soon as my sister taught me how to navigate my parents' kitchen, I became the family baker. Would there have been birthday cakes if I had not baked them myself? I doubt it, and by sixteen I had gotten pretty good at cakes. I baked this one conscientiously, frosted it carefully with pink icing, and decorated it with delicate white flowers that I had learned how to make from the instructions on the back of the Betty Crocker frosting tube. I was trying hard to conform to the idealized notion that we carried around with us of what a "sweet sixteen" cake was supposed to look like. I remember the cake, but I can't recall eating it. Did we celebrate? Who was there? Did I receive gifts?

Martha's Vineyard, 2004

Memory fails even as it succeeds. It tells the story it wants to tell even though I, as memoirist, want to convey a rounded out narrative. Here, there seems to be a theme that insists on a lonely girl, left behind in a big house. Despite my creative desires to construct a fully realized, multidimensional adolescent, the shallow themes of *Cinderella* frustratingly persist—both the pitiable girl, who I want to disclaim, and the handsome prince, who I have grown to detest. Perhaps I can only remember the baking and decorating of the cake because the loneliness I felt as I sculpted each tiny white flower overwhelmed happy anticipation. Perhaps that stand-alone gesture pierced my consciousness in an essential way. A small, self-appointed task seems to have set me apart. Had my parents, sisters, friends, and boyfriend forgotten my sixteenth birthday? Is this an instance of indifference, cruelty, or simple forgetfulness? Why was I on my own to bake that significant cake?

In 1964 in San Marino, most mothers were still stay-at-home moms, their only outside interests their charity *du jour.* My mother was different. She had a career, one that she was extraordinarily good at and that she loved. She poured her energy into it and graciously succeeded. I do not want to speak of her work with any tone of resentment, for as a women's studies professor, I have ardently supported women with children *and* careers and argued fiercely that working moms, myself included, deserve dependable childcare. I have preached from this particular soapbox with such ardor that it would be impermissible for me to whine about my lonely adolescence. And yet I would come home from school so hungry for company that I learned how to call myself on our black, rotary dial telephone in order to have long imaginary conversations with the dial tone. And even I resort to the oldest cliché in the world—when we remember childhood unhappiness and feel its repercussions in the present, we account for it again and again by blaming our fallible, overwhelmed mothers.

Try as I might, I can offer no reliable version of the delight I must have felt as my birthday cake was sliced, served, and eaten. Were candles lit? Was "Happy Birthday" sung? Perhaps that celebratory moment refuses to surface because it fit the generic "sweet sixteen" narrative. Whatever it was, it was not remarkable, hence not memorable, and the self-pitying descent into this sad birthday cake memory strikes me as somewhat petty and peevish. Perhaps my birthday wasn't even overlooked. Perhaps I was filled with joy and gratitude, and it is probably only my limitation that I can't recalled the significant ways I was sweetly acknowledged.

It's not the cake; it's the girl frosting the cake for whom so many moments live on—going braless at the graduation party, walking Caroline around and around outside the Pasadena Civic Auditorium, fumbling passionately in the back of Alec's car, smiling for Richard Nixon. Layer upon layer I thumb through the phantasmagoria, trying to find the consummate element, the pea in the mattress that then and now keeps me awake at nights. My memories remind me that although I was typical, I was also different, and so achingly separate that I became desperately attached.

As my teenage angst intensified, my cheerfulness waned and my disobedience became more reckless. I can see now that my parents were rightfully apprehensive and annoyed. It was almost impossible for me to be the docile daughter they expected. Instead, I was a determined, moody stranger, still wanting to please, but unwilling, perhaps unable, to keep up the kind of performance they wanted. They could already tell that I was much more than they signed on for. Perhaps they heard familiar echoes of someone from their past.

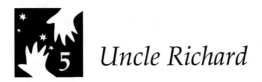

5 Uncle Richard

BEFORE I WAS BORN, my sisters had an Uncle Richard, Aunt Betty, and two cousins, Richard Jr. and Caroline Jean. Richard was my father's younger brother. Only a year separated the two. My father grew up good at everything. He was smart, athletic, well behaved, and handsome. He went to the University of Michigan where he joined a fraternity and eventually became the captain of the track team. Richard followed devotedly in his footsteps, at least as best he could. When my father went to Michigan, so did Richard. When my father started running track, so did Richard, becoming an outstanding hurdler in his own right. I know all this from my own detective work, from piecing together a still-incomplete puzzle. I found a few paper clippings about the track successes of the two brothers in the depths of the huge bottom drawer of my mother's ancient desk that she calls the "Gunston Hall Secretary" because George Mason, who like Katharine Hepburn is one of our highly visible relations, is said to have composed the model for the Bill of Rights while sitting at it.

My sisters filled in some bits and pieces from what they could recall for me, and my mother has been willing to tell me a little, but my father has only mentioned his brother twice when I have been within earshot. Once when I was a teenager, before I knew anything of Richard's existence, my father was telling a story about canoeing, and offhandedly he said that his brother was in the canoe. I remember the jolt I felt when I heard my dad say "my brother." "What brother?" I said to myself, for I somehow knew this was not a question I could ask as we sat with company around the dining room table.

The other slip was a few years ago, again at the dinner table where many were gathered, this time at Christmas. This time my father was telling a rare story about his boyhood, about waiting up to see Santa Claus . . . with his brother. This time I knew more about Richard, and I longed to softly interrupt and say, "Dad, tell us about your brother." But I knew that even such a gentle suggestion was forbidden and respected the fortifications my father had placed around this part of his past.

Nonetheless, even unseen and unspoken of, Uncle Richard was a significant part of our family. He was missing, but he was definitely a presence. His shade hovered over family gatherings, over moments of crisis, over days of depression and hours of uncertainty. It was Richard who had kept my father awake when Tammy failed to come home from our school dance, haunting him through that long night. Maybe it was Richard's ghost that put my mother on edge; we had to be careful around her, be calm, be cheerful, and especially be in control. How did one man, one lost man, hand down such a legacy? I was to learn how his lasting influence lay in the incommensurability of his crime.

My father was twenty-nine in 1942—the year following Pearl Harbor. The pressure to enlist must have been intense. My mother had just given birth to their second daughter, my sister Anne, and my other sister, Katie, had just turned four. My mother had repeatedly begged my father not to enlist, but late one afternoon, without consulting her, he and a friend went to the Navy recruiting office and signed up. When he came in that evening and told her what he had done, she was nursing the baby.

She left him almost immediately and moved with my sisters to Tucson, where her own mother and father were living, but my parents' marriage survived the only impulsive step my father ever took in his life. My mother stayed in Tucson for a few weeks and then, missing my father terribly, she began to follow him across the country, little girls in tow, as he was moved from Jekyll Island, Georgia, to Cape Cod, Massachusetts, and finally to San Clemente Island, California, where he taught Navy pilots how to use radar.

Richard, as had been the pattern throughout his life, tried to follow my father's example. He too was married and had a son, Richard Jr. But when he went to enlist, he was turned away, stamped with a humiliating "4F" because of a testicular hernia. He desperately wanted to join up, but not one branch of the military would take him. Instead, he had to remain in civilian life, walking through the streets for the rest the war without donning the uniform he coveted. Inextricably tied to his manhood, his exclusion nagged him. Despite his relentless efforts, he could never equal the brilliance of his older brother. Apparently his disappointment was vast and deep.

When the war ended, my father decided to move his family from Michigan to California, and he went successfully about the business of buying a home for my mother and sisters in South Pasadena, passing the California bar exam, and landing a job practicing law in Los Angeles. As if on cue, Uncle Richard followed him and, likewise, moved his family—my Aunt Betty, Richard Jr., and now a new baby, Caroline Jean—also to the San Gabriel Valley, where he rented a house in Topanga Canyon. There the mystery begins.

Although Richard came to Southern California with several thousand dollars from the sale of his house in Michigan, the money soon disappeared. He never found a job; in fact, it's not clear he even looked for one. When Betty's parents visited, Richard complained that he felt the city a dangerous place, so his father-in-law gave him a gun. But where did the money go? Did he drink it away in the seedy, dark bars near the Green Hotel in Pasadena? Did he gamble it away at the Santa Anita Racetrack? Did he have a secret mistress, the mystery woman whose letter they found amongst his belongings? Nobody knows. However, it became clear that Richard was not going to prosper in Southern California. My grandparents wired him money to buy train tickets so he and his family could return to Michigan, and Richard made eccentrically secretive plans for their departure.

My mother and father were puzzled, fearful. My mother has told me what she can manage of that day, sixty years ago, in her own words:

> I knew something was very wrong. Richard wouldn't tell us anything. Your dad didn't go to work. Instead, we decided to go to the train station to see for ourselves that they all got safely on, but Richard wouldn't tell us which station they were leaving from. Your dad decided he would

drive into Los Angeles, to Union Station, and I would go to the Pasadena station. I was the one who found them there, in the station. But Richard had not purchased the tickets and all the money was gone again, mysteriously gone. They would not be able to leave. I took Betty into the women's room and begged her to come with me and let Richard follow. For some reason, he still had his car. But Betty refused to leave Richard. So I begged her to at least let me take Richard Jr. and Caroline Jean with me. Betty said "No." She wouldn't change her mind. They would all go with Richard in their car to our house in South Pasadena, and then they would decide what to do next.

My mother says she helplessly watched them with great misgivings pull away from the curb. Betty would not let her do anything, to help in any way. She walked back to her car alone, drove home dejectedly, and waited for them to pull up. She sat with my sisters on the front steps, watching for the car to come rolling down the palm-lined street. My father returned from Los Angeles. They continued to wait.

There is an undercurrent here—something was going on that my mother will not or cannot tell. Why did Richard keep the time and place of his impossible departure from my parents, from his brother? Why go through the charade of going to the train station at all? Why did he still have his car? Had he planned to put only Betty and the children on the train? Did my mother's unexpected appearance on the scene cause him to change his plans? Surely there must have been tension between the two brothers, perhaps even outright quarrels. My father would not have sat by quietly while his brother's life fell apart. He undoubtedly would have offered interminable advice whether asked for or not and with it, incessant disapprobation. There is something here that will always be a secret, which because of some sense of dread will never be articulated. What happened next could not have just come out of the blue.

The following is information I gathered not from my mother—she wouldn't have told me this—but from a Pasadena police report, submitted on November 11, 1947:

Leaving the train station behind, Richard drove the car to a deserted road near the Rose Bowl and parked under a bridge. He shot Betty in the head. (She lived, but was blinded for life.) He shot his son in the head as he sat in the back seat. (Richard Jr. died as he was being transported to the hospital.) Then he held Caroline Jean in his lap and killed her instantly by firing a bullet into her temple. He then put the gun in his own mouth, fired, and died.

My parents waited all night long, drifting in and out of an anxious slumber, only to be startled at dawn by a police officer's knock on the door, the bearer of the unthinkable.

My parents will never fully recover from this night.

In their fierce attempts to do so, they barred all mention of Richard, Betty, and the children from their lives. My grandparents destroyed all their family pictures that included Richard, and so there are no baby or childhood pictures of my father. In all our family albums, his life begins when he met my mother. It is only then that we see him for the first time, a dashing, tall athlete, her first and only love. There is only one surviving photo of my parents' large, elaborate wedding, and it is only my mother and father. Since Richard was my father's best man, all the other family photos taken that day were thrown away. The only wedding picture that displays my mother's entire family on her crowded wall of family photos is of her sister's wedding. It can hang as a permissible record of the past because Richard was not a member of that wedding party.

My parents and grandparents drew a line around the murders, the suicide, and Richard, a line so clear and real that even though I was shocked the first time my father crossed it by referring to his brother in a canoe, even though I had no part in the pact not to talk about this man, I respected it. I knew intuitively not to ask the most obvious question in the world, "What brother?"

Can they be blamed? My mother must have been devastated by sorrow, mixed with guilt, mixed with powerlessness. Surely she must still ask herself, "Why didn't I insist that Betty and the children come with me?" "Why didn't I just grab the children and run with them?" My father must be haunted by the questions a suicide leaves: "Why didn't I know?" "How did I let it go so far?" "Why didn't I act sooner?" "As his older brother, how am I to blame for his self-loathing?" But Richard's suicide must have paled in comparison to the murders.

On my copies of the front pages of the *Los Angeles Times* and the *Pasadena Star News*, headlines scream the sensational story along with our name. It's from these accounts that I get more information. I learn the gun was a German Luger. I learn where each person died and that my aunt, when she regained consciousness, told the doctor her husband had "slugged" her. She still did not know that she had been shot. She did not know her children and husband were dead. He must have shot her first. What a word—"slugged"—a word I would never use. Does it suggest that he had "slugged" her before? Just one little word, a word that implies a kind of hard-boiled detective novel, makes me suspect vast differences between my mother and Betty. If my mother were ever to report something like that, she would have said "hit," as in, "He hit me." But my father would never hit my mother; he reveres my mother. His lifelong task, or so it seems to me, has been to protect her, to quell her overwrought emotions, to soothe her distress. To make her happy.

It is from the newspapers that I learn about the "mystery woman." She is not mentioned until the second day's article as the investigation gears up. A love letter is found in my uncle's belongings, but it has no signature—only "'Nite Darling." I am eager to find out more, as were undoubtedly most of the population of Pasadena and even greater Los Angeles must have been. But the story stops there. The only follow-up is a small article days later, reporting that the coroner's inquest had been held—the case was ruled a double murder/suicide and closed. There would be no further investigation. Perhaps my father and grandfather had somehow intervened. The mystery woman's identity would never be uncovered.

The publicity must have been horrifying—murder, suicide, adultery. Such possibilities in life are so far removed from my unfalteringly conventional, protectively bourgeois, and intensely controlled upbringing that I am still taken aback as I am irresistibly drawn to this sensational chain of events. I know the aftermath. I know how completely the past was obliterated. But no matter how much my father denied his brother's life and death, it was never enough. No matter how formidably my father constructed the family battlements against a tragic past, Richard lay siege to our lives with a relentlessness that finally exhausted us all.

Martha's Vineyard, 2004

I was to be the child to heal their sorrows, to bring life where there had been death, promise where there had been tragedy, sweet dreams where there had been nightmare. I was to provide the balm from the River Lethe. My mother loves to tell the story of my father coming home and announcing with pride that they had enough money to join the country club. My mother replied, "If we have that much money, I think we should have another baby." I wonder now if she feared the country club would not admit them, given that the *Pasadena Star News* had not long before reported, "Richard Ellerby, brother of Tom Ellerby of South Pasadena, attempted to murder his wife before killing his six-year-old son and three-year-old daughter and then turning the gun against himself." Although my mother would later love to jest throughout my adolescence and on into my adulthood, "We should have joined the country club," I was welcomed into the family less than two years after my uncle's stunning exit. Like most of their generation after the terrible devastation of the war, my family had longed for the peace of normality. Instead, an emotional war waged on with unthinkable horror, suffering, and death.

For awhile, for almost sixteen years, I was the sweet surcease my parents had sought. I was an agreeable child, either eager to please or willing to remain unnoticed. If I was mischievous, it was something funny—like eating the dog's cookies or meticulously filling the fishpond with spoonful after spoonful of sand from my sandbox. I was a bit of a bother when at six I was roller skating too fast down our steep, curvy sidewalk and fell and broke my wrist. They were exasperated again when I said no to caution and broke the same wrist a few months later, falling out of a backyard tree. They were truly annoyed when at seven I recklessly ran in front of a girl on a rope swing, my collarbone snapping when she careened into me. This time my parents warned me: "Accidents happen because of carelessness." Chastised but still undaunted, at nine I organized a game with neighborhood friends to see who could jump from the highest tree limb in our neighbor's front yard. I won the contest and hobbled home with an aching foot.

I was so determined not to displease my parents that I waited hours to tell them I had hurt myself again. I sat in our huge downstairs playroom watching *The Mickey Mouse Club*, my foot propped on my doll's rocking chair. I was sure the pain would subside, but then I had to stagger upstairs to the dinner table, my foot blue and swollen. There could be no disguising that I had done it again, and I haven't forgotten my parents' irritation as they once again had to drive me to the emergency room at the Huntington Hospital so that I could have another cast molded to yet another limb.

As I look back at the little girl, sitting in front of the television, trying to ignore a broken bone in an effort not to displease her parents, I'm impressed by my resolve. It's notable that at nine I dreaded my parents' displeasure more than the pain of a bad break. But I see now there was an instructive ghost keeping me down there in the playroom, urging me to choke back my tears as best I could. Long before I ever heard his name, Richard had cast an aura of anxiety over our house. Invisible but almost palpable, my uncle's shadow made it clear to me and my sisters that we were not to upset our parents, to overwhelm their low tolerance for disruption with our antics. "Be a good girl," "Be a quiet girl," "Be an obedient girl," were the mantras whispered in my ear.

In one night before my birth, my parents had had their life's quota of grief. It filled all their reserves. I couldn't add more; I couldn't disappoint; I couldn't make my mother cry; I couldn't disillusion my father by revealing any tendency to be out of control, to be unpredictable, to be unhappy. "They've drawn the lines clearly," Richard whispered. "Obey—or disappear."

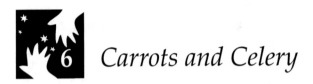

6 *Carrots and Celery*

South Pasadena, 1950

IN A PHOTOGRAPH OF ME at age two at our house on Fair Oaks Boulevard in South Pasadena, I am squatting in the sunny driveway with a small chalkboard and chalk. My hair is still a wispy baby blond; I'm wearing red corduroy pants and a tiny University of Michigan sweater—dark navy blue with a big, gold "M," the symbol of my parents' alma mater. They've dressed me with the confidence that I will be like them. Their career goals are written on me in the shape of that mighty "M," and I am already complying by "writing" industriously on my chalkboard. Innocently, I practice for the career my father will later choose for me when he sends me off to a large West Coast university. At two, I am their willing student of a certain life, and although my mother doubts my memory, I can still recall the comfort of that sweater and the attention I unfailingly got when I wore it. Even then its symbolic significance was not lost on me. I knew how pleased they were when they saw me in it.

Martha's Vineyard, 2004

Sixteen years later, upon entering college, I told my father I wanted to major in art, that I wanted to be an artist, but he rejected that choice posthaste. If he was going to send me to college, he wanted a good return on his investment; therefore, I was to opt for something more practical. He acknowledged that I might have some artistic talent, but to him, painting was a

Janet at two with Michigan sweater, 1950.
Photograph by Harold Thomas Ellerby. Courtesy of the author.

hobby, not a profession. Besides, he maintained no good could possibly come from spending four years in art studios under the sway of suspicious, bohemian professors. The thought of me spending hours at an easel, wearing sloppy, paint-bespattered clothes, with my hair falling long and lank down my back, made him shudder. He wanted to see me in neat skirts and crisp blouses carrying my tidy, well-organized notebooks to large lecture halls where long-winded, professorial men would pass on no-nonsense, pedestrian skills. At eighteen, still trying hard to win back my parents' favor, I was more than ever that wispy-haired little girl in her Michigan sweater who loved to please her father. So I quietly gave up my dream of an artist's life and obediently checked the box marked "Teacher Certification" on my "Declaration of Major" form.

San Marino, 1953

On my fifth birthday, May 18, 1953, we move to a big Mission-style Spanish house at 860 Winthrop Road, San Marino. This move—our family's transition from middle class to upper middle class—might have provided my parents with their first inkling of the extraordinary frustration I would provoke in my teens. I would not happily adjust to the change of address.

I was terrified of this house. I had seen its previous owner, Mrs. Bishop, when my parents took my sisters and me to see our new home. She was ancient, and my sisters, already eleven and fifteen, told me that she locked herself up in her bedroom every night, in fear of the ghost of Mr. Bishop who had died in the house. I can still recall sitting at the bottom of the marble staircase, crying miserably because I could not find the kitchen where I knew my mother was. I was told I was an ungrateful child, a crybaby, a bother, but I could not quell my fear of this new, uninviting space. I whined for our old house; no amount of reassurance would pacify me. I became fretful, clingy, unwilling to sleep in my very own bedroom, wanting back the security of my sister sleeping across the room from me. She, of course, was delighted to have a room of her own.

The beautiful red-tiled house, built solidly into a terraced hillside and surrounded by silvery olive trees and droopy eucalyptus, was a marvel, but it would always scare me. When I went back recently to see it, not much had changed, and I couldn't help but feel sympathy for the twin girls who live there now and will have to grow up listening in the dark to its nighttime creaks and groans. The house made me fearful, but it became a major dimension of our family's identity, so much so that when it came time for my parents to retire to San Diego, my eldest sister would purchase the house from them so that she too could be defined for awhile by its well-appointed rooms and lovingly groomed gardens.

The house's "great" room is at the bottom of the marble staircase. It's actually two huge rooms, divided by a bathroom. When I was a child, the smaller room contained a ping pong table and a dartboard. The larger room was the playroom, as it is now for the twin girls. Their flat-screen TV is still in the same corner that once held our massive old Motorola in its maple cabinet. Back then, as now, couches, tables, lamps, and shelves full of books and board games lined the walls. What's missing is the spooky, dark wooden chest that Mrs. Bishop had left behind, sitting in one corner, a forerunner of today's entertainment center. My father rigged it to contain our record player that eventually evolved into a stereo. It was there

I would play my records, listening for hours to *Peter and the Wolf* at age five, to the Beatles at fifteen, to Dylan, the Stones, the Doors at eighteen, nineteen, twenty. In the middle of the room, facing the capacious fireplace was a huge, forest green chair that we named quite simply the Big Chair. This room was perfect for making out.

Martha's Vineyard, 2004

By the time I inherited the playroom from my sisters as my own domain where I could invite my own boyfriend, it had already been witness to their teenage sexual experimentation. As a nosy kid sister, I had crept on socks down the stairs to spy on each of them as they sat in the Big Chair, kissing their boyfriends hungrily. My parents, who tried to contain our sexuality with an exceptional severity, had ingenuously purchased a home with a special room that begged for adolescent intimacy, one that was separate from the rest of the house, that muffled ardor, that gave us all time to straighten our blouses and pull down our skirts as soon as we heard someone coming down the noisy marble staircase.

My parents battled with my sisters bitterly over the boys that came and went at 860 Winthrop Road, though their fierce remonstrations never directly addressed anything more serious than "necking," my mother's term for those passionate kisses. Though left unsaid, my parents were surely thinking of those girls who got "in trouble." After all, they were faced with reining in three striking, nubile girls, one after the other. My mother insisted we dress in plain, loose skirts and sweaters, but despite her best efforts, nothing we wore could really hide our developing bodies. Like our mother, we were hopelessly robust, unconsciously sexy. Still, I don't think our parents believed we would dare to actually have sex.

Katie is ten years older than I am, which means that she was twenty-six in 1964, when I turned sixteen. While I was pummeled by a myriad of conflicting desires—mine, Alec's, my parents', and my friends'—she was already happily married and a mother. Anne—six years older than I—was already twenty-two and about to marry a man my parents despised. Each sister had been rebellious in her own way, but it seems to me that they had limited choices.

After all, when Katie was sixteen, it was 1954. Although the iconic sitcom *Leave It to Beaver* wouldn't come to television for three more years, popular culture was already constructing the highly circumscribed values and scripts that white, middle-class, suburban families like ours would adhere to. Katie skipped the upheaval of the sixties, when everything changed for me. After one disastrous foray into independence, she remained under the spell of the stultifying fifties and the protective shield of our parents' world. She welcomed the security of marriage at twenty-two to her San Marino high school sweetheart. They bought their first home in neighboring San Gabriel and had two babies—a boy and a girl. Katie agreeably adjusted to packing her husband's lunch before he left for the office with neat carrot and celery sticks that she kept crisp in gleaming bottles of water in her well-stocked refrigerator. Fifties ideology lasted well into the sixties, and by the time change might have touched her world, she was so inculcated into San Marino's unproblematic priorities that it could not have occurred to her that there was anything worth rebelling against. She wanted my parents' world; their values were hers without question.

Anne too was solidly influenced by the fifties. In 1960, when she turned eighteen, the civil rights movement had begun, but it was far, far away from Southern California. There was no Vietnam yet, no hippies. Her heartthrob had been Elvis. It would still be four years before the Beatles would appear on Ed Sullivan, five years until Bob Dylan would sing "Like a Rolling Stone." When she did marry Bill without our parents' consent, she was being rebellious indeed, but women had been eloping for a long time. Her bid for freedom was not tied to an era. She did this one radical thing, marrying a man who thumbed his nose at the financial security and material comforts my parents believed were the vital ingredients for a happy life. Nevertheless, despite their enduring disapproval, Anne settled into a domesticity not unlike Katie's, leading a conventionally mainstream life throughout the sixties.

But before that, back on Winthrop Road, I turned twelve in 1960, and by then, both my sisters had left home for good. I was effectively an only child in a big house with parents involved in their gratifying careers. I know now that an only child, rather than suffering a disadvantage, is supposed to benefit from her status as the focal point of parental atten-tion, from the lack of competition with siblings, and from the undiluted material stability of the family, but this was not the case for me. With the house to myself day after day, I had too much time to brood in those lovely, quiet rooms. As I write this, I know I sound ungrateful, as I was so often accused of throughout those years. No, I am not ungrateful, but I am struck by the contrast between my family's material wealth and my emotional neediness.

Today we hear that kids are overcommitted, driven to distraction by dance lessons, piano lessons, followed by gymnastics, followed by soccer practice and games galore on the weekends. I am not sure this distrac-tion is a bad thing. Not much was required of me during my adolescent afternoons other than to remember to put the meatloaf in the oven. Such languishing left me too hungry for people. I planned a lifetime of escapes, longing for the life-affirming bustle I seemed to find everywhere else but home. My lonesomeness let friends like Jackie hold much more control over me than I should have allowed them. Pop music became a steadfast friend and teacher that I turned to with an avidity that if not extraordinary for a teenager, was too intense. And eventually, Alec became a much more necessary companion than he should have been.

7 The Assassination

San Marino, 1963

I CAN NAME THE DAY when I began to mistrust my parents' values. It was momentous for America: Kennedy's assassination. My parents had loathed JFK, and when he defeated their champion, Richard Nixon, they believed the country was in real danger. He was a Democrat, a Catholic, young, untested, untrustworthy. (How ironic this sounds given the deviousness of their candidate, though that would take another ten years to expose.) They made fun of Jackie Kennedy, of her "accent" and mannerisms when she gave her televised tour of the redecorated White House. They loved to hear and tell the latest anti-Kennedy jokes. Back in 1960, they had objected to my sister Anne dating a boy because he had a "Kennedy for President" bumper sticker on a car. I listened and assumed they were right. And then, suddenly, the president was dead.

All of us, of a certain age, can remember where we were.

Friday, November 22, 1963

I am at school, and it's lunchtime; I'm standing in the outside lunch court in line to buy a hamburger that I will then take to a low wall by the girl's gym where Alec and I meet everyday for lunch and between classes. The principal, Mr. White, comes over the loudspeaker to tell us that the president has been shot in Dallas. My friends and I are surprised but not overly concerned. We take it for granted that the president of the United States could not be in any real danger. We are at the age when our bodies feel invincible. We've grown up with nourishing food, antibiotics, x-rays, vaccinations. We get sick only to get well. We break a bone only to have it heal neatly. We have no idea yet how easily the human body can be torn apart, how fragile the cerebrum is the instant the skull has been pierced, how easy it is to cross the irrevocable line from alive to dead. We still don't think of death as inevitable. To us it's always preventable given "the wonders of modern medicine."

It is only minutes later and I've almost reached the front of the line at the cafeteria window when Mr. White is back on the PA system, his voice husky. He struggles to make his terrible announcement: "Our president is dead." I can't remain there now with the other bewildered students. Instead, I leave the line and head for the wall where I know Alec will be waiting for me. When I get there, we ponder together the enormity of this catastrophe. Alec accepts the broadcast, but I refuse to believe Mr. White's words. I insist that they will bring the president back from death. It will be one of those miracles—dead for thirty minutes only to be revived. Kennedy himself will tell us later of not being ready to go down that long tunnel toward the beckoning white light. Of all men, surely the doctors will save this man. Such faith is testimony to my adolescent sense of indestructibility, though my naïveté will be shaken in the days that follow.

Sunday, November 24, 1963

I am sitting on the floor in our playroom, reading the Sunday comics. My brother-in-law is sitting in the Big Chair, watching TV. On the screen we see Lee Harvey Oswald being walked down a crowded corridor as he is moved from the jail in Dallas to the courthouse. "Bam!" My brother-in-law jumps up and starts shouting: "He shot him! That man—there! He just shot Oswald!" I saw it too, but again, I deny the possibility of any real harm. Such things just can't happen in the world as I know it where presidents are invincible and assassins cannot murder assassins.

Monday, November 25, 1963

Again I am in the playroom, this time by myself, curled up in the Big Chair. The entire nation is at home today to watch the funeral on television. I watch the caisson move slowly down Pennsylvania Avenue. Jackie is sheathed in black with Carolyn and John-John in front of her. When I see John-John salute his father, the world shifts. My universe is remade. Death awaits even the most powerful. Kennedy died just as surely as Oswald did. His body was nothing extraordinary; it surrendered life just as inexorably as his killer's did. And this man, who my parents had denigrated, who they had told coarse jokes about, this man was good and moral; he was a man to be respected, revered, and mourned. My parents were wrong.

Martha's Vineyard, 2004

Kennedy's assassination ushers in for me with searing lucidity my parents' fallibility. It is a remarkable transition, for now I judge them with disdain for their myopia. They seem small and petty and hardhearted, and I see myself as different. I don't know quite what I am, but I know for the first time and for sure that I am not like them. And, more importantly, I do not want to be.

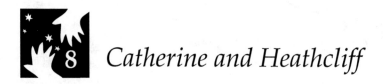

Catherine and Heathcliff

THE BEATLES. Their arrival changes everything. Sitting in the Big Chair, I watch them on the *Ed Sullivan Show,* and for some weird reason, I too want to scream along with the shrieking girls in the TV audience. At age ten, I had seen clips of girls screaming over Elvis and had scorned their hysteria, but now it was happening to me. I fell hard for the Beatles, especially George. Everyone else was in love with Paul, but from the beginning, I loved George. He was already the "Quiet Beatle," and I identified with his marginality in the midst of wild popularity. I bought all their records and, tucked away in the corner of the playroom, listened to them over and over again for hours. Jackie, Caroline, Tammy, and I bought tickets to watch them on closed-circuit TV at the Academy Theater, and we screamed mindlessly for the entire two-hour program. I wallpapered my bedroom with Beatles posters, although after I got caught trying to get into the Civic Auditorium with Caroline, my mother tore them all down and put them out with the trash.

She was troubled by my passion, my zeal for those four young musicians who to her looked sinister. She didn't want me to feel that much for anything. As I look now at their first album cover, all four of them look so utterly respectable in their expensive French suits and their trimmed bangs and skinny ties. It's almost inconceivable that she found them threatening. But at the time they were very different from anything in Southern California, and her daughter was clearly and perversely under

49

their spell. Why were they so foreboding to her? Did she presciently know just how much music would influence our generation? We hadn't yet heard a protest song, although Dylan was already singing "Blowing in the Wind." That spring, it was all about the Beatles and we were passionately in their thrall.

For my mother, the Beatles were emblematic of my undoing. Like many parents then and now, rock and roll was her scapegoat. She could blame it for everything. And truly I relinquished all levelheadedness and succumbed to the hysteria that these four mop heads could whip up. The door to outside influences was wide open. At the same time that I was listening to "Love, Love Me Do," I was also listening to "Cast Your Fate to the Wind," and it wouldn't be long before the tambourine man would be beckoning as well.

I knew other girls that spring that had steady boyfriends, but I couldn't imagine they were having sex. The only female folksinger I knew was Joan Baez, and although she seemed to be a free spirit with her long hair and bare feet, she also appeared to be virginally pure as she sang so ethereally her mournful love songs. It seemed to me that if I finally gave in to Alec's importuning, I would be the only sixteen-year-old in San Marino to have had intercourse, to have lost my virginity—so young, so young!

Alec and I talked about "it" shyly. I told him I feared the consequences, that if he "got what he wanted," he would despise me afterwards. Though I couldn't articulate it effectively, I understood intuitively the way the exchange would work: he would gain masculine capital, and I would be "used goods," unappealing, maybe even ruined. He assured me over and over again that that would not be the case. I can still remember him sitting in the Big Chair asking me to marry him—some day. We would be married, he said; we would go to live in New Zealand, a faraway island that fascinated him; we would have scads of children. He described our cottage, its roses, and its garden path. It was a dreamy adolescent fantasy, and I came to believe in it. I thought he did too.

So my surrender, I rationalized, would not be a downfall. It would be more like a consummation that would seal our love forever. And I had my role models. I had been reading *Wuthering Heights* in Miss Fenner's class that semester. I'm not sure this wildly romantic novel is a sensible choice for adolescents with not an ounce of skepticism. Completely swayed by Catherine and Heathcliff's romance, I was so eager for them to consummate their love that I, like Hollywood, completely ignored the second half of the novel. Young Catherine and Hareton's love—Emily Brontë's sensible, balanced answer to the reckless tragedy that was Catherine and Heathcliff—was completely lost on me. Miss Fenner added more fuel to my fire by assigning *Romeo and Juliet* after we had all seen *West Side Story.* At least, I thought, Romeo and Juliet and their modern-day versions, Tony and Maria, had one night together before they had to die for one another. I thought I should keep my virginity but at the same time I was moved by "carpe diem." So it seemed necessary that I had to ecstatically relinquish my virginity to my one true love in order to ensure that our promises would last forever.

Our country was deep into the Cold War by this time, and we had been having civil defense drills since I was in grade school, getting under our desks and curling into a ball, absurdly warned not to look at the windows because if we saw the nuclear flash, it would blind us. My parents never prepared a fallout shelter for us, but the Penningtons up the block had stocked their basement with canned foods, powdered milk, medicines, first aid kits, cots, blankets, huge plastic jugs of water, flashlights, and a complicated-looking radio. I liked that shelter, mostly because I liked the idea of a secret place, like a clubhouse with fantastic provisions to hide away in, but the prospective of catastrophic destruction and my own death never registered.

Once I fell in love with Alec and we began our ongoing sexual foreplay, I did worry that if the bomb were to fall, I would die without having experienced our ultimate destiny—what finally we all were here for, or so it felt. Again, contradictory cultural voices were pulling me one way, then the other: "Do it! Do it now before it's too late!" and "You will pay; you will pay dearly."

The other compelling reason for capitulation was that Alec was graduating and would be leaving in the fall for the University of Hawaii. He wanted to be a marine biologist and a surfer. What better place to pursue both careers? I had two more years of high school, four more of college, and then, only then, would we be able to marry. Kids from San Marino did not marry upon graduating from high school. We all went to college; there were no other options.

So, with zeal and determination, I worked out a quixotic theory for romantic completion: Catherine had made her fatal error by failing to make love to Heathcliff as they roamed the moors as teenagers. Had she done so, that would have sealed their love forever, and she would never have married Edgar and died of a broken heart. I would not be Catherine. Alec and I would be "one." I don't believe in that kind of transcendence now, but at the time I believed the "act" would be accompanied by a blinding conflagration of body and spirit. Like Catherine, when she declares herself to Nelly, saying, "I am Heathcliff," I would be able to proclaim, "I am Alec." We would be "married" physically and spiritually for life. Better to risk heartbreak than nothing. This echoed another cultural lesson learned from Miss Fenner's classroom to feed my newfound convictions, one that high school sophomores still ponder and probably act on today when they read that line in Tennyson's "In Memoriam": "Better to have loved and lost than never to have loved at all."

Was I foolish? Yes. Was I naïve? Utterly. Was I impressionable? Definitely. Was I in love? Hopelessly.

Martha's Vineyard, 2004

Of the spring of '64, I have to write about love because whether it is socially constructed, chemical, spiritual, or magical, by the time I turned sixteen, I was genuinely, ardently, and absolutely in love with Alec. I use those superlatives because they apply. My parents wanted to brush off my attachment to him as insignificant. My mother dismissed it as "puppy love." I am still not sure what that would be, since I have always fallen "head over heels" in love "at first sight" with every puppy I've ever had. "Puppy love," as my mother would have defined it, is feeble, uncomplicated, and limited by immaturity and lack of experience. But my love for Alec was none of those. It was formidable, complex, and unconditional for a long time. I gave myself over to a degree of love that no one but me would finally believe in, not even Alec. Such an overwhelming attachment is puzzling for a young girl, and perhaps can only be explained by my loneliness and my unquenchable craving for affection and approval. I needed him everywhere and always.

And in the ardor was lust. I do not intend to mislead by playing the role of the put-upon naïf. Alec was not simply the unrelenting, unappeasable aggressor, and I was not simply the innocent, unwilling victim. True, I was unprepared and uninformed. We both were. But the fervor he felt for me was no more than I felt for him. I wanted him to hold me endlessly, to sleep in my bed, to kiss me again and again forever.

Despite the rumblings of a sexual revolution in the offing, such an upheaval of long-held, sacred ideals had not yet reached San Marino. The intact hymen was still the symbol for the essential marker of female value. I had believed for a long time that my virginity was something that should only be offered up on my wedding night. If only figuratively, the bloody sheet still had to wave outside the bedroom window the next morning. But this law was yielding under the persuasive rhetoric of my various advisors: Paul McCartney, George Harrison, Emily Brontë, William Shakespeare, and Alfred Lord Tennyson. My own desire, the fiery rush that would wash through me whenever Alec took me into his arms, let me hear their words as corroboration for all that I thought I would ever want or need. Foolish and misled, there I stood, poised on a dream precipice, ready to dive into what I madly trusted was a pool of bliss eternal.

The Avocado Couch

San Marino, Early Summer 1964

AND SO THE NIGHT in late June arrives. Alec is ill, recovering from pneumonia that developed from a bad cold he caught at the all-night graduation party. His parents are away. His sister is somewhere else. I can drive myself to his house now, having only that week passed my driver's test and gotten my license.

Although I have had a great deal of abstract preparation for this moment, I have not been prepared in any practical way on how to prevent pregnancy. I have never had that conversation with my mother, with a teacher, not even with my older sisters. I have whispered about it with my girlfriends, but they know next to nothing—even Caroline, whose doctor father made her write a report on the dangers of alcohol poisoning. I do know that conception occurs when a sperm penetrates an egg, but I do not know when this would most likely happen during a menstrual cycle, which means I don't even have a basic understanding of the rhythm method. What I do have is classic erroneous folklore, somehow circulating in adolescent subcultures then and now. Jackie must have gotten some bit of advice reversed because she has told us that you can't get pregnant right in the middle of the month. We all believe a girl can't get pregnant "the first time." Our only sex education had occurred four years prior, in the sixth grade when we were twelve: the girls went to see one film about menstruation and hygiene and the boys a film about—well, I don't know, but certainly not birth control. By the time we got to high school, those brief and vague films with their embarrassing diagrams were no defense against reality. There I was: fertile, passionate, and unprotected.

I would like to make this part of the story humorous, or dramatic, or poignant at least. I would like to say it exceeded all my romantic expectations. But if truth be told, it was a seedy and loveless night, one I stumbled through submissively and without any sense of self-direction or choice. In my mind's eye, the night is colorless because the only lighting was the black-and-white TV that stayed on during our hour together.

Alec greeted me at the front door and we got right down to the serious task at hand. Because he was ill, he undressed me but he remained dressed. This was not unlike the way we usually made out. He would explore my body. I would passively acquiesce, a fairly typical sexual arrangement of the times. That night he had on a white button-down shirt and a blue mohair v-neck sweater. He hardly had any need to shave yet, but I can remember the little facial hair he did have tickling my upper lip and the astringent smell of the white acne medicine still visible on his chin.

We were lying on the family couch, gray in the half-light of the TV but actually avocado green. The textures of the evening come back with amazing clarity, and I can still feel this ugly couch, nubby, almost warty—weirdly appropriate in its toad-like hue. This time Alec did actually manage to enter me by prodding, pressing, and pushing slowly but persistently as I lay very still beneath him. I was too shy to touch him, to guide him, too scared to respond in any way; instead I just held still like an obedient child, focused not on the romance I had anticipated but on the discomfort of it all. Rather than passionate, I was fixed on the idea that we must be doing something wrong. This was just too painful. And then suddenly he pulled out and I realized that moisture was seeping into the couch. We both scrambled up; trembling, I turned my back and pulled up my underpants and jeans. I never did see his penis; I was too inhibited to look, more ashamed than curious.

When he turned on the unforgiving, glaring lamp, I could see a large wet spot of what looked like blood on the couch. Alec ran for two towels and we scrubbed at the offending spot. Zealous in our concern over the couch, we did not acknowledge what had just happened. He said he would tell his mother he had turned over his TV dinner by accident, an excuse that seemed much more plausible than the reality.

Time for me to go home. He walked me to the side, louvered door, hugged me, and murmured that he loved me. Then he said something puzzling: "We can never do it *like that* again," and then he added, "Go home and take a hot bath, as hot as you can stand it."

What did he mean by *"like that"*?

I drove home shakily, already lonely and full of trepidation, but it wasn't until I got into that excruciatingly hot bath tub and watched the thin stringy blood seeping out of my sore vagina that I realized what might have happened. Had he "come" inside me? Is that what he meant by *"like that"*? And all the blood on the couch, in my underpants, and now this! I put on a clean pair of white underpants and fiercely scrubbed the ones I had been wearing, hoping maybe that it was menstrual blood. In the morning there was one more spot of blood, and then, it stopped—no more blood, none at all.

I was just sixteen. It was 1964. I was sheltered. Neither Alec nor I knew know how to talk about sex. We were brought up in a culture where sex was never articulated. There were layers of inhibition, self-conscious-ness, and shame that kept me from asking Alec the simple question, "Did you come?"

So that was it, the first time. No transcendent melding of body and spirit, no conflagration of souls, no unbreakable seal that would now bind us to one another forever. I was not Catherine and he, ill in his fuzzy sweater, was surely no Heathcliff. We had fumbled through an awkward, embarrassing overture to sex, not atypical in its gracelessness, not un-usual in its uncertainty. But its consequences for me would be profound and enduring.

California Girl

California, Summer 1964

BY THE SUMMER OF 1964, I had only left California for classic family vacations—at three, for a cross country trip to my grandparents' home in Michigan; at six, for a summer excursion to British Columbia; at eight, for a camping trip in the Oregon Cascades. These privileged forays offered few glances of what "the other" might be. I was as seamlessly woven into a Southern California stereotype as one possibly could be. It was a hypnotic time for teenagers and called for absolute allegiance to a particular script. When the Beach Boys sang about Del Mar and Doheny Way (*Surfin' USA*, 1963), they were singing about the beaches my friends and I went to; when Jan and Dean made lighthearted fun of "The Little Old Lady from Pasadena" (1964), they were singing about my extended neighborhood. We had all seen the movie *Gidget*. I had read and reread the dog-eared *Gidget* paperback (Frederick Kohner, 1957) that Jackie had gotten her hands on and passed among us. I was fascinated by Gidget's sexual adventurousness, impressed that she spent the night in a surfer's hut on the Malibu beach with the "Great Kahoona." I was growing up in the middle of a pop culture phenomenon that fascinated a nation that was full of teenage boomers.

A friend from Georgia recently told me that when she was a teenager, her girlfriends and she envied the tanned, beach girl adolescence I was living. But cultural ideology often blurs self-consciousness, providing us with little perspective and, therefore, almost no conception that one's moment in history is somehow remarkable. To me, everything seemed natural. Steeped in the self-centeredness of adolescence, it seemed as if the Beach Boys were singing about my town and my friends, which only normalized our lives and made it even more important that I measure up to the "California girl" iconography. Once the hit song came out about a shy girl's "itsy-bitsy, teenie-weenie, yellow, polka-dot bikini" (Brian Hyland, 1960), we all knew that we had to have such a bikini—two-piece bathing suits that hid our belly buttons were hideous. For that important summer of '64, my mother refused to buy me a bikini, but Jackie had two and her blue one fit me perfectly. With school out for the summer, we could take the little ferry from her parents' house in Balboa over to Newport Beach for the entire day, wearing nothing more than our bikinis. We were long and lean with golden tans achieved by hours in the sun slathered with baby oil mixed with Mercurochrome.

There are many privileges that go with being raised by successful professionals, among them a family beach house in Balboa, and long, lazy summers with no need for a summer job. I loved the beach and Jackie's company, but the other welcome opportunity for me was the chance to go to summer camp. I had been going to camp since I was eight. It was a way for my parents to keep me occupied in the summer, and once I entered adolescence, it must have been a relief for them to see me off on the train, safely away from the temptations of Balboa, Newport, bikinis, and surfers. The train took us from LA to San Francisco; there we would board a bus for Plantation Camp, about one hundred miles north, close to Sea Ranch and Mendocino. I loved it there. I learned to ride horses, milk cows, paddle canoes, start camp fires, sing dozens of camp songs, square dance, and revel unabashedly in my tall, strong body that at home felt embarrassing and ungainly. I had always been self-conscious of my height, and I was never skinny. I looked at my petite friends enviously, but at camp my athleticism was appreciated; it was there that I could take pride in my energy. The counselors and my fellow campers valued vitality and endurance more than docility.

This particular summer was going to be special. Rather than stay in camp for the entire month, a group of us would travel to the High Sierras where we would backpack into the wilderness area with our sleeping bags and food. Knowing I would have my period while we were gone, I conscientiously packed sanitary pads in my backpack—tampons were only for "married women," I had been told. As we tramped up and over the pristine Sierras, my period did not start. As I lay awake in my sleeping bag after everyone else was sound asleep and allowed myself to consider the possibility this signified, I was filled with mind-boggling dread. While gazing at billions of stars, I would pound my stomach, kneading, squeezing and gouging at the space where I imagined my uterus lay. I hiked at a frantic pace, always in the lead, always volunteering to take on more weight so that my backpack would be agonizingly heavy and demand too much of me. When we stopped to swim, I would plunge into the crystal-clear snowmelt, allowing no time for my body to adjust to the frigid water. When we completed the backpacking trip and returned to camp, we rode horses bareback. I kept my horse at a trot, bouncing off her backbone rather than lead her into the gentle gait of a canter. I tried to eat as little as possible, but I was ravenous and the camp food was irresistible. Nonetheless, despite all the melodramatic treatment I inflicted on myself, when it came time to return to San Marino, I had to throw all the unused pads down the outhouse toilet.

At home, the remaining weeks of summer passed slowly. The consequence that I had feared most about having sex with Alec had come true. While I was away at camp, he had found a new girlfriend. Her name, absurdly but appropriately, was Candy. She was his age and already had a "reputation." One night, after dark, as I accompanied my parents home from dinner out, we passed Alec's car at an intersection, and there was Candy, smoking a cigarette and sitting close to Alec as he drove one-handed, his right arm draped around her shoulders. I knew my parents had seen them too, but we all said nothing, though they must have suspected how devastated I was by what the flash of the headlights had revealed.

But was I devastated? Did I even want to see Alec? Did I want to confront him with the possible consequences of doing it "like that"? I was certainly sad to see him with Candy, but I was also relieved. I felt safe peering out from the dark backseat of my father's car. Had Alec been waiting for me upon my return to take up where we had left off, I might have had to tell him what I feared might be happening to my body—and to do so, I would have had to say to him and to myself, "I think I'm pregnant." That was impossible. I hadn't gained a pound; my stomach was still flat and taut. I never felt like throwing up. I had no cravings. Surely pregnancy had to feel like something.

I would see Alec two more times that summer. The first was a chance encounter while I was again staying with Jackie in Balboa, still wearing her blue bikini and looking slim and lithe. Alec was staying in Newport, and we watched each other warily from a distance at the beach at Fifteenth Street one day. That night, Jackie and I ran into him and his friends at the small fairgrounds in Newport. He took my hand and led me out to the beach and into the darkness under the pier.

"Can we do it one more time?" he asked.

Alec did not want to talk; he did not want to apologize about Candy; he did not want to comfort me. He wanted to have sex again before he left for college. Silent and unyieldingly, I extricated myself from the embrace I thought I had been waiting for. Unconsciously I must have known that any demonstration of concern on his part, however calculated, would have released a confession from me that I could not have borne. Stunned by his heartless request, I walked alone back to the fairgrounds, crestfallen and confused.

Martha's Vineyard, 2004

The California Girl—caught in a web of messages that ranged from sleeping with the "Great Kahoona," to hiking like a demented banshee through the High Sierra, to looking slender and golden on the sandy shoreline. The allure is still there. Even now in my fifties, I want my hair long even when everyone tells me, "You'd look so much younger if you cut it." I ruefully apply the SPF 30 and resentfully plop a hat on my head before heading outdoors. I still want that flat, taut stomach and jog miles a week (in vain) to keep it so. I have wisely given up bikinis, miniskirts, and those dark suntans. I've managed to relinquish many of the accouterments of the "California Girl." And Southern California will most likely never be my home again. Still, I cannot bow out completely. I can still see her—my adolescent idol—looking out over her blue Pacific as the sun sets gorgeously into the west.

Why hold onto such trappings? After all, when I tempted fate by taking my own "dead man's curve" (Jan and Dean, 1964), I collided with a realm of intimacy I had no idea how to interpret. Blinded by both a blitz of freewheeling messages and a bubble-like naïveté, I clung as long as I could to a kind of beatific vision of romance and to an iconic girl, who was, in fact, about to crash to the earth, wings melted by a daring, foolish faith in love eternal.

11 *San Marino—Mid-Sixties*

SAN MARINO IS LOVELY. The streets are immaculate; the yards are meticulously groomed. There are no apartment houses, no duplexes, no bars, and only a handful of restaurants, none of which serve liquor. Huntington Drive, with its wide expanse of well-kept lawn and carefully pruned trees, meanders down the middle of this small, "bedroom" community of doctors, lawyers, and executives, the more subtly well-off of Los Angeles's workforce. And, of course, their wives and children, mirroring their environs, are also immaculately groomed and polished.

Heading down Huntington Drive from South Pasadena and Alhambra, past Twohey's and Ralph's Market and entering San Marino, you sense a difference immediately. There's little ostentatiousness in this community. It is not well known for its zip code, like Beverly Hills; few movie stars choose to live here; but it does have its own rituals of decorum, understated but rigid. In 1964, there were no African Americans, no Asian Americans, and no Latinos living in San Marino. They came in old trucks or by bus to mow the lawns and clean the houses. There was one Jewish family that I know of, though they were quite secular; there were very few Catholics. Of all the children in my class, only one, Sandra, had parents who had divorced. Sandra's mother, a chain smoker, lived up to our version of the stereotypical divorcée. She seemed rough and unpredictable to us. She yelled at Sandra and her sisters in a community where no one else we knew ever raised their voices.

San Marino was the epicenter for the Protestant, nuclear family, a place so relentlessly white bread that the unswervingly conservative John

Birch Society chose to locate its headquarters there. Though there were no perceptive gates cordoning off the community from its neighbors, its boundaries were unmistakable. My sisters and I were so "protected" from difference that our occasional forays to neighboring, "exotic" Pasadena for Mexican food or to downtown LA for my father's annual office Christmas party seemed like perilous sorties.

Traveling toward the San Gabriel Mountains on Huntington Drive, you'll first pass Stoneman School, still a quaintly beautiful stucco and tile California gem, which I attended from kindergarten to fourth grade. It was there that I first felt like an outsider. Already big for my age with a noticeable speech impediment and hand-me-down clothes from my older sisters, I knew immediately I didn't have the polish of my fellow classmates. I was excruciatingly shy, so fearful of my first-grade teacher, Mrs. Quigly, that I wet my pants one day rather than ask to be excused to go to the bathroom. The result, a large, startling puddle under my chair, was immediately noticed, and my mortification was even more absolute when that school nurse made me wait outside her office in the hall for my mother, my dress wet and clinging to my thighs as my snickering classmates traipsed by for lunch.

As you continue down Huntington Drive, you'll see the Shopping Basket, where we stole the vodka, the pharmacy, where we went for Heath Bars and Sugar Babies, the Colonial Kitchen, where my family sometimes went for hamburgers and I was allowed to order a black-and-white sundae for dessert. You'll pass Catherine and Tammy's neighborhood before coming to Huntington School, my junior high school. Huntington School remains in my memory as significant for two things: long division and puberty, neither of which I would traverse with ease.

In fifth grade, Mrs. Eerie made me stand at the chalkboard until I either solved the long division problem she had written for me or I cried. If I cried, then I had to memorize another verse of "The Midnight Ride of Paul Revere." Up to this point, I had only felt marginalized by my height, my speech (which by now, after considerably therapy, passed as normal), and my hand-me-downs. But now Mrs. Eerie made me feel stupid, too.

Desperate to gain any measure of status, I told my classmates—Joanne, Christy, Ellen, and Cindy—that I was going to try out for the Mickey

Mouse Club. This falsehood was excessive and unsustainable, an indication of the depth of my ingenuousness that I thought I could get anyone to believe me. I had never had a dance or voice lesson in my life. I knew nothing about how a ten-year-old would even begin to enter the competitive world of television, but I longed to be a Mouseketeer like Karen with my own Mouseketeer costar, Cubby. The other girls caught on quickly that I was fabricating an impossible counterlife, but my own life seemed so unsubstantial and flawed that I persisted in finessing the story until my would-be friends refused to play with me at all. I can't help but wonder if those girls, now women with their own grown children, remember my pitiful gambit for acceptance. Can they now sympathize with the needs of a child who thought that she could gain a place in their clique with such a foolhardy tall tale?

Huntington School embodies the lingering frustration of my failure to fit in, but it also stands for puberty. It seemed to happen quickly, almost in a matter of weeks. Not my period, not that for a while. First, breast buds, tender and embarrassing; then oily hair and tiny pimples dotting the entire surface of my forehead, which I covered assiduously with greasy bangs that I scotch-taped to my forehead every night to get them to lie straight. I went to a swimming party at the twin's house—Lynn and Leslie—and was confronted by Caroline, naked, her pubic and underarm hair so obvious. I stared. Wasn't she ashamed of this perverse turn of events? She seemed to be flaunting her new body. None of that for me. Jackie was the only girl I knew who actually wanted to start her period, but she was also my only friend whose mother wore lingerie and whose father had a collection of paperback soft porn. Only what I saw as family corruption could account for her unnatural desire.

Most of us wanted to be tomboys forever. I played hard with the boys and girls of my neighborhood, trying to be as daring as possible. I was twelve when I was caught breaking windows in an old estate near Winthrop Road that was soon to be torn down to make way for more suburbia. A police cruiser swept up to the house, and we took off, running to the four winds at full speed. But I, who have never been able to get away with much, stepped on a small piece of wood with a protruding nail that went straight through my sneaker and into my foot. Unable to run with the block of wood attached to the rubber sole of my shoe and the nail in my heel, I had to stop, sit down, and try to pull it out. The police officer caught up with me there on the ruined tennis court, frantically trying to pull out the piece of wood as my sneaker filled with blood. Everyone else had escaped over the wall, but I was caught and in tears. He drove me home in the police car and rang the doorbell at my house.

Before he left and my exasperated mother took me once again to the emergency room, this time for a tetanus shot, she insisted I give up the names of the kids who had been with me. Oddly enough, I didn't betray the friends I was with. Instead, I told on Douglas, who wasn't there at all, the boy on whom I had my first secret crush. Douglas told me later that the policeman came to his door, but his mother told the officer that Douglas never played on the grounds of the old estate. In fact, I don't think he did play there. He was an obedient boy in school and had no reason to pull madcap stunts that could get you brought home in a police cruiser. Maybe I wanted Douglas to be bad too, to do whatever it took to resist our percolating hormones with my ferociousness, but he remained disciplined and in control all the way into manhood—never once disappointing his mother, who had so quickly come to his defense when the policeman I had sent came knocking.

That year my mother took me to a dermatologist who earned his fee by explaining that not only did I have to wash my hair more often, I had to wash my face morning and night. I'm not sure why my mother or sisters had neglected to teach me these details of personal hygiene—but somehow they had been overlooked. Well past childhood and on into adolescence, I had been allowed to go for days without bathing. That I had to be taken to a doctor to learn about the benefits of cleanliness seems unusual given our milieu. Maybe my sisters were just so glad to get their bothersome little sister into bed at night that a bath was easy to overlook.

I hated my pimples, so I followed the dermatologist's regimen and they slowly disappeared. But there was no stopping my expanding breasts and hips, and thick brown blood that showed up one day in my underpants shortly after I turned thirteen. I asked my mother for a pad and belt, a horrible contraption I'd seen my sisters fiddle with, and was mortified when the first thing she said nervously to my father when he came through the door that evening was, "Janet started her period." Were they already worried about this marker of my sexuality? Did my transformation from an impish, reckless child to a worrisome, reckless teenager happen in one afternoon? I think so, for from then on we all seemed on different terms.

As you continue up Huntington Drive, you pass St. Albans Drive, a street lined with huge pines that each Christmas are strung by professionals with colored lights—nothing garish for San Marino, but lovely, every year, so lovely. If you turn left on St. Albans, you will arrive at Lacy Park, and with just a few more turns, at Oxford Road and the Huntington Library. Both were havens of my childhood.

Lacy Park was where I went to Brownie day camp. Recently, I took the opportunity to walk through the park. Astoundingly, forty-five years later, the shady grove of trees where my troop gathered on summer mornings was still there and still a favorite spot, judging by the children playing under the grove's protective beauty. Even the public bathrooms in the park had not been remodeled, and I was reminded of our peals of laughter when we crept into the boys' bathroom, fifty years ago, to see a urinal for the first time. In the spring of 1964, I would walk through the park after school with Alec. By crawling into a thick clump of bushes, we found a private hollow where we could be alone. Lying flat on our backs, looking up together through the tangled branches of the overgrown bushes and into the pallid evening sky, felt like a state of grace. We seemed blessed by the privacy of our little woody sanctuary. Perhaps not Catherine and Heathcliff on the moors, but we had found our own retreat in a place that didn't feel closeted and wrong like the cramped back seat of his car or the tempting but risky playroom at home.

When I came home with my sweater covered with grass and twigs, my mother readily accepted my excuse that I had been climbing trees and rolling down the hills. She wanted to believe me, as all parents want to believe their children, and, in fact, only months before I had indeed been rolling down the hills of Lacy Park, screeching with delight at the twirl of the barreling world as I picked up speed. My fabrication was not implausible, but I knew it was necessary. I had a secret life now that couldn't include my mother or father.

After leaving Lacy Park, you keep an eye out for Oxford Road; that's where you'll find, discreetly marked, the entrance to the Huntington Library. When I tell people that my favorite place in my hometown is a library, they are always dubious unless they have visited it themselves, for this Versailles-like wonder is hardly a neighborhood library. You can't check out books there, or even sit quietly and read unless you are a scholar with special permissions. Instead, it is a series of amazing gardens and palatial galleries.

As a child I always wanted to go to the library when we had visitors in town. Until I was ten, I was not allowed to enter the galleries, but the grounds were enough to absorb me. My parents loved the Cactus Garden and would dawdle over each exotic plant, but what I wanted was to get to the Japanese Garden. The garden itself spans two hillsides that meet at a series of lily ponds interlaced by sculpted, concrete stepping stones and winding stairs that meander up the far hill to the Japanese Tea House. There is a huge iron gong that I could hit with a swinging piece of wood, and the deep commensurate BONG would reverberate thrillingly through me and then the garden. I badly wanted to be able to cross the ponds by way of the arched red wooden bridge, but it was roped off because a woman had slipped on it and broken her leg. When I turned ten, I was finally allowed to enter the galleries, and I always tried to seem impressed by the Gutenberg Bible and Poe's manuscript of "Annabelle Lee." But it was to the largest, climate-controlled and carefully lit gallery of paintings, in front of Mrs. Siddons that I always wanted to return.

Everyone expected me to be enchanted by Lawrence's *Pinkie* and Gainsborough's *Blue Boy,* which face one another in that gallery, and I did like them, but I was disappointed to learn that they didn't actually know each other. It was Joshua Reynolds's *Sara Siddons as the Tragic Muse* that captured my imagination. The painting is dark—done almost completely with a pallet of browns. Only Mrs. Siddons's pale skin, pearls, and white sleeves offer any light. Her gown falls in dense, velvety folds; her eyes look fearfully upward, and behind her, two natives dance in dim firelight. But Sara Siddons's skin glows and each individual pearl is radiantly lit. I asked my mother why she was there, deserted in the jungle. What had she done to be abandoned so? To me it appeared she was about to be cooked, for I had read a child's abridged version of *Robinson Crusoe* and knew something about cannibalism. I had also seen *King Kong* on TV at the neighbor's house, and knew that the jungle was a place where savages and monsters coveted beautiful women. My mother explained to me that the painting was symbolic; Sara Siddons was not really in a jungle. She was an actress, and the dark, naked men behind her stood for tragedy in drama—Pity and Terror. At the time, my mother's explanation was lost on me, but now I find it insightful and informed. Perhaps she too identified with Sara Siddons. She must have been haunted by the dark tragedy of Richard's murder/suicide, always lurking in the lambent firelight of memory. At the gift shop, she let me buy a postcard of the painting, which I kept in the little drawer of my bedside table. I would study it night after night until I was told to turn out my light. Sara Siddons and her besieged setting still fascinate me, and whenever we visit the library, I am still eager to visit her first.

I must have been a peculiar girl at ten, so drawn to a woman made vulnerable by perilous shadows. Why not Pinkie on her lovely sunlit hillside, stroked gently by a light, warm breeze with her Blue Boy gazing fondly at her from across the well-lit room? Already the unknown and the illicit must have attracted me. Even now, I will conjure up Sara Siddons when I'm sleepless or agitated. She fears the darkness behind her, that which will overtake and consume her, yet she does not cower or cry. Instead, she patiently and beatifically sits in her grand chair. Her endurance gives me a model of stoicism and with it a measure of peace. Sara Siddons continues to ward off the unthinkable even as it eternally lurks just over each shoulder.

In 1964, I took Alec to the Huntington Library and found myself confounded by his lackadaisical response to Sara Siddons and the Japanese Garden. There are guards all over the grounds and no secret burrows to crawl into. With apparently the only thing on his mind thwarted, Alec was ready to leave, to stop "wasting" the day we had together, he said, eager to head back to our private warren in Lacy Park.

Continuing up Huntington Drive, you will pass Sierra Madre Boulevard. On your left, you'll see San Marino High School. When I passed by there not too long ago, I could not calm a shudder even though it has been forty years since I graduated. It is unfortunate that my memory has let sorrow and regret overshadow the good education I benefited from in those classrooms. I had first-rate teachers. There were no willful, disobedient students to distract us from our learning. Our preparation for university was excellent, but, of course, high school culture is so much more than academic achievement.

I wasn't an entirely unpopular girl. I was invited to almost every dance, asked to be in the girls' service club, accompanied to school activities by friends, encouraged by my teachers. But the pedestrian flotsam and jetsam of high school life did not assuage my feelings of inadequacy. Objectively speaking, my failures there were insignificant given that my opportunities were clearly so substantial. Even as I recall them, they sound absurd. For one, I was never chosen for the drill team. That this mattered greatly is testimony to the solipsistic cocoon of adolescence. Second, for the senior class play, I was only good enough to be in Chorus II, which meant we huddled anonymously (without a costume, which was unbelievably disappointing) in a small, darkened balcony in the back of the auditorium where no one could hear too clearly the sour notes we regularly hit as we belted out "Brigadoon." That I interpreted what should have been minor disappointments as utter failures is indicative of my downbeat frame of mind at the time.

I was never the best student in the class, but I never failed a test. I was shy and awkward. I hovered between the poles of adolescent unconsciousness and awareness with little success when it came to examining critically the hierarchies of high school's hermetic universe. I drifted between a group of girls who were daringly mischievous (Jackie, Caroline, and Tammy) and those who were obedient and focused (Karen, Virginia, and Sharon). And then there was Alec.

I met Alec on a church retreat. Although my parents were unswervingly secular, I had become quite religious as a young girl and had even been confirmed at St. Edmund's Episcopal Church, which I started attending with my friend, Helen, and her family. In order to be confirmed so that I could receive Holy Communion on Sundays, I had to be baptized, something I found mortifying since by then I was already eleven, and I knew I was supposed to have been baptized as an infant. But my parents agreed to attend these rites of passage; my mother even bought me a red felt hat for my confirmation because I was expected to cover my head in church. I accepted it all wholeheartedly and eagerly joined the St. Edmund's choir with my friend Karen, though my weak voice, neither soprano nor alto, was probably anathema to the patient choir director.

My parents' Sunday mornings were spent quietly, one might even say reverently, in their large, intricate gardens. That they did not feel the need to provide me with a church-going routine should not suggest they were relaxed in my moral upbringing. They were staunchly devoted to a propriety that I would eventually find stifling and unforgiving. Even my religious friends would see my parents' later inflexible attempts to control me as harsh and dictatorial. Church was appealing because week after week, there was always forgiveness, unlike at home where so much of me was becoming unpardonable. My grateful devoutness was in full bloom at the church retreat at Big Bear Lake where Karen and I met Alec and his friend, Terry. We were charmed by them and their efforts to catch a fish, and they, in turn, seemed taken with us.

One week to the day after the retreat, Alec called me and awkwardly but sweetly asked me out. I was his first date and we went to see *Bye Bye Birdie*—at the Academy Theater. He was a junior and I was a freshman, but he was young for his grade, not yet having arrived at his full height, skinny, pimply, growing toward handsome but not there yet. I had just celebrated my fifteenth birthday. We quickly moved from shy ingenues to boyfriend and girlfriend status. He gave me a yellow St. Christopher medal to wear on a long silver chain around my neck—the marker in our circle for going steady.

My sophomore year was almost entirely taken up by my devotion to Alec (and the Beatles) and was not unlike my religious zeal. Should I remember it, my first love, as blissful, blithe and pristine? I don't. I shudder when I pass San Marino High School because it reminds me of laying myself on a different kind of altar, committing my selfhood to the hormonal needs of a seventeen-year-old boy.

One day as Karen and I walked down the school hall by our lockers, Karen told me that I was too submissive. I was surprised by "submissive," which sounded like too important a word to apply to someone as uncomplicated as me, but I am impressed today by her youthful insight. She was right, I was simply overly compliant. Though she had no idea just how heavy the petting was getting, I was agreeing to each step in our sexual passage, even as I castigated myself for each capitulation and for my own passion. I wanted to be a good girl, a well-liked girl, a smart girl, but I wanted Alec to love me more than I wanted all that. So with complicated lies and guilty duplicity, I secretly removed myself from the protective embrace of my family and placed my well-being in his care. That I was so needy is still dismaying.

To recall San Marino circa 1964 is to recreate a town that seems almost magical—not unlike the Brigadoon we sang of. There, beneath the snow-capped mountains, it surfaced from the orange and lemon groves of the San Gabriel Valley, a lovely, protective enclave inhabited by people lucky enough to have been able to spin hard work into gold. The homes they built were all unique—no Levittown here. Instead, all were designed as decorously spacious and well appointed, with a room for each child, a garage for two cars, a yard for a dog, and a "family room" for the television. The children walked on safe streets to the corner where the school buses stopped for them; they were fed nutritiously and sensibly. They went regularly to their pediatricians, to the library, to horseback riding lessons, to ballet and art lessons; they were sent to sleepover camps and accompanied their parents on family vacations to Palm Springs and Enci-nada. There were no truants and few slackers. All were bound for college, if not Stanford or USC then for small liberal arts colleges or respectable state universities (though not Berkeley, which was already suspect). High school sweethearts never married right out of high school. None of the young men went directly into the service. In 1964, the Vietnam War was escalating, but it was understood that San Marino boys were not groomed for the military, unless it was later, as part of their college experience in ROTC. There were other young men from communities like Pacoima, Tor-rance, and Pico Rivera who would fight this war.

Though there were class bullies and cliques of pretty, rich girls, all the children were cared for with such vigilance that emotional problems, just like physical ailments, must have seemed improbable. *The Valley of the Dolls* would not be published until 1966, so we had still not heard of

Dexedrine or Seconal, though our mothers may have already been falling under their spell. So many middle-class women came out of the fifties medicated, yet we heard little of terms like depression, anorexia, bulimia, or substance abuse. These maladies were for later years. In San Marino in 1964, we were expected to thrive. Unhappiness was invisible in the landscape that we walked through.

Propriety was everything. Even our language was monitored, our word choice a source of concern. My mother continuously corrected my grammar. When I answered the phone and someone asked to speak to Janet, I was taught to answer with the hypercorrect, "This is she," a habit I've never been able to forego. I was unfamiliar with swearing, though occasionally I would hear my mother say, "Hells Bells" in a singsong, good-natured voice. I had never heard anyone say "Fuck." One time I heard Jackie's father say "Crap!" but that was extraordinary. My parents never shouted at one another. I can't remember them having an argument. Occasionally my mother would raise her voice at my sisters, but for the most part, we were all unfailingly polite to one another. My father was an attorney, and his commanding presence and persuasive voice precluded any attempts at debate or even discussion. Dinnertime conversations had nothing to do with politics or the news of the day beyond our insular community. We paid little attention to national or international imbroglios. There was no place for contention, no room to try out a stance or take a side. Our day-to-day activities were our only fodder for conversation, so we obediently, cheerfully, and gratefully reported no more than the surface events of our lives.

"Either put a smile on your face, or go to your room." "If you can't say something nice, don't say it at all." "Wipe that smirk off your face, young lady." "Count your blessings." "Put your napkin in your lap." "Never eat with your fingers." "Stand up straight." "Enunciate you words." "Slow down!" "Say 'Please.'" "Say 'Thank you.'" "Say 'Pardon me,'" and above all and constantly, "Calm down!" These were the admonitions of my childhood—the way we three demonstrative daughters were expected to handle our appetites and emotions. There was no language for anything but positive feelings. I learned to hold back, deny, smother, check, and repress. Not unpredictably, the phrase chosen to go under my senior picture in my high school yearbook reads, "My, oh, my. What a wonderful day!"

Anne did scream at me one evening when she discovered I had cut up all the blue construction paper she had brought home from school to make tiny Titan shields for an upcoming football game. My father took her in her room, closed the door, and punished her. I don't know what he did behind that door, but I remember my sister's puffy eyes the next morning, and I knew I was responsible. Her unjust punishment made me fear my father even more. I went through childhood trying so hard to please that I never actually got a spanking. I would be disciplined for not eating my dinner, left alone in the spooky dining room to sit at the table with a plate of cold vegetables in front of me while the rest of the family went off to other warm rooms of the house. But other than a steadfast unwillingness to eat the food that was deemed necessary to my growth and well-being, I was an acquiescent child who did not need much discipline.

In fact, my one and only spanking came when I was fifteen, after my mother got the phone call from Catherine's mother about our disastrous attempt to get into the dance at the Civic Auditorium. My mother and father marched me into my room, threw me face down on my bed, and then the two of them thrashed me. I was astonished by their loss of control, humiliated more for them than for myself. I knew I had done something very wrong, and they could have made me feel unbearably guilty, but their uncharacteristic physical reaction made me hold them in disdain instead. Their desperate rage suggested that I was now traveling out beyond their control.

In 1963, I had still lived consistently and conscientiously according to the prescriptives of my parents and their community. I had not known there was any other way to be. But in 1964, I stepped at least part way out of their bubble into a risky, ill-defined defiance. Attempts were made to reign me in, but I had found a new script of teenage rebellion to follow. It was no less codified perhaps, but it was one my parents could not fathom and, therefore, they couldn't follow me until I was rendered so helpless that their power was restored. Only then could they reach into the whirlpool, where I surely would have drowned, and yank me back to the protection and control that only their well-defined shore could promise.

 ## 12 *Banished*

San Marino, Summer's End, 1964

A FEW DAYS BEFORE I was to start my junior year in high school and Alec was to depart for Honolulu to begin his freshman year at the University of Hawaii, we saw each other one last time. My mother had already taken me to Robinson's for new school clothes, and I had finally convinced her to buy me my first miniskirt to wear on "free dress" day when we were granted a temporary reprieve from our knee-length gray skirts and jumpers—the school rule being hems must touch the floor when we knelt. After much pleading, she also bought me a green corduroy jacket that seemed especially hip, a coat Joan Baez might have worn, I thought.

After the calamitous experience I had at twelve when I got caught fooling around in a deserted estate, it would have made sense for me not to go on a nighttime foray to a local "haunted house" (aka large home about to be demolished) in Pasadena. But, when I heard Alec was going to be there, I jumped at the chance and told my mother I was going to the movies. Before she could ask too many questions, Jackie pulled into our driveway, tooted the horn, and I was out the door and into to the car. Once again my mother watched us drive off into an evening adventure. She must have intuited that we were bound for trouble, but somehow I wriggled through her grasp once again.

The haunted house was genuinely frightening. By the time we got there, it was already dark. We hadn't brought flashlights. We knew that Alec and his friends were in the house because we saw their car, but when we called out to them, they would not answer or show themselves. We crept up to the house on our own, crunching on broken glass, stumbling over refuse. It was too dark to identify much when we actually entered through a large, downstairs broken window, but the boys were there, darting around us, whispering, jostling, tickling, and luring us deeper into the house. There were five boys there, and four of them were having great fun making us scream. We were perfect targets, ready to shriek at the slightest rustle. But Alec would not play the game; instead, he disappeared mysteriously into the depths of the house alone. Was this a test to see if I would follow? I didn't have the nerve for the hide-and-seek game; in fact, I was too afraid of the dark, ominous house to even go past the foyer. I went back out to sit in Jackie's car alone, hoping Alec would come find me there. I waited there a long time, but he never came. Finally my girlfriends returned to the car, sweaty and exuberant. They had been having a great time while I had sat weeping in the car, hurt and bewildered once again by Alec's rejection.

I got home safely and undetected from this second escapade in a deserted house. No wounds, no police cruiser. Nonetheless, I was much more distraught than I had been when I had actually gotten caught trespassing. I went straight to my bed, sobbing. My mother came into the room, asking for the first time in a long time, "What's wrong?" I told her that I had seen Alec and that he had ignored me; he wouldn't even say hello. I didn't tell her that I was also crying because just days before, he had spoken to me only long enough to ask me to have sex with him on the beach. I had kept so much from her in the past months. Nonetheless, she knew to ask the next question, which is still hard to record, even today, more than forty years later. I cringe as I type her words: "Janet, are you pregnant?" I answered her with the only information I had: "I don't know."

She turned around immediately and left me alone in my room. I knew she was going to tell my father. Exhausted, fearful, yet also with a paradoxical sense of relief, I waited in my well-lit yellow room. Finally we would all have to confront my situation, whatever it was. My father called to me to come into the living room and I went cautiously. My mother asked me if Alec and I had had sex. Again, I answered the only way I knew how: "I don't know." I was not lying. I was still not sure if what Alec and I had done back in June counted as sex. He had said afterwards, "We can't do it 'like that' again"; but it was our one-and-only time doing it "like that." It had been so painful and embarrassing. Surely this could not be the way a baby was conceived. There were no more questions that night. Only my father's curt, "Take her to the doctor first thing Monday morning." I was not asked to relate any of the details of that June night, three months earlier. They knew more than they wanted to know for now.

That was a Saturday night. The next day was a bright, sunny, unusually smog-free September Sunday, and I went to a track meet with my father at the LA Coliseum. To be asked to accompany my dad on an outing was more than unusual. Looking back, I think he decided it was best to keep me out of my mother's sight for the day, and it gave her time to put their plans in motion should the worst prove true. That day we saw Mike Larrabee break the world record in the quarter mile, my father's race when he was a track star at the University of Michigan. We saw several men run a four-minute mile, a feat that was still unusual. My dad told me that people had once thought it was impossible for a human being to run that fast, but Roger Bannister had done so, and now others were able to as well. My father told me to remember witnessing those races, and I always have, but mostly I remember how much it meant to me to be there with my father that day, how good it felt to be sitting next to him, how handsome he seemed, how much I loved him, how much I wished he spent more time with me.

For that day, he was not the disappointed parent or the controlling patriarch. On that day, he was an inexplicably kind and loving father, a father who wanted to tell me something about hope and effort, even if he had to do so by way of Mike Larrabee's forty-four-second quarter mile and Roger Bannister's four-minute mile. Perhaps he was thinking that there should have been more days like this one. Perhaps if he had been more engaged in my life, I wouldn't have drifted beyond his protective reach. But it was too late, already too late.

When we returned home that evening—tired, sunburned, and strangely jubilant—the phone rang for me, but I was not permitted to speak to anyone, nor did I want to. I heard my mother saying to Alec and then later to Jackie, "She can't come to the phone." Unexpectedly, this new wall she was erecting around me felt like a welcome shield rather than a restriction. Overnight my wish to choose my own course had evaporated. I wanted nothing more to do with being a free agent. I wanted only one thing—to be an obedient daughter, if I could only have one more chance.

The next morning, my mother and I were on the doorstep of her obstetrician's office when it opened. Dr. Cook ushered us into his book-lined office and now, finally, the explicit questions were asked: "Was his penis inside you?" "Did he ejaculate?" "Did you bleed?" My answers were inconclusively vague. My mother was seething, disgusted, and mortified. Dr. Cook said the only way to find out what had really happened was to examine me. My mother rose to follow us into the examination room, but he asked her to wait and we went into the room alone.

This was my first pelvic exam. I knew that doctors helped women give birth, but I had no preparation for the table, the stirrups, the position, and the instrument. I followed each of his nurse's instructions: taking off all my clothes, putting on the huge paper gown, placing my heels in the stirrups, scooting down on the table and arranging my legs in a way that felt degrading, obscene. As Dr. Cook inserted the cold speculum, he tried to cheer me by commenting on my beautiful suntan. Then, with the gloved fingers of one hand inside me, he pressed hard on my stomach with the other hand. I squeezed my eyes shut, but tears still spilled out, sliding down my temples into my hair. Slowly he removed his fingers, rose from the stool, took off the gloves, washed his hands at the sink. The nurse silently left the room, carefully shutting the door behind her. He walked to the head of the table where I still lay. And then he said it: simple, blunt, devastating: "You're pregnant."

Was I brave? Did I receive the news stoically? Not really. My tearful reply reflected my steadfast denial: "No, no; I can't be; it was only that one time." But he was adamant: "Janet, you *are* pregnant. Get dressed."

From here on out, I would make no more choices. I would do only as I was told. I mechanically redressed myself. The nurse returned and led me back to the doctor's office where he and my mother, now pale and drained, waited. My mother asked him if there was anything he could do.

"No—nothing," he answered. "It's much too late for that. If she had come to me immediately, I could have given her something. But not now. There is nothing I can do." It was September 13, 1964. Roe vs. Wade was still nine years in the future (January 22, 1973). And I was three months pregnant.

Martha's Vineyard, 2004

Where was I that morning? In complete psychological and emotional re-treat. I became no more than a watcher, a listener. If anyone had thought to ask me, "What do you want?" I would not have known how to answer. I observed the adults around me as they began making important decisions for me, and I put up no resistance. I was so shocked by what was happening to my body, that I had no control over it, that it was doing something monumental without my knowledge or consent. I could not process my pregnancy, much less wonder about my future. Since I had let my parents down by giving them such an insurmountable problem, my only recourse was to comply with anything and everything they decided.

My body was not my own; perhaps it never had been. When it had escaped my parents' control, Alec had immediately taken it up, and when he had abandoned it, a baby had claimed it. It may sound as if I am unwilling to take responsibility for my actions, but, in fact, I did not completely understand that my body was my own dominion, that I could say what did and did not happen to it. In significant ways, women were not led to believe that they owned their bodies—the state, their husbands, or their fathers did. I definitely had no inkling that the baby I carried was mine. I willingly handed my body and my future back to my parents. Their money and authority took over, and I surrendered all bids at self-control. I would not be allowed to make another decision for months.

What about an illegal abortion? My parents certainly had the means to pay for the travel and the procedure, but it is here that our hermetic life in San Marino prevented them from knowing how one might proceed with such a plan. When I tell people who grew up in working-class neighborhoods this story, they are always amazed that no one considered that option. But there were no back alleys in San Marino, nothing illegal whatsoever, and my parents' principled moral rigor would have prevented them from considering anything unlawful in the first place. If an abortion had been obtainable, would I have been able to make my own informed, thoughtful decision? Regrettably, no. I was in my parents' hands entirely with no more free will than a newborn. The baby I carried was theirs too, to do with as they saw fit. I must confess that I would have agreed to anything.

For years I wondered how they launched the intricate maneuverings of my new secret life so quickly. The very next morning, instead of starting school, my clothes were packed, and I was on a plane for Cleveland, Ohio. I understand now that their alacrity was the result of prior practice in managing a catastrophe. Years before, they had erased Richard, his family, and his complicated crime from their lives with such exacting precision that the details of sending me into exile must have been easy. My mother's sister agreed to care for me throughout the pregnancy, and so others took up the secret burden that I had been carrying alone for three months. I said good-bye to no one, not my grandparents, not my sisters, not my girlfriends, and especially not Alec. No one would know the truth except those who would play a part in the secret drama now being constructed.

Excuses were proffered: First, I had been running with a wild crowd. By San Marino standards, this was plausible enough. Second, I would benefit from making a clean break, by putting distance between my wayward friends and me. This was also true. Third, I needed to improve my grades for college; one's junior year was the most important. Also reasonable. Fourth, the best way to get a fresh start was to spend a year with my favorite aunt in Ohio. Apparently credible, at least enough so that neighbors, teachers, and friends would not press the issue.

The words that had fed my dreams just days before—*sweet sixteen, boyfriend, going steady, prom, kiss, charm bracelet*—instantly lost their magical potential to depict anything about me or the life I would now lead. The words that I had found deliciously scandalous—*surf-bum, bitchin', shoot the breeze, bikini*—held empty promises. I avoided them. They felt soiled. The lingo of Southern California 1964 had beckoned me to enter a world of hedonism and chance. I had willingly followed, but now the penalty seemed extreme indeed.

My sixteenth year would become something else entirely—the year of my leaving, my shame, my loss. The words that gathered around me—*scared, melancholy, homesick, alone*—were the opposite of what I could have imagined for myself. I gathered them within me, hidden and remote, only trying them on when I was alone in my new room. On the outside I still needed to appear positive but penitent, regretful but eager to make the best of a bad situation. No longer did I turn to the ironically like-minded role models I had found in *Wuthering Heights* and *Gidget;* Heathcliff and Catherine had set a dangerous example; Gidget had led me astray.

Now I needed a way to survive a year that I was utterly untrained for. I would find a new set of feminine ideals in the long novels I began to read voraciously: Scarlett O'Hara would teach me how to repress when she said "I'll think about that tomorrow"; Marjorie Morningstar would try to persuade me "there really was more than one man in the world"; Jane Eyre would offer me a kind of hope: "Reader, I married him"; Eustacia Vye would serve as a warning against desperate rebellion; Tess Durbeyfield would give me a name for my baby, "Sorrow"; *Jude the Obscure* would confirm for me there was far greater tragedy than mine to endure. The consoling identification, the peace, the escape, the redemption that these novels offered me would turn into a lifelong means of personal comfort and a professional commitment to the healing power of narrative.

When my parents and I arrived at the terminal gate at LAX where I would board my plane for Cleveland, my mother was nervous, hurried, and her voice was clipped. She was still very angry with me, and her anger helped her avoid any signs of grief or reservation. I wanted to get myself out of her sight so she would not have to be so disturbed, so tense, so furious. But my father seemed defeated and unsure. I was amazed when I noticed him crying. I had never seen my confident, controlled father, a celebrated Los Angeles attorney, in distress. The image of him standing there, tall at 6'4", but for the first time noticeably stooped and weeping as we said our goodbye, still makes me cry. I was and still am thankful for his tears. They remain a permanent sign of his abiding love for me even though I was suddenly a shameful burden. Despite his great disappointment, he was suffering from the decision to send me away—a necessary banishment, he must have reasoned, but exile just the same.

I turned, leaving them there watching me, and started up the ramp and into the plane. The die was cast; I knew there was no turning back. I found my seat and stared blankly and utterly empty out the window as the plane accelerated, bearing me into a far-flung life that no one could have anticipated.

 *Pepper Pike*

Cleveland, Ohio, Fall 1964

WHEN I EMERGED from the plane in Cleveland, my Aunt Jo was waiting for me at the gate, smiling and seemingly happy to see me. In 1949, married with three small children, Jo had survived a devastating case of polio. Her body was left paralyzed but through excruciating months of physical therapy, she had regained the use of her upper body. She went on to have another child, and lived her life full throttle from then on. She walked with crutches, swinging along so quickly that I had to quicken my pace to keep up with her. I was to live with her, my Uncle Bill, and their two youngest children in the Cleveland suburb of Pepper Pike in a large house on Fox Hollow Road, an affluent community very similar to San Marino. I loved the names of my new home. When I said "Pepper Pike" and "Fox Hollow" to myself, they gave me the impression I was going to live in a sheltering forest, like Christopher Robin's "One-Hundred Acre Wood" or "Toad Hall" of *The Wind and the Willows.*

And I was to have companions in my new setting. My cousins, Clyde and Betsy, were fifteen and thirteen. The two older children were out of the house: Chris, married and with a child, lived nearby; Steve was in Vietnam. Before I arrived, my aunt told Clyde and Betsy that I was pregnant and that this was a secret they had to keep. Since I didn't look or act pregnant, they quickly ignored the matter, as did I, and we became instant friends. The morning after my arrival, I was enrolled in the public high school and started immediately. My aunt told the school administrators nothing about my condition. If they had known I was pregnant, I would not have been allowed to attend and the truth of my circumstances would have been difficult to evade.

But that was not the case. I was tall with plenty of room to hide my pregnancy. When my stomach began to pooch out, my aunt bought me the tightest girdle she could find, and I wore it until January. She gave me appetite suppressants that worked remarkably well, so I did not put on weight. The first time I felt tiny flutterings in my stomach, I was taking a test in my European history class. I attributed the new feeling to nerves, later to indigestion. When the kicks against the tightly bound girdle became more insistent, I told no one and ignored them as best I could, maintaining with an unwavering resolve the unreality of my pregnancy.

I did everything my cousins did: horseback riding, sledding, ice skating, even tobogganing one winter day. My cousins either forgot or didn't stop to consider the real reason I had moved into their home; instead we were friends and playmates. "Play" may be a strange word to use to describe the activities of three adolescents, but that is what our time together felt like. My cousins were sheltered, as I had been, by their parents' privilege, but their protective walls were even thicker. They each attended prestigious, private, single-sex schools. Betsy went to Laurel School where sociologist Carol Gilligan would later do her renowned study of teenage girls (*In a Different Voice*, 1982). Their interests revolved around their schools (soccer, field hockey, service clubs) and their church (choir, youth group, more service clubs). The midwestern insulation of Pepper Pike, Ohio, so far from California beaches and Greenwich Village, kept them detached from the burgeoning cultural changes. Neither the Beatles nor the Beach Boys had captivated them; they were not interested in dating or drinking. To be daring was to gallop their horses full speed through the woods beyond the riding stables. Clyde and Betsy wanted to please their parents, not defy them. To follow their lead was an enormous relief, since I wanted nothing more than to redeem myself, to be "good." I loved being part of this family. The three-and-a-half months that I lived with them were filled with lighthearted fun; I was seldom alone; I was busy; I studied; I pleased my teachers; I pleased my aunt and uncle. The angst of the preceding perilous year dissipated into an idyllic reprieve.

On my first day at Orange High School, my California tan and my green miniskirt impressed my new peers. I could see boys turning their heads as I walked self-consciously down the aisles and through the halls. But attention was the last thing I wanted, and I never wore that skirt again. When friendly students approached me, I was shy and inarticulate. I ate my lunch alone and found my way to the school library during breaks. I did make one friend, a girl named Nadia, but we only saw each other once outside of school, and that turned out disastrously when she drove her father's car into the drainage ditch outside my aunt and uncle's home. My aunt kept me occupied with errands: driving my cousins around Cleveland and babysitting. I baked dozens and dozens of cookies (though I didn't eat them), attended church, studied with my cousins. I had no need for friends at school; I didn't want to be noticed; I sat quietly, paid close attention to my teachers, and began to excel academically.

This was a surprise. I had been a fair student before—mostly As and Bs, a C in French, even a D in algebra—but I had never taken school seriously. Now I did, not because I wanted to earn As but because I wanted my parents, my aunt and uncle, and myself to forget what else was happening to me. My only report card from Orange High School boasts straight As. My teachers' comments read, "It's a pleasure to have Janet in Biology II"; "Janet has quickly established herself as the best student in my junior English class." This was another new facet of myself, one I had not known I even possessed, but I liked feeling smart and I liked school. Furthermore, I found I could concentrate with unwavering attentiveness. This became a game for me: How long could I sit quietly and memorize dates from my history book? How long could I read my biology chapter without my mind wandering? How many hours could I put in reading *Great Expectations*? All of these newfound skills made it possible for me to pay so little attention to my pregnancy that I could almost entirely refute it.

When I first arrived in Pepper Pike, my aunt thought I should see a psychologist, and I went to the appointment prepared, I thought, to talk about what was happing to me and what was going to happen to me. First her assistant, a young graduate student, gave me a Rorschach test. After I had identified each of the inkblots as best I could, he told me how he was interpreting some of my responses. For example, two vertical lines with big blobs on their tops that I had identified as flagpoles, he said, represented the authority figures in my life—my mother and father. Teenagers love these reductive games, and I was no exception. Rather than doubt his interpretations, I was impressed and fascinated, naïvely believing that he could read my mind by way of inkblots. But then it was time to meet the psychologist herself. I am sure she was a kind woman. Her office was pretty and she spoke softly, asking me to tell her how I felt about my pregnancy, about eventually giving birth, about the baby I carried. She was the first person to ask me these questions. Confronted with her questions, I burst into unstoppable tears. I cried for the whole hour as she murmured consolations and handed me tissue after tissue. On our way out, she told my aunt we had had a good start. In the car, exhausted but still inconsolable, I begged my aunt not to make me return. As long as no one asked, I could remain in the safe realm of denial—no one need know I was pregnant, not even me. We did not return to the psychologist.

The months passed; my denial remained unshaken; the girdle and the appetite suppressants did their job. When I had left California in September, I had weighed 129 pounds. By Christmas, I weighed 128 pounds. Nonetheless, when I removed the girdle at night and slipped with relief into my long Lanz nightgown, my stomach was obvious to my aunt and me. No one at Orange High School or in Pepper Pike could know, so I needed to disappear once again. The truth about me was so shameful that it had to be kept secret even from strangers.

My aunt told the school administrators I was returning to California. She embellished the secret by claiming I was to have back surgery. Earlier she had pulled me out of physical education because changing in the locker room would have meant revealing the girdle and what it hid. The excuse she used then had been a back injury that prevented me from participating. Now she could elaborate that excuse: I was going home to have necessary surgery on my back. There was even a small story about me and my injury in the Orange High School newspaper after I left. A fellow Orange High School student who lived across the street showed it to my cousin Betsy, but Betsy had not been let in on the fabricated back injury and was dumbfounded by the article. My aunt and I should have learned then that the best secrets are kept uncomplicated, but keeping the secret had become an idée fixe and we were much too inventive to consider simple excuses, much less simple truths.

Throughout my stay in Pepper Pike, my aunt encouraged me to write to my friends in California, telling them about my happy new life. My own embellishments began immediately after I received a letter from Alec in Hawaii. I opened the letter with conflicted feelings. I was overjoyed to hear from him but full of trepidation as well. As I read the letter, my heart sank. All was for naught. There were stories "going around" at home, he said, that I had been sent to Cleveland because I was pregnant. Jackie had written him to let him know what people were saying. He knew this couldn't be true, but he wanted me to know the rumors "my friends" were spreading. In tears, I took the letter to my aunt, and with her typical ability to turn bad news into good news, she took the letter as an opportunity. My task was to write Alec back, claiming that of course I could not be pregnant, reiterating again why I had been sent to Cleveland and finishing with a vivid description of the school dance I had just attended. There had been no school dance, but encouraged by my aunt, I began my foray into the creation of the fairytale existence of a sixteen-year-old darling, a confabulation of tall tales to hide behind.

I made up marvelous stories, fantasizing a dream world that reflected my real life in only cursory ways. First, I replied to Alec; my aunt read over my letter before I sealed it to be sure that it revealed nothing. I would be so successful in my storytelling that two years later, when I finally confessed to Alec that I did have a baby, his baby, he refused to believe me.

Martha's Vineyard, 2004

One of my San Marino schoolmates I corresponded with throughout my time away is still a dear friend. Remarkably, through all the moves and upheaval of her own life, Karen held onto the letters I sent her for more than thirty years. Not long ago she gave them back to me. This has been perhaps the most surprising and illuminating gift I have ever received. How often can we travel back to our distant past, meeting a familiar yet deeply remote version of ourselves? The first letter lays out the foundations of the fabricated counterlife that was meant to deliver me unscathed from ignominy:

Sept. 23, 1964

Dear Karen,

I guess you're probably curious why I was sent here. Well, the week before school started, I got into some trouble down at the beach. My mom found out what happened and decided she didn't want to send me back to San Marino High School. I left Sunday morning for Cleveland.

I'm not really sad at all. I have picked my own friends. Tonight I'm going to see *Hamlet* with Nadia, my best friend back here. She is so sweet and cute and she makes me feel much so much a part of school and the social life. Saturday we doubled to downtown Cleveland. My date, Don, is the co-captain of varsity cross-country.

I've already been riding 3 times. We ride English and I even got a pair of jodhpurs.

The stories in this first letter lay out some of the parameters of my invented world, peopling it with some plausible characters. But how hastily I have created this new world! I have been in Pepper Pike for less than two weeks, yet already I claim to have a best friend with a circle of chosen friends, a "popular" boy to date, and a classy hobby.

In fact, there was no double date with Don and Nadia, and as marginalized as I was, no one introduced me to the "social scene." Although I did go horseback riding with my cousins, there were no sleek, tight-fitting jodhpurs. Instead, I wore a baggy sweater that hid the unbuttoned waistline of my Levis.

On October 8, I write Karen about an imaginary date to the homecoming dance, but I do not elaborate other than to say it was "really fun." In this letter I seem more introspective. I tell her I received a letter from Alec, though not about the rumors he has heard. I do confess the following: "I still love him. I guess I probably always will in a certain way. I won't be seeing him for so long though. Maybe my heart will straighten out by the next time we meet." Although these comments about Alec are honest, they will prove as naïve as my school-life fantasies. My "heart" will take years to "straighten out"; in fact, it will take decades for me to recognize that my devotion to him was a delusional and damaging fixation.

On October 17, I write to tell Karen about going to a "semi-formal dance" and to a "real fun" party after a rainy football game: all make-believe. I also tell her about falling in love with a horse named Gwen, who does, in fact, exist. Yet Gwen, a gentle but worn-out stable horse, was finally only one more extension of my groundless daydreams. I spent hours fantasizing about buying her and taking her back to California with me, imaging myself traveling with her in a special train car and feeding her sweet grass and apples across the country. This aspiration was hopeless, even ludicrous; my parents would never have consented to my owning a horse, much less shipping Gwen from Ohio to California. Now, in hindsight, I find it bittersweet that even in my dreams, I could only imagine feeding, caring for, and bringing home a broken-down horse. How far this substitution of horse for baby was from my deepest and still wholly unconscious desire sadly reinforces how close I still was to childhood.

On November 15, I write to Karen about another new make-believe girlfriend and what we all do together. My imaginary leaps are becoming more and more extravagant. "Betsy Bridges was over and she loves the Beatles as much as I do. Betsy is really darling and she works as a model downtown. She is the new Miss Cleveland for Miss Teenage America. It's too bad she didn't win." I must realize I cannot make my imaginary friends too remarkable. Betsy Bridges can be Miss Cleveland, but she cannot have won the statewide competition to become Miss Ohio because Karen might watch the televised Miss Teenage America pageant. There will be no trim and pretty Betsy Bridges on the runway, for she only exists in my letters.

One truthful and constant subject throughout the letters is my enchantment with and longing for snow, a fascination that I carry with me still and that must somehow be related to the snowy night of my daughter's birth. In a letter dated December 16, my desire for snowfall is irrepressible. I exclaim, "Guess what the high is going to be tomorrow? Ten degrees!! It snowed all last night and a little today and this weekend I'll probably try my hand at skiing again." I never actually did ski while I was in Ohio, though I make up several elaborate stories about my clumsy attempts and funny falls for Karen. Because I will return to California still never having skied in my life, I create a kind of cute but klutzy character for myself in anticipation of my ineptitude should I ever actually visit the slopes.

In another letter, I describe in great detail an imaginary dress I will be wearing to an assembly ball at my aunt and uncle's country club: "It's green silk and I'm going to wear a little necklace with a Christmas tree on it. It's real simple but it's beautiful." The boy I create to escort me is even more remarkable: "I'm going with a boy who looks exactly like Paul Peterson on the Donna Reed Show. He's so-o-o good looking." I also add: "Back here, I've become the kind of girl I want to be." The ironic poignancy of this affirmation was lost on me then, but today it stops me cold.

As I reread these adolescent fantasies, I am struck by how young I was. My extraordinary flights of fancy are evidence of my naïveté and childishness, and, given the reality of my actual situation, the contrast seem melodramatically pathetic. For example, in almost every letter, I ask Karen about Hildy, her dachshund, and I often close my letters by sending Hildy hugs and kisses. I am also young enough to be still experimenting with my handwriting; in some letter my words slant to the right, in others to the left, obviously paralleling my unstable sense of who I was and which way I might lean. When I tell Karen what I miss most, it is my dad's pancakes.

I am also impressed by how readily I retreat from the edgy counter-cultural steps I had only just begun to take in California away from my parents' values. Although I do mention that I still like the Beatles, all other aspects of rebellion have been erased from my new incarnation. My correspondences sound like letters that my oldest sister would have written about her high school adventures in 1954. My frame of reference is *The Donna Reed Show* (1958–66), which is not as infamously oblivious as *Leave It to Beaver* (1957–63), but which conformed just as strictly to what were accepted as wholesome fifties' values.

Although I was given free rein to invent a counterlife of my own as I wrote, I was clearly limited by the cultural and psychological codes of conventional suburban America. I couldn't imagine myself rebellious anymore since breaking rules had left me in exile. Gidget no longer held any allure. Instead, I retreated back to a hodgepodge of fairytale characters that had one thing in common: they were all good, and ironically, as I fabricated shamelessly, they were all innocent of deceit. I constructed myself as a teenage Snow White, an ingenuous girl who had escaped the evil temptations of wicked role models and poison apples in order to live happily in her own new enchanted village, one that even had a guileless name—Pepper Pike—one that was peopled with jolly friends and family, fine-looking horses, soft snowflakes, and my pick of handsome princes.

14 *The Florence Crittenton Home*

Akron, Ohio, Winter 1965

AS PART OF THE ONGOING and now multilayered narrative of secrecy, on the day after New Year's my aunt ostensibly drove me to the Cleveland airport to return to San Marino. In fact, she drove me to the Florence Crittenton Home for Unwed Mothers in Akron. I was well into my seventh month of pregnancy but still wearing the tight girdle under a loose beige wool jumper, the last article of clothing roomy enough to disguise my vanished waistline. I was scared of this latest move but resigned to its inevitability, eager to remove the girdle but apprehensive about what my body would do next.

The home looked like something out of the nineteenth-century novels I had been reading, a massive, three-story brick "home," surrounded by a forbidding brick wall with a wrought-iron gate. When I saw it for the first time, surrounded by its snow-covered grounds, the place loomed dark and ominous behind its menacing bars. We drove up a short driveway to the solid front door and parked. My aunt pounded the knocker and the door swung open. In the foyer a tiny, gray-haired woman, the housemother, greeted us.

I realize this sounds like a hackneyed beginning to a horror movie, and I was indeed horrified during that initial introduction, but the home itself turned out to be quite benign. I fell in love with that ponderous, vast old house with its heavy, dark wood paneling and ornate fixtures that impressed me greatly after the relatively unadorned stucco homes of

Byron Robinson residence, Akron, Ohio, ca. 1906; later the Florence Crittenton Home. Photographer unknown. Courtesy of the University of Akron.

Southern California. It was the perfect setting for my ongoing fairytale, my very own castle where I would be kept from all harm. In fact, rather than acknowledge to myself the whole point of my being there, I pretended I was entering a Victorian boarding school. That I was there to have a baby still did not register.

There were many such "homes" for unwed mothers at that time. It was a place where privileged girls were sent. There were no African American or Hispanic girls at this Florence Crittenton residence, at least not while I was there. Approximately thirty girls, all white and middle class, lived there at a time. Their parents, like mine, had sent them there to protect everyone from the shame of their pregnancies and to facilitate the adoption process. It was a rule that every girl who came to live at Florence Crittenton would "give up" her baby (the words we used then) for adoption. Although the Florence Crittenton Home of Akron no longer exists, the house still stands today, I've been told, as headquarters for an insurance company. The Victorian values that fed its business finally lost their grip on middle-class America. Abortion became legal and cultural ideology shifted so that girls could decide "to keep" their babies; the pill became readily available. All these progressive social changes have erased much of the need for such "homes," and the need to hide unwed mothers from view is no longer a priority.

Mrs. Williams, the housekeeper, gave my aunt and me a tour of the downstairs first. There was a large, dimly lit living room. Soft comfortable couches lined its walls and a grand piano stood in one corner. Next door was a cheerfully wallpapered pink dining room where long tables were being carefully set for lunch with linen, flatware, and china by obviously pregnant girls who glanced at me nonchalantly. I shyly looked away, not yet identifying with them. I just took it all in, passively, obediently.

Next, Mrs. Williams showed us her private office, an ill-omened room (the oft-repeated scene of heartbreaking relinquishment), but on first glance that day, it looked intriguing. It was an ornately decorated study with thick maroon carpeting, velvet burgundy drapes, an elaborate oak desk, and deep easy chairs gathered around a gas fireplace. Mrs. Williams's secretary, who was also the receptionist, had a conventional outer office with a metal desk, phone, and typewriter. That office opened out onto the front hall where there was a pay phone for our use. And there was my favorite room, a solarium that looked out on the fresh snow and allowed in some warmth from the weak winter light that was blocked off by heavy drapery in all the other rooms. The solarium had a cushioned window seat, shelves stacked with games and puzzles, and a player piano against one wall. That room would become my refuge; I would carefully load roll after roll of music onto the player piano and pound away on the pedals for hours. Or I would spend entire afternoons reading, secreted away in the window seat like the young Jane Eyre.

Part of the basement had been converted into classrooms. That was where I would attend school on weekdays for the next three months. Another large room held the laundry where I would wash and iron my clothes as well as the bed, bath, and table linens for the home when that was my particular chore for the week. The old washing machines had wringers, something I never seen before and loved to operate. When weekly chores were posted on Monday mornings, I would always try to trade if I got dusting, vacuuming, or kitchen duty for laundry responsibilities so I could feed dripping pieces of laundry through the wringer as I vigorously turned the handle, watching with satisfaction as they emerged unharmed and ready for the hot iron press.

This was not a home run by the infamous Magdalene Sisters of Ireland; there was no slaving over bleach-infused boiling vats. Mrs. Williams was kind to all of us, and perhaps because I was the youngest girl in the home for those months and certainly the most naïve, I became a favorite of the home's full-time nurse, Mrs. Reilley, who lived in an attached garage apartment. My ancient teachers, all retired from full-time teaching for years, were capable and caring, and because the student/teacher ratio was no more than four to one, I got a kind of focused, individual attention I had never before received in school. My teachers quickly saw that I wanted to work hard, so they eagerly assigned me extra reading and writing projects. My French teacher, the peculiar Madame La Pierre, taught me third-year French. She was much like my own loveable grandmother, whom I missed but who had to be protected from the truth about me. I was drawn to Madame, and she clearly liked me and was eager to teach me. Her kind regard for me was one small but treasured instance of validation in that winter of adult disapproval. My instruction for those three months was of an unexpectedly high quality, and rather than fall behind, I continued the focused academic progress I had begun at Orange High School.

Continuing her tour on the day of my arrival, Mrs. Williams took us up the wide staircase to what would be my room on the second floor, the small room at the end of the long hall that I shared with Tina. Tina, who was expecting her baby in May, had been a senior at a Catholic high school in Ohio, and when her school found out about her pregnancy, both she and the baby's father had been expelled. I laid my empty suitcase (empty because I had no maternity clothes to pack) on my bed and looked rapidly around. The room was tiny but warm. My bed was pushed up against the wall, which I liked; the bedspread was soiled, but a stack of clean, pressed sheets waited for me at its foot. There was a tiny dresser and sink that Tina and I were to share. The toilet and tub were down the hall. Our room was prime locale, I later learned, connected by another door to a room with a big table and chairs for studying and beyond that, the much-inhabited TV room, where girls vied for comfortable spots on three shabby sofas.

Mrs. Williams explained the daily schedule and the rotating chores we would do every morning. After chores I would go to school for two hours, Monday through Friday. Lunch was served promptly at noon. In the afternoons after French and on weekends, I would have free time and fill it as I pleased: doing my homework, my laundry, taking a walk, reading, writing letters, knitting. Girls were responsible for setting and clearing the dining room tables once a day. The meal they were assigned depended on whether they went to school or not. Because many of the "girls" were in their late teens or early twenties, attending school was not automatic, but since I would be going to school daily, I would always be assigned dinner duty. In the evenings after dinner, the girls gathered in the TV room, where smoking was allowed, or downstairs in the living room to play cards or work jigsaw puzzles while listening to old-fashioned pop music on the home's single record player. As Mrs. Williams showed us the workings of my new home, my fears were slowly diminishing. It seemed possible that I could live here safely.

Mrs. Williams took us back downstairs to the living room where girls were gathering for lunch. More than anything else, I had been afraid of meeting these girls. Surely they would be tough, streetwise and brash. Not surprisingly, like most of mainstream culture, the image I held of an "unwed mother" was someone who was "cheap," someone who had casual sex with lots of boys. I expected the girls at Florence Crittenton to have a hard-heartedness and cynicism that would leave me silent and friendless. But like most stereotypes, this was far from the mark: most of the girls were not intimidating at all; in fact, I could be characteristically cheerful among these girls. They were much like me. I was not alone.

We could leave the home during the day, signing out with our destination noted. We would go for long walks into downtown Akron where we would do the kinds of things most teenage girls were doing then—buying candy, shopping for makeup and nail polish, listening to 45s in the record store sound booths. Sometimes we would see "real" high school girls also poring over the makeup counters at Woolworth's or examining scarves and mittens at the J. C. Penny's, but we would hurry away with our heads lowered, fiercely aware of our jutting stomachs. The girls who were from Akron never accompanied us on our walks and were allowed visits from their parents only. Although I would make friends at Florence Crittenton, I also felt keenly detached, severed from my family, far from the familiar, and acutely homesick. Was this place a safe haven for lonely girls or a necessary banishment for the disgraceful? I could not tell.

For a while during my stay at Florence Crittenton, I would call for a taxi on Sunday mornings and it would deliver me to the Episcopal Church across town. There I would listen intently to the sermon, sing the hymns, repeat the prayers reverently, bow and cross myself at the right moments in the ritual, take Communion, and beg silently for forgiveness. Although my aunt made sure I had pretty dresses to wear to church, I never removed my big, bulky winter coat during the service. My well-meaning aunt had let the minister of the church knew who I was and why I was there, so young and alone. One morning after services, he saw me emerge from the church and took the opportunity to ask a couple to give me a ride home so that I would not have to call for a cab. As he opened their rear door for me, he did not tell them where they were to deliver me, only that I lived in their neighborhood. Embarrassed and unsure how to proceed, I gave them the street address of my "home," but not its name. Did they know? Could they tell? The couple made small talk with me as we crossed town, asking about school, what was my favorite subject, did I plan to go to college. When I told them to stop at the Florence Crittenton gate, I could see their expressions turn from mild interest to surprise and unease. It was clear that they had not known "who" I really was. Silent now, the man stopped the car at the curb, and I hoisted myself gracelessly out. Profoundly self-conscious, I mumbled a weak thank you and goodbye. Whatever the first impression I had might have made, it had been thoroughly erased by my real address.

My aunt was right: even strangers had to be protected from my condition. Humiliated and sad, I recommitted myself to keeping this mortifying interruption in my life a secret forever and from all. People wouldn't be able to handle the truth about me. And despite my aunt's urging, I refused to return to the Akron Episcopal Church.

Each of us had to take a new name when we came to Florence Critten-ton; we were told not to reveal our "true" identity or where we were from. I became "Jan Mason," the name my aunt had chosen for me when she signed me up for my stay. To me, "Jan" seemed flat and plain; I resented it. And, to this day, I cringe when it's used to address me and immediately correct the affable, unknowing people who think they're just being kind and familiar when they shorten my name from "Janet" to "Jan."

I wanted a name like my friend "Bernadette." Bernadette herself ex-plained to me that she had chosen her name specifically because it was the name of the Catholic saint to whom the Virgin Mary had revealed herself with the words, "I am the Immaculate Conception." Now her choice seems weirdly ironic to me, but at the time I found it wonderfully dramatic and perfectly fitting. Immaculate conception seemed as reasonable as inter-course to me. None of us ever talked about the actual circumstances that had brought about our pregnancies.

On that first day in Akron, after I had been introduced to Tina and a few of the other girls, my aunt took me shopping for maternity clothes. I assume this was her way of cheering me up, in case I was forlorn and clinging when it came time for her to leave. We bought smocks and pants with big elastic waists and those pretty dresses for church. The mater-nity clothes were nice looking and pleased me. I brought them back to the home, eager to try them on, looking forward to organizing my new belongings in my new room.

Although I did cry when my aunt left, and spent several of the follow-ing afternoons in my bed, listless and homesick, I did come to adjust to the routine at Florence Crittenton. I learned how to keep busy and continued to suppress any real consciousness of why I was there in the first place. And on that first evening, free now in some strange way to be myself, I thank-fully peeled off the girdle and stuffed it in the back of a drawer. Afraid of making my way downstairs for that first, awkward meal, I locked myself into the old-fashioned bathroom and ran the fabulously huge, claw-footed bathtub—another prop for a captive princess in an enchanted castle—to the brim with steaming water. After my ablutions, I finally dared to take a look at myself in the long, speckled mirror on the back of the bathroom door and sighed, deeply dismayed by the reality before me. Complicated blue veins crisscrossed my swollen breasts; a darkly visible brown line extended down from my distended belly button into my pubic hair; and my round stomach seemed impossibly to be growing hair on it. Disbelief was difficult to suspend given this reflection, so I quickly pulled on my underpants, fastened my bra, donned one of my new smocks and a pair of elasticized slacks, combed my hair, and headed down to dinner, nervous but ready to be introduced to more of my new peers. I was determined to be good, no matter what, and my uncomplaining forbearance worked to make this newest phase of the secret easier on everyone.

Martha's Vineyard, 2004

Why were we girls at Florence Crittenton disposed to keep our secrets? Were we all so driven by guilt and shame that we could not comfort one another's broken hearts? We might have compared "war stories," consoling one another over the boys who made love to us only to abandon us. We might have daydreamed together about our babies, how they might look and how we would feel about them. We might have talked about our futures, but our prospects were so befogged by the event looming ahead of us that such dreaminess seemed senseless and strangely out of place. Many of the older "girls" at Florence Crittenton whiled away the hours while the rest of us were in school by knitting. I too learned how to knit while I was there. One would think we would have knitted booties, sweaters, or Afghans as gifts for our babies, tender mementos they could remember us by. But such gifts were against the rules. They would be unappreciated; adoptive parents would not accept something that would stand as a reminder of our part in this drama. "An exercise in futility," we were told. So we spent our time knitting scarves for our mothers or afghans for our grandmothers. I took on the knitting of a fabulously complex cable-knit sweater for my mother—turquoise yarn with silver buttons. It turned out misshapen and small, but it occupied me for weeks.

This was a secret time to be gotten through, a shameful present that would became a forgotten past. We all thought if we obeyed the rules, we would emerge from it untarnished and free. We believed in the rituals and wisdom of the adult world. If only we followed these elaborate procedures, then surely our salvation was around the corner. Why become attached to one another? None of us wanted to know anybody who was a player in this scrupulously scripted charade.

Only Tina would become my cautious confidant during those three months. Our circumstances were similar. She too loved her boyfriend deeply and believed they would marry someday. But unlike Alec, Tina's boyfriend knew of her pregnancy and her whereabouts; in fact, his parents were paying for her room and board. She had been exiled just as thoroughly as I; even though she was not due until May, his parents had insisted she enter Florence Crittenton in late November (before she started "to show") and had forbidden any correspondence between her and their son. Naturally, they held Tina responsible and had told her outright that she would never be welcome in their lives again. I left Florence Crittenton long before Tina, but before going I furtively told her my real name and how to contact me, and she called me, five years later. Her baby boy had been born with such serious birth defects that he was unadoptable. Ironically, it was this misfortune that let her bring him home instead of giving him away. Her boyfriend's parents were forced to relent, and the two were married immediately after her return from Florence Crittenton. Tina passed her GED easily, and her boyfriend graduated from a public high school a month after they married. The next fall, they began college together. When we talked, she had just given birth to their third son. How paradoxical that it took a so-called damaged baby boy to bring about what seemed to me a gloriously happy ending.

One night as I sat in the television room watching *Bewitched* and playing hearts with three other girls, the subject of hymens came up. One of the girls, Linda, who would pass on the black dress with orange and white flower sprigs to me, was older, twenty, and seemed much more informed that the rest of us. We were all regretting that we had lost the chance to be virgins for our husbands-to-be on our wedding nights, but Linda proffered the following theory: "If a girl does not have sex for seven years," she said, "her hymen will grow back."

I listened intently and calculated: "You mean, if I'm sixteen now, I can get married when I am twenty-three, after I graduate from college, just like I'm supposed to and I'll be a virgin again?"

"Yes," Linda replied.

What a reprieve! I would not be "damaged goods." I would still be able to offer up the "bloody sheet." That most essential part of me would have been restored in order to be lost again. He, whoever he was, would never even have to know that I had ever had sex, much less a baby!

That I desperately wanted to believe Linda's theory demonstrates that although it was 1965, not 1955 or 1855, virginity still felt like the necessary ingredient for a "real" marriage. I adhered fervently to a worldview constructed in the fifties, and for years after, I remained unequipped to critically examine neither the demeaning assumptions about women that stood behind my secrecy nor the absurd mythologies about sex that have circulated among girls for centuries. I believed Linda and began to plan my life accordingly.

I continued to write to Karen while I was at Florence Crittenton. My letters were still postmarked Pepper Pike because I scrupulously abided by all of my aunt's maneuvers to ensure the secret of my whereabouts. I gave my letters to her when she visited me in Akron, and then she would mail them from Pepper Pike. My imagination was still unmoored from the restraints of the ordinary, and I continued the stories of Betsy Bridges and my ball gowns, fabricating details with abandon, although I was also making some errors: "Betsy Bridges, my best friend, got the girl lead in our Junior class play, *Teahouse of the August Moon*, and she is Lotus Blossom. I decided not to try out because I'm already too busy. The Assembly Ball was so much fun. I wore a green velvet dress. It really was a 'Cinderella ball,' and I'll never forget it." In my December letter, I had told Karen that my dress for the ball was green silk. By the time I wrote the January letter, I correctly remembered the imaginary dress's color, but had mixed up its material. Now it was velvet rather than silk—a small detail, but representative of the difficulty of sustaining consistency in make-believe lives and a harbinger of the adult reality that fabrication eventually unravels. Karen did not catch my slip. In fact, she said she never once doubted the faraway Ohio life I was creating for her.

In late February, when I was beginning my ninth month of pregnancy, I wrote to Karen about a planned ski trip, but I no longer had the imaginary fervor to dream up details such as a fashionable parka, a comical spill, or a princely rescuer. I ended up telling her that the imaginary ski trip had to be cancelled for want of snow. I followed this disappointment with a lackluster report of a downtown shopping expedition with unnamed girlfriends with whom I found nothing to buy. My subdued tone was a change from the earlier exuberant letters whose audacity was being tempered by the actual gray textures of winter in Akron and the heavy, impending reality of my condition. I also told Karen about the real death of my grandfather on New Year's Eve, poignantly exposing my lonely feelings of faraway seclusion and growing unsuitability: "I wanted to come home so much then, but I guess it's better that I stayed back here and didn't add to all the confusion and tears." I would not write Karen again for six weeks.

When girls went into labor at Florence Crittenton, they would sit in a special wooden rocking chair in the TV room. It was a house rule that you could not sit on an upholstered chair or couch while in labor in case your water broke. I had always kept my distance from these proceedings, but other excited girls would sit diligently, timing the patient's contractions until they got to be about fifteen minutes apart. Then our nurse, Mrs. Reilley, would bundle the girl up and deliver her safely to the hospital. Girls would return in two or three days, pale and quiet. Either in denial or childish obliviousness, I simply assumed the tired cheerlessness I saw in their faces was the natural aftermath of giving birth, and that I too would simply be "sick" for a while after my delivery. I imagined it as something akin to having the flu.

My aunt had taken care of all the arrangements concerning the adoption procedures and my medical care in Akron. Although all the girls at Florence Crittenton were required to attend a one-hour class to prepare us for childbirth, I still could hardly believe I was pregnant with a baby. Aunt Jo encouraged me to think of "my condition" as a kind of temporary setback—like a badly broken leg or a serious appendicitis attack. When I did think of giving birth, I pictured a bright day with my aunt by my side in complete control of the situation. She would take me to the hospital and hand me over to my doctor's superior care. I imagined myself sleeping peacefully while he carefully monitored my contractions because I would be unconscious. Aunt Jo told me, and I believed her, that I would feel very little pain and would later be unable to recall the ordeal because she and

my doctor had agreed to have me as heavily sedated as was safe throughout the entire labor and delivery. We never actually talked about the baby
itself. My aunt must have believed that by avoiding that reality, I would
continue to discount the baby's actual presence in the world forever. It was
common practice at the time that an unwed mother never see the baby or
even know its gender. That was the plan for me. I would have no recol-
lection of the birth or the baby. It would be removed and then whisked
out of the room and out of my life. My trespasses would be forgiven, the
secret would be ensconced, and I would return to life as a sixteen-year-old
junior in high school who had taken a momentary rebellious swerve but
had recovered well. It was a nice way to anticipate the event, but as often
happens in life, these plans would go terribly wrong.

 ## 15 *Sorrow*

Akron, March 1965

AT SEVEN O'CLOCK on the evening of March 19, I began noticing a tightening of my stomach—no pain but definite contractions. This was a surprise since I was not due to deliver until the end of the month. Mrs. Reilley, our nurse, was busy dispensing Milk of Magnesia and other medications to girls who needed them. When I told her what I was feeling, she dismissed the mild contractions as false labor. In fact, no one was due to have a baby in the upcoming week, so she had arranged to squeeze in some off-duty time and visit her daughter in Youngstown for the next three days. She assured me I'd be fine, finished her tasks, and hastened out the door and into her car. Snow was in the forecast and she wanted to get to Youngstown before it began.

False labor or not, it was my turn to sit in the special rocking chair, and in the tradition of the home, other girls sat cheerfully around me, timing the irregular intervals between contractions. It was exciting until we all had to go to bed at eleven. It was expected that the girls at Florence Crittenton would be in labor for at least twenty-four hours, if not longer, so if I actually was in labor, everyone, especially me, assumed that I would spend an uncomfortable night, but that the next morning would find me back in the rocking chair, conscientiously timing my contractions. Mrs. Williams would then calmly call my aunt, and she would drive down from Cleveland to make sure everything went as planned. We were all very wrong, and a long, forsaken night ensued.

Instead, alone in my bed that night, I kept checking my watch with the flashlight my aunt had given me so I could read after lights out. At 1:00 A.M., my pains were ten minutes apart; at 2:00, eight minutes; at 3:00 I decided to stop counting, willing my body to halt a process that was escalating all too rapidly. The little illuminated hands on my watch were approaching 4:00 when, in the middle of an intense contraction, my water broke, seeping into the mattress, warm, plentiful, and alarming.

According to another rule of the house, given this new development, I had to notify Mrs. Williams, which meant waking her. I reluctantly knocked on her door, apologizing for getting her up. She was clearly tired and annoyed by the disturbance; this part of her job must have been one of the most unpleasant. She sent me back to my room to dress and grab my overnight bag, which we had been instructed to pack with necessities and keep ready under our beds. Since Mrs. Reilley was far away by now, Mrs. Williams had to call an on-call nurse. Mrs. Williams could not take me to the hospital because she could not leave the house unattended, and again rules forbade that she just call for a cab and direct the driver to deliver me to the hospital. Instead, a nurse I was unfamiliar with had to come from across town to get me. As if to deepen the melodrama, it had been snowing heavily for several hours; the nurse called back to say that rather than try to drive herself, she had decided to call a cab. I was to wait for her in the downstairs hall with my coat and overnight case ready. Mrs. Williams went back to bed.

I waited for her alone for over an hour, wondering how I would live through this nightmare unaccompanied. The pains were shocking; I could not help but cry out every time one gripped me, so I kept stuffing my mittens in my mouth to muffle my insuppressible yelping. The house was cold, dark, and profoundly still. Above me on the second and third floors, everyone slept. My stifled cries and subsequent whimpering awakened no one. I kept looking at the pay phone. I imagined calling my parents. I needed them then more than at any other time in my life; this was my hardest thing, and I was completely alone. Early on my aunt told me that it was too upsetting to my parents to hear about the details of the pregnancy. We were all in denial—until now. But I did not dare call them in the middle of this Dickensian night and draw them into my panic and pain. I just sat there and imagined dialing the phone, and then I could hear their phone ringing next to their bed in San Marino and my mother's concerned "Hello?" and then my inexcusable begging to please, please help me.

Finally, a little after 5:00 A.M., a woman I had never seen before but had to assume was the on-call nurse walked in the big front door and hustled me out to the cab waiting in the snow. She seemed inexplicably angry and entirely unsympathetic. She was exasperated by my tears and moans. When the cab driver showed concern, she irately dismissed him, snapping that there was plenty of time, and that I was just acting like a baby myself. My labor pains were by now coming one on top of the other, yet I was unable to convince her that they were valid, that I was in actual, desperate pain. Completely distraught, I frantically begged the cab driver to help me—which infuriated her; she shouted at me, "Shut up!" and slapped me hard across the face. I was dumbfounded by her malice and utterly helpless. When we finally arrived, she shrilly cursed me when I told her I couldn't walk and hauled me out of the cab. More afraid of her than of the pain, I hobbled up a ramp, across the entryway, through the doors, and into a brightly lit hall. She yanked off my snow-covered coat and pulled me along beside her, gripping my arm like a vise. Later, I would watch the imprint of her fingertips, four little purple bruises each with a small cut at the top from her fingernails, slowly disappear from the inside of my arm.

The kind cab driver did help me; he had run ahead and found an orderly who now moved swiftly to guide me into a wheelchair and we quickly moved down a long white hallway. I assume the on-call nurse, from whom I was so glad to escape, checked me officially into the hospital. Hugging my coat and overnight case to me with one hand and the other gripping the wheelchair's arm, I gratefully let the orderly whisk me into an elevator, up a few floors, down another hallway, and finally into a room where that gentle hospital nurse was waiting to help me undress. I handed myself over to another stranger, unable to do anything else. This time, thankfully, the people who would lead me through the next steps of this long, grim night were sympathetic. Just as I have never forgotten the off-duty nurse's inexplicable fury, I have also not forgotten those others that helped me: the cab driver, the orderly, the nurse, and the intern. With compassion, they saw me for what I was, a lost child in baffling pain, and they cared for me accordingly.

•   •   •

I give birth to Sorrow a little after 6:00 A.M. Because of the lower-body numbness brought on by the saddle block the intern administered, I do not see or feel my daughter being born, but I immediately hear her crying. Even before she completely emerges from my body, she's crying. She is not placed on my stomach, like most newborns are, but when I ask, I am allowed to look at her for about a minute. I am allowed to touch her rosy, glistening cheek and her wet, dark hair. I see that the umbilical chord has been cut; its small, yellow-gray stump extending from her navel is all that is left of our lives' intimate connection. Her tiny perfect hands are furiously grasping at the new, shockingly cold air around her, so different from the peaceful, watery warmth of my body that had rhythmically cradled her. She won't stop crying, and I know that I can soothe her, if they will just let me hold her. Her wails are infectious; her entire body quivers. My crying resumes, this time much like hers, those same big, gulping, cadenced wails. I realize that this is my one and only chance to claim her. I beg the nurse to let me hold her: "Please, please, just let me have her. Please give her to me. Please."

The resolute nurse shakes her head: "No, I'm sorry; I can't." I am left with an image I will always carry, a terrible burden yet a treasured memory: my baby is crying so hard, her fists and legs frantically beating the air—her high, shrill command to me to comfort and suckle her. My arms are outstretched; they extend before me, supplicating, ready to receive her forever. And then she fades from my line of vision. I push up, panic-stricken, trying hysterically to free myself, to get off the table, but I cannot move my deadened legs that are still tied to the stirrups. A male voice, probably the intern, says, "We're going to let you sleep now." I feel the puncture in my arm of the injection that will sedate me; the room warms; my sobs ebb, the waves of shuddering fade, and the tiny hiccups stop. Slowly I succumb to the warm drift away from that night.

Martha's Vineyard, 2004

How was it that I was fated to meet the cruelest person of my life on that portentous night? I would see the on-call nurse one more time. When I returned to Florence Crittenton, I told Tina what had happened. Apparently, she told Mrs. Reilley, who must have questioned the nurse's conduct. A few days later, she came back, slamming into my room, livid, hissing at me to keep my mouth shut, that I didn't know what I was talking about. I was terrified. This was my first lesson in how crucial it was that the details of that night be left to my dreams. As I write it down, I am confounded by how much the cab ride itself reads like an overdone, theatrical nightmare. It also astounds me that my parents, my aunt, and Sorrow's father were all sleeping peacefully while I, at my most vulnerable, was being mistreated by a stranger. To protect me from trauma, they had made complicated and expensive arrangements. But I still ended up alone at 5:00 A.M.—helpless and terrified. It remains a paradox that this thing my parents did because they wanted to safeguard me from the cruelty of people did just the opposite. Instead, despite good intentions, they sent me defenselessly into a night from which I have never completely recovered.

As the tranquilizing shot was administered, I knew that I was finally being granted that promised unconsciousness that was supposed to have shielded me from the acute pain and cruel separation. I did not know that a door was closing that I would not be able to reopen. I would not see my daughter again.

Because there had not been enough time for my regular doctor to get to the hospital to deliver the baby, and because I was fully conscious for her birth, some of Aunt Jo's instructions had not been carried out. How grateful I am to the people in the delivery room for giving me that minute with my baby, no matter how much anguish, no matter how many nightmares that moment has evoked. Sorrow's tiny image still abides with me. It has clarified rather than faded over these years, and though I might now have difficulty picturing my mother's face even though I have only just visited her, my wailing baby girl remains crystalline in my memory. I cherish her endurance.

I know now that Sorrow's birth was an irreparable tear in the fabric of my adolescence, a rent that became the most meaningful and consequential event of my life. The night of Sorrow's birth ignited the implosion of a self I had only tenuously pieced together by sixteen. The center that had provided the centrifugal force that held me together—a bold, bright, sunny girl—was obliterated that night as I turned into a helpless, unfamiliar, straining body consumed by unimaginable pain. I had no idea what was going to happen to me, who would finally find me in that lonely hall at Florence Crittenton. That I was found and delivered to the hospital did not make it easier to cope with the knife in my heart—surrendering the baby I loved instantly and completely. She was, I believe, the only thing in the world that might have repaired me, recentered me after the pain and terror of that night, but she was taken away. And so my selfhood imploded into fragments of hysteria. The tranquilizer the doctor administered was simply the first of thousands more I would take in order to quell the pain, to silence the screams, to restrain my Sorrow.

When I woke later that day, a metamorphosis had occurred: the girl I had been was gone. I can remember that first girl. She was so unformed and so insubstantial that looking back, it is easy to see how easily she was erased. In a way, I was like my daughter. Indeed, two births could have been registered that day. Sorrow begins her life, and I also had to begin my life anew. But this time, I had to start over hobbled by a complex psychological wound, shell-shocked from a night that had shattered an irreclaimable girl.

Expected to emerge from the ash like the phoenix, my fledgling identity was painfully complicated by the duplicity that had to be a critical part of the new me. Not only did I need to construct a new self, but it also had to be necessarily split: one half was the more genuine but deeply wounded child who emerged from a secret trauma; the other, the counterfeit teenager, pretending to be that other, sunny girl, the girl I was before Sorrow. But I would never find her optimism again.

Later, I would spin an intricate personal narrative, weaving my memories, constructing a passable identity, but I would never faithfully incorporate within it either the actual events of Sorrow's birth or my inner, inextinguishable grief at her loss. In fact, I would create tangled, conflicted layers of self, a complicated orchestration that consistently failed me. An inexorable past would always insinuate itself into my present, and I would break apart, falling into sloughs of depression so deep I feared I would never climb out.

Now I can appreciate why these periods of deep-seated unhappiness kept returning. When Sorrow was taken away, a multitude of overwhelming emotions were created. Most of the time I can pretend those repressed emotions are not there, but inevitably I return to them as surely as the tides ebb and flow. The triggers are not always the same, so I have never been able to identify exactly what provokes a recurrence, but inevitably I find myself drawn back to the same terror, helplessness, grief, even the transforming hysteria. The anesthesia I have pumped into my system through years of hard work—my busy family and demanding career—always wears off, and I lose control, falling into inconsolable melancholy.

Thirty-five years after Sorrow's birth, I will find Merideth, the beautiful, accomplished woman that Sorrow became. One would think our reunion would eradicate all sorrow, self-doubt, and emotional susceptibility. But a shadow remains. Certainly, the shadow is not Sorrow, whom I have always accepted, always wanted, always treasured. Nor is the shadow my parents or my aunt, all of whom I love. I know that they wanted more than anything to protect me. The fateful events of that night were caused by a tangled confluence of circumstance and random bad luck. There was no demon, not even the tired, abusive nurse. Nevertheless, the shadow endures.

What I did for too long was to deny that it should have any significance in my life. But denial is a failed strategy. Despite my aunt's and my parents' unspoken dicta not to feel and not to recall, the night I lost Sorrow remains always. I encounter the memory over and over again: the icy delivery room; the precise sounds of Sorrow's cries and my own wailing; my dead legs in the stirrups; the image of my tiny baby, so vulnerably naked except for the whitish, chalky substance that covers her; my own outstretched arms. Despite my earnest, most concentrated efforts, I am inundated by the flood of feeling this memory releases, leaving me, even now as I write this, in disarray—discomposed, stranded, utterly alone.

THE JOURNEY

16 The Gray Room

Child with a child pretending
Weary of lies you are sending home
So you sign all the papers in the family name
You're sad and you're sorry, but you're not ashamed
Little green, have a happy ending
           —Joni Mitchell, "Little Green," *Blue* (1971)

Akron, March 1965

I STAYED IN THE HOSPITAL for two days. Babies were bundled up and brought from the nursery to their mothers every few hours. On that first afternoon, after awakening from a deep, death-like sleep brought on by the intern's sedating needle, I waited for my baby too. The nurses bustled about, delivering swaddled babies here and there. I waited and waited, but, of course, Sorrow never arrived. Too shy to ask why and apprehensive that this might be "policy" for girls like me, I faintheartedly hobbled down to the nursery to see her behind the glass partition. I gave my name, "Jan Mason" to the attending nurse, but she only shook her head, "No," from her adjoining office. I tried again. Maybe I needed to say "Janet Ellerby"; I wasn't sure who I was here. This time she emerged to explain tersely that according to Florence Crittenton procedures, the baby had been placed in a nursery on a different floor; none of these babies were mine.

Slowly, holding back a flood of emotion, I made my way back to the miserable isolation of my room, trying to avoid all eyes. The last thing I wanted was to be noticed. Enveloped once again by my now-agonizing difference, I knew kind words or gentle gestures would be torture. Perhaps I made myself invisible enough as I tottered down that corridor, or perhaps people were familiar with lost girls like me because no one approached me that day other than to deliver or collect a food tray or brusquely attend to my minor medical needs. From my window, I watched the wet snow, still falling profusely, blanketing Ohio, preventing my aunt from traveling, keeping me isolated from everyone. I did not telephone my parents nor did they call me.

I had assumed my adolescent California body would be restored to me after giving birth, but for days it would remain foreign territory. Stitches, apparently sewn after I had been sedated, had left me sore and swollen, but I was much too reticent to ask about them and too fearful to examine what had changed "down there." A nurse administered a shot, telling me it would cause my milk to dry up, and she bound my chest with long lengths of white flannel. Such measures had very little effect; my milk would flow plentifully the next day, leaking through all the tightly bound layers, leaving me nervous and embarrassed for having to disturb a busy nurse to ask for dry flannel and a dry gown. As she shook her head, sighing with frustration when she realized that even the bed sheets would have to be changed, I blushed with guilt over this body of mine that I still couldn't control.

My hospital roommate arrived that evening—an enormous woman who had just lost her premature baby. She was already the mother of five, and she was sympathetic when I told her tearfully that I had to give my baby up for adoption and was not allowed to see her. Although she too must have been grieving, she seemed resigned to her loss. She told me something important: that I would someday have my own babies, and they would make up for the pain that now seemed so unbearable. Her assurance gave me a glimmer of hope, if not solace. Her priest came to see her and I watched enthralled as he gave her the Host to eat. They sat quietly, whispering arrangements, and when it was time for him to leave, she kindly asked me to pray with them. Together we prayed for our lost babies. Her husband came next, rotund, ruddy, and astoundingly cheerful. I remember him telling her doctor confidently, "It won't be long 'til we're back here again!" The doctor grumbled to him to be sure that his wife took off some weight first, but I had no doubt that they would be back, and I could picture their pink, chubby, angelic babies waiting to be born. Her husband left with the priest but came back shortly, sneaking contraband chocolate milk shakes in for both of us. I knew I wasn't supposed to have that treat, having been told that drinking milk would only produce more milk, but I couldn't resist the sweet consolation of that creamy dessert, not that evening nor the next, when he arrived again, this time with strawberry shakes. They endure still as my comfort food.

Aunt Jo arrived on the second day; the blizzard that had made my journey to the hospital so frightful was finally over. When I saw her, I dissolved into more inconsolable weeping. Aunt Jo admonished me gently, repeating what I already knew: I should feel relieved that "it" was over and thankful for all my mother and father were doing to get me out of this secret trouble. I believed her and felt more guilt for my thanklessness, yet I could not authentically summon either relief or gratitude. Neither emotion was available, no matter how sensible my aunt's remonstrances sounded, but I pretended to calm down, just for her.

While she was there, seated by my bed, an official-looking woman came into the room and asked me to fill out my baby's birth certificate. *My* baby's birth certificate? I could still be asked to do that? I scrambled up, reaching eagerly for the clipboard. It was almost as if she had brought me the baby herself. But my aunt instantly intervened, lunging to intercept the proffered clipboard. This was no concern of mine, she scolded. Quickly, she gathered her crutches and ushered the surprised woman out of the room.

Left alone, I dove under my pillow and gave in to what were now all-too-familiar tears, gulps, and shudderings. But this time, as the sobs abated, I defied my aunt in the only way available to me: secretly I bequeathed upon my lost baby girl the name that Hardy's Tess had given her lost child: "Sorrow." I committed the details of her birth to memory: Name: *Sorrow*; Weight: *6 lbs. 4½ oz.*; Time of birth: *6:04 A.M., March 20, 1965.* I inscribed everything I knew about her on my heart. Slowly my breathing regulated; my tears subsided. Obsessively I began to whisper a refrain I would intone in secret for decades, "*My* Sorrow; *My* Sorrow."

When my aunt buzzed back into the room, business completed, she saw the wet pillow, my wild hair, flushed face, and reddened, swollen eyes, and heard what to her sounded like some crazy mantra. Disconcerted, she bathed my face with a cold washcloth, shushing me sternly, demanding I get control of myself—now! I complied. Looking back, I think I must have briefly descended one more time into the hysteria that had engulfed me in the taxicab and later, in the delivery room. But this time, Aunt Jo pulled me back to the surface with common sense. No slap or tranquilizer was needed to curb my strange performance, only brusque directions and practical advice.

Toward the end of my aunt's visit that day, she had me write a letter to Karen, which she then took back with her and mailed from Pepper Pike. I could only manage an apologetic, brief note that read, "I'm really sorry I've taken so long in answering your letter. But you can't imagine how busy I've been with testing and everything." I was pretending to refer to school tests, but in fact, I had just been through the most grueling test of my life. My summing up with "and everything" was the only way I could account for my descent into trauma. In this note, as I had done before, I used a holiday to structure passing time and dutifully made up a perfunctory report of decorating for a St. Patrick's Day dance at school. However, I included nothing about attending the dance itself and demonstrated none of my past inventive flare. As Aunt Jo instructed, I added briefly that I was leaving the next day on a school trip to Washington, D.C.

In fact, this convoluted stratagem was one my aunt had worked out weeks before, and it enabled her to have postcards of the Jefferson Memorial at cherry blossom time sent off to my California friends at the time I delivered Sorrow. In case Alec had told his friends that he had sex with me in late June and they had been counting the months, these postcards were meant to silence any remaining conjectures about my abrupt disappearance. I could not possibly be having a baby in late March or early April because here was proof—I was a tourist in Washington, D.C., with postcards to prove my whereabouts.

Now that Sorrow was born, the postcard ruse was launched. I had conscientiously written them out weeks before, and now my aunt had them mailed to California from D.C. by a willing friend of hers so they would have the correct postmark displaying the exonerating date. The postcard of frilly pink cherry trees that Karen received is postmarked March 24 and reads, "Dear Karen, Isn't this beautiful? Having a wonderful time. Just got back from seeing the White House. It is really gorgeous. Saw Kennedy's grave too. See you soon—Janet." In actuality, I would not visit Washington, D.C., for another six years, and I have yet to see the cherry trees in bloom, visit the White house, or see Kennedy's grave. Nevertheless, it is fitting and revealing that I mention visiting a huge old house, for when I had dutifully written out this postcard, I myself had been buried behind the thick, though finally unprotective, walls of Florence Crittenton. That of all the places to visit in D.C. I chose Kennedy's grave, where I knew he lay buried with the baby that he and Jackie had lost, is also telling. Losing my own baby was a withholding that would always feel like death to me.

On my third morning in the hospital, I dressed one more time in the black dress and was released to Mrs. Reilly, who had only just returned from her visit with her daughter. Silently she drove me back to Florence Crittenton for a required ten-day postdelivery stay—another regulation in the home's procedures. At the time, I thought it was to ensure my healthy recovery, but now I understand it had much more to do with adoption requirements.

I was not allowed to go back to my cozy little room and Tina. In fact, a new girl had already taken my bed. There was a special room for girls who had given birth, a ward-like room with four white institutional beds lined up side by side. No longer pregnant, I seemed an interloper at Florence Crittenton. Because of another Victorian rule, "newly delivered" girls could not go up and down stairs. I was expected to remain in that dull, lifeless room, enclosed by its four gray walls, my meals brought up to me on a tray. Unlike the rest of the house, this room looked and felt like a dismal cell. No other girl gave birth during my ten days of incarceration. What may have been welcome privacy to others was for me bitter loneliness. I had no roommate, no confidante. In retrospect, it is clear that I was in desperate need of any gentle commiseration, but there was no one to ask. All the other girls, all of whom were still pregnant, avoided me just as I had avoided the downcast girls who had preceded me in this special room. I lost the will to wash or eat, and sleep was almost entirely elusive.

Alone in that room, laden with a barrage of grief I could not restrain, I deteriorated in ways too deep to express.

• • •

After ten days of alternating listlessness and silent despondency and ten nights of tearful, debilitating insomnia in the gray room, I was asked to bathe, dress, and come downstairs. Ushered into Mrs. Williams's darkly formal office, I was introduced to a social worker and a representative from the adoption agency. I was handed a pen and showed where to sign the requisite adoption papers. I mutely and obediently acquiesced and was then excused. The formality was ominous, and again complete loneliness and utter helplessness overwhelmed me. No one informed me that I did not have to do this, to sign away my baby. In fact, I did not understand that until I signed those papers, she was *my* daughter—that no one else could have her unless I consented.

I thought I had lost her when she was taken from me in the delivery room. After all, it was then that the nurse had said I could not hold her. And the next day, another nurse had told me I could not see her, that she was in another nursery. I interpreted these refusals as meaning that I had no right to her. That she was already gone. My signature was only the last step of a fait accompli. For years after, I excoriated myself for my ignorance, but I have since learned that this was a common deception. Girls were deliberately not informed of their parental rights—not informed that keeping their baby was an option, even if they were not yet adults, even if their parents did not consent. I realize now that I was coerced by well-meaning people into doing something that for me was deeply unnatural, aberrant. But then, at sixteen with no sense of self-reliance, no means of self-support, and no informed legal council, there was no other conceivable option. I had never been encouraged to be decisive or to think for myself, and my previous tries at independence had gotten me into grave trouble.

There was an adoption "plan." The representative from the adoption agency told me that "the" baby (never "my" baby) would now be the daughter of a professional couple who could not have children of their own. She told me that "the" baby's parents (not her "adoptive parents") were stable, smart people in their thirties, both in the medical profession. Their occupations would ensure that "the" baby would be raised in a home free from financial worries; in fact, she would have the same kind of upbringing that I had had. Her adoptive mother was going to stop working and they planned to adopt at least one more child. At some point in her life, she would be told that she was adopted. The "plan" provided me no comfort. It was meant to sound like a soothing, rational plan, but it was hiding a terrifying, traumatic, and oppressive experience. The plan allowed Sorrow to be taken away from me and any of the ways that might have brought her back to me were hidden once it was set in motion.

I remember Mrs. Williams searching for me after the signing—and again I found myself apologizing to her, this time for worrying her by hiding in a remote part of the house where I could mourn undetected. I had not known that I did not have to sign; I had not known that I had a right to my child, not just to hold her but to feed her with the milk my body was still producing just for her, to bathe her, clothe her, to comfort her with my healthy body that did know what to do with itself and would not stop pining for her. My body ached for her touch as hers must have ached for mine, but all I could do was to leak the milk, tears, and blood that I wiped shamefully away. If she was anyone's, I believed, she was my parents'. And they did not want her. What I wanted was so irrelevant that I did not even hazard asking it of myself. I was shattered even though I was told over and over that I should feel relieved, fortunate, that the worst was over. That was cold comfort. It would never be over. And that loss, that chasm, that split in my very being, would never heal.

Martha's Vineyard, 2004

In February 1965, one month before I gave birth to Sorrow, Joni Mitchell gave birth in Ontario to a daughter, and although her circumstances were different than mine, the result was the same. Alone, broke, and unequipped for motherhood, she too was forced to place her daughter for adoption. Not until 1994, almost thirty years later, would she tell *Vogue* magazine that she had lost this secret child, though she would cryptically sing about her and the decision to relinquish her as early as 1971 in her song "Little Green." Mitchell's story provides me with some solace: someone so talented and famous was as vulnerable as I. In the winter of '65, she too was forced to make the same decision that had been made for me.

For girls like Tina, Bernadette, Joni Mitchell, and me, "choice" was not a concept, not even a word in our vocabulary. If we had been poor girls or girls of color, most likely we would have been required to marry as soon as our parents found out about our pregnancies, or our mothers or grandmothers would have taken on the responsibility of raising another child. But illegitimate children and "shotgun" marriages with a full-term baby coming only six or seven months after the wedding date were anathema to our parents. We were smart, healthy, middle-class girls, meant to succeed in college, and only then to settle down to promising marriages and children. Adoption was the only solution for girls like us, and there was definitely a market for our healthy, white babies, as there is today.

There were businesses like Florence Crittenton in every large city in America to hide us, and hundreds of adoption agencies to take care of the sought-after product of our fruitful nine months. No one thought about social programs that might have created homes for us to return to with our newborns, places where we could have learned how to be competent mothers. Cultural codes were so punitive that such a solution to unplanned pregnancies was unthinkable. We had to agree to a stunningly simplistic, unexamined agenda: to be secreted away, give birth without a fuss, willingly relinquish our babies, and return—grateful, contrite, and unscathed—to the lives that had been planned for us. Because our promising futures could not be blighted by stained pasts, we had to agree to an imposed secrecy and follow it with a rigorousness that still surprises. We agreed to adoption, we agreed to our own unsuitableness, we agreed to a shameful interpretation of our actions, we agreed to take on the secret of our lost babies because we had no means to question the values that informed those decisions. Still influenced by the cultural rigidity of the fifties, we had no means to become the loving, responsible, proud, and capable young mothers we might have been.

Looking back now at those incomprehensible, lonely gray days at Florence Crittenton after giving birth, I can understand the new, forlorn girl I was, pacing around that bleak room. Now I can appreciate and account for her confusion and dejection. Now I can take the word *trauma* and apply it to that night of solitary physical pain, which I had been in no way prepared for, and to my unanticipated, inescapable agony in that cold delivery room. I know now I was feeling the torment any new mother feels who loses her baby. When a woman loses her child after carrying it for nine months, when her baby dies, we feel tremendous sympathy for her. It seems the worst possible misfortune. We wonder how she will cope with her grief; we hope she will become pregnant again soon so that her loss can somehow begin to heal. Yet I was expected to feel happy, relieved, unburdened after losing Sorrow. No wonder I was baffled. In the struggle between nature and culture, I lost. I had been told what to anticipate—unconsciousness—but my actual experience had invalidated all predictions. Furthermore, I had to keep my grief deep beneath the surface because if I showed it, such indulgence would be perceived as ungrateful and unreasonable. After all, I had been saved from lifelong humiliation, hadn't I?

In retrospect I see now that my long days and nights in the gray room occurred at the worst possible time psychologically. I was cut off from everything familiar immediately after a night of overwhelming trauma. Rather than intervening with kindness and sympathy, the standard prescription was a kind of incarceration with isolation—no family and no friends. I was even removed from the society of the other Florence Crittenton girls. And so, I crawled into a hole for ten days and while I was down there, no one looked for me. I was supposed to be healing—as if I was getting over the flu—but, in fact, a dangerous ignorance about trauma intensified my pain and caused irreparable damage. And many other girls must have suffered as I did. Where are they now? Do they still subscribe to the "it's for the better" theory? I can't believe that could be true.

Perhaps there are those who believe the decisions made for me made my life easier; that I had more choices, or different choices, because my daughter was given away. Returning to California at sixteen with a newborn to care for would have dramatically changed the direction of my life—at least for a few years. Instead of the supposedly burdensome responsibilities of motherhood, I was allowed to return to a presumably carefree adolescence, a seemingly untroubled university education, as well as adventurous trips to Europe, Hong Kong, and Japan. My daughter's adoption into a safe and stable home is a kind of testimony to the well-meant intentions and the sensible decisiveness of the adults around me. For my parents, it was the best possible outcome for an onerous obstacle; for her adoptive parents, it was a longed-for wish finally granted; for my daughter it was a dependable future: a reliable mother and father.

I am the one who could not, cannot, will not find release from my sacrifice. My remaining adolescence was careworn, my university education discordant, my world travels lonesome. I was a mystery to myself, confused by waves of solitary brooding and a recurring sense of difference, separation, and loss. I was haunted by my tiny daughter and prone to fits of inconsolable anguish over her loss. Rather than safeguarding me, secrecy worked to sabotage me. Rather than free me from disapprobation, secrecy shackled me with guilt.

By telling the secret, renarrating the story, I have been able to reinterpret the characters, and in so doing reexamine my fellow players and myself on that faraway stage. I have come to see that I was not the innately bad girl who did the unpardonable. I was temporarily blown off my parents' course by the first winds of a cultural revolution that would oppose and eventually obliterate many of their values. My parents set me back on their course in the only way they knew how, and over the years, I have come to regard their decisions for that year with forgiving eyes. They were not just driven by a commitment to superficial appearances. They too were pawns in a cultural ideology in which secrecy and denial were the putative antidotes to stigmas such as suicide, murder, unwed mothers, and illegitimate children. My parents believed in the remedies, but once the secret was ensconced, it became the substructure of who I was. Keeping its intricate complexities would demand my ongoing, scrupulous attention for the next thirty-five years.

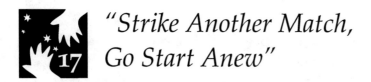

"Strike Another Match, Go Start Anew"

San Marino, April 1965

THE DAY AFTER THE ADOPTION was finalized, Aunt Jo came to get me. When I walked down the stairs to meet her, I could tell she was pleased by how flat my stomach looked behind the pleated wool skirt I had been unable to squeeze into three months ago. My like-new maternity smocks went into the box for incoming girls; I washed and ironed the precious black dress and passed it on to Tina. As my aunt drove me back to Pepper Pike, I timidly tried to tell her some of my newfound fears. I wasn't sure, I said, that I would be able to keep the secrets. Surely I could not hide all that marked me now. The man who might want to marry me someday would surely sense my transgressions, and I would have to tell him about the pregnancy. And how could I deny the baby?

I had been told to think of "it" as nothing more than useless tonsils or an unnecessary appendix, and, trusting this interpretation would be possible, I had not anticipated her beloved, heartbreaking realness. Her birth had turned me into a different girl. The fact that she would go on living in this world without me and I without her had made me someone who would live from here on out with an undeniable patina of sorrow.

Aunt Jo replied to my questions instantly and forcefully with complete self-assurance, "Absolutely not! You don't have to tell. You should not tell. Everyone has secrets. Whoever you marry will have secrets. You will have the right to keep yours. He will have the right to keep his." I accepted her pronouncements as correct; secrets were not only protective, they were inevitable. Keeping them, I rationalized, was a way to exercise my free will—something I did not have then but was beginning to realize I wanted.

As we approached Fox Hollow Drive, she reminded me that all the neighbors had been told that I had returned to California after Christmas; therefore, I would have to get down on the floor of the car until we got safely inside the attached garage. I numbly complied. So many people would have to be protected from the truth about me! That night all the curtains were drawn so no one could look in and spot me. My cousins were still in on the secret, although they tell me now that they did not, nor could not, comprehend what that really entailed. But they were allowed to see me, and thankfully and gamely, I tried to be "the same" for them, chatty and cheerful. Alas, I could not manage it. Exhausted and forlorn, I went up to my bed right after dinner and cried myself into a fitful sleep. The next morning, my bags repacked, I once more got down on the car floor so that my aunt could drive me out of the neighborhood and to the airport. I was returning to Southern California for my "spring break." And so the bizarre narrative continued as I stumbled through the role written for me by conventional codes and protective adults unaware of the emotional trauma of their maneuverings.

Like kids all over the country, I was ostensibly on vacation from school for a week. This chance for me to come home for the first week of April was considered a lucky break. I had delivered earlier than anyone expected; I looked so slender. Surely this visit would quash any lingering rumors. Physically I could play my new part well, since I actually weighed less on my return home than when I had left California in September. When I had been weighed at Dr. Cook's office on that ill-fated September morning six months ago, I had felt a momentary relief ("I can't be pregnant") because I was still my normal weight—128 pounds. The last time I was weighed at Florence Crittenton, a few days before I gave birth to Sorrow, I weighed 135 pounds. The appetite suppressants my aunt had given me had worked. When I had checked out of Florence Crittenton after my ten hopeless days in the gray room, I weighed only 120 pounds. When I arrived in California, no one could have guessed from my appearance that two weeks earlier I had given birth. That I remember all of these varying weights so precisely is indicative of just how obsessed I had become with the size of my body and how hard I would forever work to keep it slim.

I began to cry as soon as I saw my parents waiting at the gate at LAX, but they were quick to hush me; my tears had always made them uncomfortable, then and now. They were so brisk and officious as we gathered my luggage and headed for the car that I was able to stop crying and work once again at looking happy. In fact, they were delighted to see me. Even though I was pale, we were all proud of my slim figure, especially my flat stomach.

On the way home, I earned temporary permission to cry once more because they had to tell me my dog had recently died; in fact, they had accidentally poisoned him with snail bait. "Sorry," my dad said, "but the dog was stupid to have eaten that bait." I meekly accepted his interpretation and blamed the dog—never my father—but losing both my dog and my grandfather while I was gone gave me certain amount of leeway for the tears that would not easily subside. As we exited the Pasadena Freeway and neared Winthrop Road, I was admonished to wipe my eyes, blow my nose, and look around at the beautiful California evening, to be grateful, as my father put it, that I was home "all in one piece." Indeed, this literal truth was the antithesis of my shattered psyche.

It was important to my parents that I be noticed on this visit so that those people who might have been counting months could see me—this slender girl—and dismiss any suspicions about my absence since fall. I was not only allowed to see my girlfriends but encouraged to—even Jackie, Catherine, and Tammy who were also on their spring break. Depleted and blue, I did not want to join up with these girls, who now seemed to me both mindless and dangerous. But my parents pressed me cheerily: "Time to get out of the house"; "Have a good time"; "Come on now—smile!" Compliantly, I went with friends for hamburgers at Bob's. Dutifully, I even spent a wary day at Newport Beach, the beacon of my girlhood, with Jackie. I felt completely dissociated from the uninitiated child I had been there just six months before and hyperconscious of my difference.

But my pensive, cheerless disposition was benignly interpreted as the newfound maturity my parents had hoped I would acquire in Ohio. My friends believed the subterfuge. When they asked questions about my life in Pepper Pike, I adroitly embellished the counterlife I had created for them in my letters home. Openness and honesty were banished; they no longer felt like options in any of my relationships.

One evening during that baffling, ragged week, I drove over to Karen's house, said "Hello" to her parents, and promptly disappeared with Karen into her room. She wanted to play a new record album for me that she had just purchased. This was before the time that song lyrics were provided on the backs of album covers, but Karen had already patiently listened to and transcribed the lyrics to several of the songs so that we could read them as we listened. She put the needle carefully down on side B of Bob Dylan's *Bringing It All Back Home* (March 1965), on a song that immediately spoke a consoling secret language to me, "Mr. Tambourine Man":

> Then take me disappearin' through the smoke rings of my mind,
> Down the foggy ruins of time, far past the frozen leaves,
> The haunted, frightened trees, out to the windy beach,
> Far from the twisted reach of crazy sorrow.

Dylan seemed to be describing my own "crazy sorrow": the night of Sorrow's birth, that foggy ruined time, "the frozen leaves," "the haunted, frightened trees." The lyrics of this legendary song have been interpreted in myriad ways. But mine demonstrates the typical egocentrism of a sixteen-year-old brokenhearted girl who can only see through the lens of her own predicament. Nonetheless, the ability to recognize in contemporary songs my own experience was salutary and sustaining.

Karen and I listened to another track, and again I was surprised by how accurately it again articulated my experience. In "Love Minus Zero/No Limit," Dylan sings of the "banker's niece" who anticipates roses, Valentines, "all the gifts that wise men bring"; I had been that naïve, star-crossed girl, and Dylan seemed to know how radically I had been changed; he could appreciate what I had become after that night:

> The wind howls like a hammer,
> The night blows cold and rainy,
> My love she's like some raven
> At my window with a broken wing.

"Broken" I was, and certainly outside the window, committed for years to come to working through the events of that cold night when the wind blew "like a hammer." But Dylan's lyrics not only captured my encounter with the blizzard, the nurse, and my helplessness; they also gave me a more buoyant, even jaunty vision of what I might become:

> Yes, to dance beneath the diamond sky with one hand waving free,
> Silhouetted by the sea, circled by the circus sands,
> With all memory and fate driven deep beneath the waves,
> Let me forget about today until tomorrow.
> —"Mr. Tambourine Man"

There was a way to be released from the past perhaps, a way to drive my memories and my fate down below the surface where I could forget about them, at least "until tomorrow." I put the needle down on the last track to find one more message: how I might begin again. Dylan advised, "Strike another match, go start anew" because "it's all over now, Baby Blue."

Certain songs and certain singers mysteriously mirror and propel the minds and hearts of a generation. Dylan's mournful twang and his enigmatic lyrics spoke directly to me and for me, as they did for millions of other boomers. Although I was obligated at least for the next few years to follow the confining parameters of my parents' values, that iconic voice of the sixties had given me both a way to start thinking and a way to stop thinking about my fateful sixteenth year.

Indianapolis, Spring 1965

The secret was launched, and we were all compelled to attend to its many faceted permutations. Like a stone thrown into a pond, the ripples of the secret moved outward with a complicated circularity that would allow no surcease, no reflection, and no compassion. I could not just stay home after my "spring break"; people in California expected me to finish the school year in Ohio, so I had to ostensibly return to Pepper Pike. But I couldn't return to my Aunt Jo's in Cleveland and reenroll in Orange High School, where I had attended in the fall; after all, people in Pepper Pike had been told I had returned to California after Christmas for back surgery. Apparently, a return to Pepper Pike in April would have been too incongruous, too suspicious; so, instead, it was off to another aunt's home, this time in Indianapolis. While I was there, the excuse for my unexpected visit would be that my mother was ill. Only my aunt and uncle, Aunt May and Uncle Lewis, would know the actual circumstances. My bags were packed again, this time with several dowdy shirtwaist dresses my mother had purchased for me at her own clothing store in San Marino. My mother was fifty-one, and these dresses were just like the ones she wore every day to work. But I did not object and would wear them dutifully and indifferently. Once again I was to be enrolled in a public high school where I would complete my junior year.

This phase of the secret had its unique challenges. When I would write to my girlfriends in San Marino, my letters could not have an Indianapolis postmark, so I had to send the letters to my Aunt Jo in Pepper Pike, and she would mail them from there so they would have the appropriate postmark. Throughout these Byzantine maneuvers, I was dazed, bashful, contrite, and simultaneously as restless as most sixteen-year-old girls. In Aunt May's house, Uncle Lewis and my new set of cousins were kind to me, but Aunt May seemed distrustful. She made it clear to me that she was doing my parents an extraordinary favor in letting a troublesome, "easy" girl like me into her home. And I seemed to confirm her reservations. Though not one high school boy had approached me for a date when I was at school in Pepper Pike, in Indianapolis I was immediately and inexplicably attractive. The phone rang a lot, and my aunt was extremely dubious as to why. I was as surprised as she and could give her no explanation for this puzzling popularity, but I wanted to get out of the house whenever I could. The day she allowed me to drive her car alone, I was so full of giddy delight that I recklessly took off, speeding around the corner. Before I could get anywhere, I ran over the curb into a large rock and flattened her tire, bending the rim in the process. Needless to say, I was not allowed to drive again during my two-month stay, and the dates I was allowed to accept were strictly supervised.

My letters to Karen continued, written on my Aunt Jo's stationery with the requisite Pepper Pike postmark. No longer pregnant and back in school, I actually did get invited to school events, so I could describe truthfully my real dates and my real prom dress. Nonetheless, my proclivity to embellish would not be bridled. For example, it was not enough for me to go to a prom; I also had to say, "Claudia Slocoam and the boy she's going with, Jim Martin, both friends of mine, were crowned king and queen." In reality, Claudia and Jim had no clue I even existed. But having been encouraged to embroider a rich, colorful life instead of the bleak realities of absence, trauma, and loss, now I couldn't resist.

Martha's Vineyard, 2004

In the years that followed, my semisuccessful survival strategies had a way of embedding themselves into my consciousness, enduring long after the crisis. I continued to offer revised versions of many of the twists and turns of my life, and my inventions gave me a veneer of protection from disapproval. I rarely felt genuine admiration from others probably because I was constructing a self on fabrication; it was never really me that was being accepted or praised. I remained vigilant and apart, concocting the explanations I thought people wanted, wearing my masks, dressing up the experiences of my life, working assiduously to maintain a chimera of legitimacy. Because I always avoided situations that might reveal my duplicities, for the next thirty years, no one who knew of my actual whereabouts for that year even had the opportunity to ask me about the night of Sorrow's birth. But even if they had, I would not have told them the real story. I would have been ashamed to let them know just how desperately that night turned out.

Now, as I reread my letters to Karen, their psychological ramifications intrigue me. Interpreting them like dreams, I play with the symbolism of the imaginary world I concocted. For instance, I wrote several descriptions for Karen about the beauty of the snow; I repeatedly expressed how much I was hoping for more and more of it. I seemed to believe in the redemptiveness of the snow, as if it covered the bare ground of my real life with a clean, soft mantle. But I was not content with a dusting; I wanted the cover to be thick and heavy. When I told her a sledding story, it was about the sled flipping over and spilling me out rather than a smooth, thrilling ride. I always portrayed myself as an ungraceful ice skater and a clumsy skier, always falling, never in control. Why did I make these narrative choices? Since almost all of my snow stories for Karen were fabricated, I could just as easily have painted myself as lithe and competent. Instead, the snow stories serve as foreshadowing metaphors. Rather than protecting me, the massive snowfall on the night I went into labor would be the cause of my lonely terror. And I am amazed by the letter I wrote from Florence Crittenton shortly before I gave birth, for in retrospect, my secret seems so transparent when I fabricate about the cancelled ski trip and the shopping trip where there was nothing to buy. My carefree adolescence had been cancelled and despite all the money my parents had invested, nothing could buy back my shattered girlhood.

Still, I marvel at how thoroughly limited my imagination was by the ideological script of my time. The letters are in their own way personalized repetitions of the reigning narrative for adolescent girls—pretty teenager is befriended by other pretty girls and wooed by many handsome young men; she wears beautiful dresses to Cinderella-like balls and rides a splendid horse. That the narrative had no historical basis in my own adolescence did not lesson its authority over me. My invented year is in some ways as telling as is the actual year I spent in ever-deepening shadows.

In late June, I diffidently returned to San Marino at the end of that long and many-layered school year with an official transcript that recorded excellent grades and, most importantly, no mention of the Florence Crittenton Home for Unwed Mothers. Though I was hesitant and wary, the secret seemed an outward success. My reasons for leaving and returning were so plausible that when I started my senior year at San Marino High School, no one questioned the veracity of my "rewarding" year away. To everyone it seemed I had returned with my priorities straight, better equipped to study hard, apply to college, and follow the path my parents expected of me. I understood the insatiability of high school gossip and knew that no matter how lonely the secret might leave me, I could tell no one. Furthermore, I felt culpable for the significant financial sacrifice my parents had made to construct the secret. I dared not risk squandering their money, and I still felt that they required protection as well. I accepted that keeping my secrets was an inextricable part of our family's integrity. It was my duty to dissemble.

I had adopted my parents' worldview almost entirely; only my deep and abiding grief contradicted their expectations. But that too was a secret. I could not let them see the sad girl behind bright eyes. I could not tell them I had seen my baby, that I longed for her desperately, that I conjured her up and cradled her deep into the night, whispering to her obsessively. Confessing my sorrow would break the implicit contract we had made: they would forgive me if I would behave like their happily reformed teenage daughter—not a young, lonely mother distraught over the loss of her baby girl. The abyss between these two selves was so daunting that I could not manage both at once. To cope, I had to relinquish my truer, grieving self, denying her existence so that the imposter might flourish. But this dance of subterfuge had its price. With it came the belief that ultimately underneath my cheerful, outer persona, I was irredeemably flawed and fundamentally untrustworthy.

And like cancerous cells, the secret multiplied, invading every aspect of my life. The trauma was never forgotten and never examined. Instead, it was internalized, embedded as a seed that would sprout into an array of irrational behaviors in my relationships with my parents, my lovers, my children, my sisters, my friends, my colleagues. The seed always carried guilt with it, but the guilt would transform itself unpredictably, depending on the secret's backdrop.

With my lovers, for example, the secret would make me inconsistent, duplicitous, and ultimately untrustworthy. The kind of intimacy that can come from honesty was impossible. With my children, it would make me fiercely possessive. I would not share them with anyone, not even with their father. With my sisters, the secret—whose details they only learned years later—would cast me as the needy and undependable little sister—the one who always caused trouble and whose life choices consistently gave them pause. With my friends, the secret would make me guarded. It had to be maintained, hence I always felt fraudulent and lonely. With my colleagues, the secret would make me fiercely committed to succeeding, as I tried to compensate for my failings, and at the same time standoffish as I safeguarded my past. Colleagues would read me as competitive, ambitious, and unapproachable when, in fact, I longed to be part of the team.

With my parents, the secret would make me feel guilty for that "difficult time" I put them through and all the difficult times that would follow. I have always felt the need to apologize to them for my failings even though I have gone on to build an admirable career and raise three loving and capable children. The guilt my parents kindled in me when I fell far short of their expectations would never abate; instead, it was compounded by the disappointment I saw register in their faces again and again when I had to tell them I had failed at yet another marriage, the key, they believed, to a happy life—a key I could not make work. I was simply unable to cast off my sense of essential impropriety in all the facets of my life.

For my parents, no matter what the consequences, keeping the secret of the pregnancy and the baby was the prime requisite. They had no idea of its latent power—that it would splinter into a myriad of other cryptic secrets, uniquely concealed. They could see that my life was unsettled, that I was driven on and on to new locales, new challenges, new men, new distractions, as if some diabolical, unappeasable daemon was prodding me on and on. But none of us would dare look back and reflect on what was compelling me, pushing me forward, away, away from the truth of the past even as that past inevitably overtook me, engulfing me, drowning me in waves upon waves of crazy sorrow.

 *Waking Up*

THE SUMMER I RETURNED from my exile in the Midwest, Los Angeles exploded into a conflagration that was so intense and pervasive, it even affected the protected citizens of San Marino. The Watts Riots prevented executives, including my father, from going downtown to work and no one seemed to want to buy a house from my mother, even in a place so safely separate from the temporary anarchy of South Central LA. Everyone paused, appalled by the unfolding pandemonium, glancing at the skyline to see if the smoke from the burning buildings would reach them. People whispered that rioters would eventually find their way to our blameless hamlet to wreak their frightful retaliation. But were we blameless? The Watts Riots made me ask that question for the first time.

A year earlier, California voters had responded to the passage of the Civil Rights Act by quickly approving Proposition 14, which in effect allowed racial discrimination in the sale or rental of housing in the state. I can recall my parents discussing their support for the initiative. My mother sold real estate in San Marino; she felt justified in keeping it a bastion of the white upper middle class. Proposition 14 would later be declared unconstitutional by the U.S. Supreme Court, but in the summer of '65, it only served to foment feelings of injustice and anger in South Central LA, a part of the city I had only passed through while traveling sixty miles an hour on the Harbor Freeway.

On August 11, a routine traffic stop by the California Highway Patrol in the heart of Watts had provided the incendiary catalyst for seething feelings. The ensuing chaos lasted for six days, leaving thirty-four dead, over a thousand people injured, nearly four thousand arrested, and hundreds of buildings destroyed.

Although I was now seventeen, I was still politically ill informed. It took the riots to show me there even was a large African American population living in Los Angeles and that they lived in conditions as segregated and impoverished as cities in the South. I had been separated from the demoralizing and disempowering poverty of LA by twenty miles of freeway and thousands of dollars of privilege.

My mother said the riots were the act of angry thugs; my father said much worse. Although they had openly supported Proposition 14, their lack of sympathy for the poor and for people of color had never before been so overt. Up until then, I had never heard blatant racist remarks in our home. Given our all-white community, any kind of interaction that might have instigated racial slurs had never presented itself, at least not within my earshot. Of course there were people of color in San Marino, but they came to town on weekday mornings by bus or battered pick-up truck to clean our houses and mow our laws and left each evening, always respectfully mindful of their "place" in the hierarchy of privilege.

Now I heard my father sound unaccountably incensed; he even used the word "niggers" when he spoke of the rioters. I was stunned, first by his angry and crude dismissal of the problem and second by the ongoing television coverage from KTLA's helicopter that captured actual rioters and arsonists in the act. My bubble-like world had left me politically asleep, but these riots woke me up. I looked doubtfully at my parents' responses. They sneered when a newscaster suggested that the riots were the results of years of joblessness, poor housing, and bad schools. Outwardly I accepted my parents' interpretations of the events ripping up our city, but inside I found their responses unfeeling, even ugly. Down in the playroom, alone, I hunched over my new stereo, a reluctant gift from my parents that I had received only when I promised them that my obsession with the Beatles was over. Little did they know that the new stereo would open more dangerous doors when it came to their values. I put the needle down on my latest record album and listened carefully to Joan Baez as she sang "And there but for fortune / May go you or I" (*Five*, 1964).

Janet at seventeen with fishing rod in the High Sierras, 1965.
Photograph by Harold Thomas Ellerby. Courtesy of the author.

The National Guard put a cordon around a vast area of South Central Los Angles, but the alarming drift of battle-torn Watts had reached even the pristine San Gabriel Valley. Since the riots kept my father from getting to work, we left the city, distancing ourselves completely from the brutality and loss. We headed for the High Sierras above Yosemite Valley where we backpacked into bucolically remote campsites where no news of the outside world could reach us. I still have a snapshot from our adventure: I am standing with a new fishing pole my father has given me, beaming for him, trying hard to be his cheerful girl again.

The wild beauty that surrounded us was restorative; my smile was not insincere. I smiled so hard, wanting desperately to please my parents, to make us all forget what I had done. The hiking trip did renew our relationship. I felt they had forgiven me, and I loved them even more intensely for doing so. But the penetrating sorrow was not vanquished. Instead, it propelled me up and down the mountains and left me lying awake late into the cold nights despite my weary body. I hid my sadness;

my relationship with my parents was so crucial that I could not let them see one more tear, not one.

After we returned home and the riots were suppressed, the three of us ventured downtown—not anywhere near Watts, of course, but to Grauman's Chinese Theater on Hollywood Boulevard. We went to see Julie Andrews star as Maria in Rogers and Hammerstein's *The Sound of Music*. My parents rarely went to movies, but they wanted to see this one, and it was important to them that I accompany them. Perhaps they wanted me to identify with Maria, the perky, virtuous girl, the girl who waited with patience in a nunnery for her handsome prince. And I did identify with Maria, but not as they anticipated. Instead, I sang to myself in the weeks that followed, "What do we do with a problem called Maria?" I knew I was still a problem for my parents, just as Maria had been for the nuns. Like her, I longed to behave and please my superiors. At the same time, I could also identify with the problems Maria posed—her restlessness—her longing to escape, to hightail it into the hills. How could they keep us contained?

Throughout my adolescence, I was forever growing my hair out. I wanted it to reach down my back to my bra strap, but my mother always complained as soon as it got past chin length. Long, loose hair was too free; to her it was unseemly, and she always pressured me to keep it short, controlled, and demure. Julie Andrews's pixie gave her new ammunition. This cropped style was so uncool in Southern California that I had successfully resisted my mother before my exile and my hair had grown past my shoulders while I was away, but she was once again relentless. Chastened now, I gave in and obediently had my renegade hair clipped away by her beautician. Did my fresh pixie cut reassure her that I would not again be prey to sexual desire?

My mother and I would continue to argue about the length of my hair for years. In 1968, when she and my father agreed to let me go to London and Paris for six months, the principal condition was that before I left, I would once again submit to her beautician and depart with yet another pixie. The second condition was that I promise not to hitchhike. I agreed readily to both and in my passport picture I sport the pixie one more time. Of course, I did hitchhike all over England, Scotland, through France,

Belgium, Germany, and a couple of times found myself in some danger, despite my shorn head. Short hair might have comforted my mother, but it did little to protect me from men or myself.

And so I moved toward adulthood, a seemingly uncomplicated daughter who agreed with my parents' interpretations of the roiling, changing world around us; agreed to haircuts, dress codes, and role models, always careful to appear cheerful and in step. Inside I was full of twists and turns, but such complexities had to be repressed. My parents never knew I was a disconsolate mother; they would not know for almost four more years that I was an awakening liberal. They might have suspected that beneath my good behavior I was still sexually curious and eager for adventure, but they went to great lengths to ensure that these yearnings would not see the light of day. I was so fearful of rejection and avid for their approval that I eagerly played the role of "Maria."

My senior year at San Marino High School would conform entirely to my parents' expectations. On the first morning of that new school year, I warily entered the girls' gym for senior orientation and was immediately confronted by a choice—my first in a long time. On one side of the gym lounged my old cohorts—Jackie, Tammy, and Catherine—watching me skeptically, their eyes harshly defined with black liner and thick mascara; their hair longer now, parted down the middle, hanging limply to their shoulders; their gray skirts rolled up; long sloppy sweaters pulled down to cover their bunched-up waistbands. On the other side of the gym sitting alone was Karen, my dutiful friend who knew well enough to avoid the likes of Jackie and her clique. Karen's clean red hair was trimmed neatly at chin length. She wore a pleated gray skirt, a freshly ironed pastel blouse, and white knee socks, as did I. She too had seen me come in, smiled warmly, and gestured to come sit by her. I glanced at Jackie, and was surprised to see her also motion casually by a slight dip of her head to join them. This was unusual for her since she typically feigned a cool, "whatever" nonchalance.

That crowded, boisterous gym is emblematic in my memory. I can see myself at the bright door, poised again on my own perilous tightrope between two potential worlds, two possible lives. I didn't hesitate, not for a moment, even though there was a psychologically complex decision to be made. The last year had been the emotional equivalent of falling off the tightrope without a safety net to stop my plunge. Cautiously, I made a beeline for Karen's prudent side.

Later that day in my English class, Mrs. Fenner announced we would start the school term with the poetry of Robert Frost. We opened our books to "The Road Not Taken," and my morning crystallized for me. Frost's poem, so heavily anthologized and read by students everywhere, uncannily reflected my decision. I had been offered two paths through the raucous gym that morning, both with their own sets of values, dress codes, and expectations. I knew that once I chose, I could not vacillate from one to the other and that I could not come back to take the other path. I never spoke with Jackie again that year. I would nod politely when we passed in the hall, but her rebellion so spiraled away from my compliance that there was no way to travel together, even casually.

The lines in our high school between good girl and bad girl were distinctly drawn, and I had made my choice: no drinking, no cigarettes, no carousing. My year would have its own kind of intensity, driven as I was by the need to please my parents, to win them back. On that morning, Robert Frost's words helped me conceptualize my future. To me, then, it appeared that I could make significant choices. Looking back, I wonder: was I exercising free will or did shame and fear propel me? Like Frost, I linger, "telling this with a sigh / ages and ages hence." I chose the well-traveled path that day, the one my parents had dreamed I would take. Rejecting the allure of the counterculture that Jackie was so eager to embrace, I chose the familiar. Nonetheless, even though I seemed to disavow her heady free fall into the sixties, the appeal of her alternative path would not vanish completely.

Without delay I became the girlfriend of a polite, studious boy from a good San Marino family. Mark had been busy as class president the year I was gone, and so entrenched in his own circle of friends that Alec and Jackie might as well have been on another planet—I doubt Mark even knew who they were. So he had missed any gossip about my year away. Kindly and without question, he accepted my carefully rehearsed and by now oft-repeated explanations of my whereabouts and devotedly escorted me to every dance of the school year. I was so grateful that he chose me, as were my parents, that I would not have dreamed of donning my black fishnet stockings and heading for the Civic Auditorium. Instead I wore pretty formals, elbow-length gloves, and the lovely orchid corsages he brought me. My miniskirt was gone along with my Beatles posters and all the keepsakes from my year as Alec's girlfriend. I went gratefully back to my knee-length gray skirts, and on free dress day, I donned the dependable, unattractive shirtwaists my mother had purchased for me.

When it was time to apply to colleges, I followed the advice of my school counselor and parents and applied to small liberal arts colleges in Southern California and to the newly opened University of California at Santa Barbara. I also begged to be allowed to apply to the Oregon universities, following my oldest sister's example. When she was eighteen and I was eight, I had watched her depart for Eugene with new clothes and matching luggage. I had loved hearing about her jaunty escapades in her dorm and later about what seemed to me to be a glamorous, sophisticated life in her sorority. Ever since, I had dreamed of going to Oregon. We had vacationed there when I was a child, and I could still remember the jagged Cascades—a range that had mountains named just for us: the Three Sisters. Unlike Santa Barbara, the foggy, wet Oregon coastline would have nothing to do with the Beach Boys or Gidget. I wanted to escape Southern California; the parts of it that had become so hip had only led me sadly off course.

Mary Ann, a San Marino girl whose father worked with mine, attended Oregon State, and she encouraged me to come to school in Corvallis. My parents were hesitant, nervous about sending me off to a place where the long reach of their careful supervision could not extend. But when they found out that Mary Ann was in one of the "best" sororities and had been chosen as the "Sweetheart of Sigma Chi," they began to reconsider. Years before, when they were undergraduates at the University of Michigan, they had been happy members of the Greek system; they wanted the same for me. Mary Ann's welcoming sponsorship calmed some of their anxieties. Since I would be required to live in a dormitory my freshman year, they made sure the dorm system had strict curfews. When it came time to decide my course of action for the next four years, they allowed me to turn down my other offers and choose Oregon State. In September 1966, I once again flew out of LAX, this time delighted to be on my way. I was, in fact, a shy, insecure, melancholy girl with a dark secret on the inside, but on the outside I was capable of conventional posing, a seemingly cheerful, buoyant girl on the threshold of promise.

Corvallis, 1966–67

I would like to be able to write here that upon arriving in Corvallis, I immediately developed a social conscience. After all, so much had already happened. The Civil Rights March on Washington had occurred three years prior. I had seen film clips of Martin Luther King Jr. calling out resoundingly to a quarter of a million people, "I have a dream!" I had watched Joan Baez lead that huge mass of people in "We Shall Overcome." I knew she had been part of the Civil Rights marches, that she had protested Proposition 14. I had witnessed the horrifying film clips of police wielding batons and fire hoses and releasing dogs on defenseless marchers. I had seen the devastating results of the Watts Riots.

I wasn't in a cultural vacuum, restricted to *The Sound of Music* and *The Andy Griffith Show.* Karen and I had gone to see Stanley Kramer's *Ship of Fools,* fervently discussing its meaning afterwards. I had gone to see *Doctor Zhivago* twice and then took on Pasternak's novel, identifying intimately with Lara, Zhivago's forsaken true love. I owned protest albums by Bob Dylan, Peter, Paul and Mary, and, of course, Joan Baez. I followed Baez's politics, marveling at her courage when, after performing for President Johnson, she had urged him to withdraw U.S. troops from Vietnam. I knew about draft card burners and the Free Speech Movement at Berkeley. But the year that I graduated from San Marino High School, not one of my classmates would begin their freshman year there. Berkeley had already earned its reputation for radicalism, and as of yet, there were no San Marino radicals. Even Jackie got only as close as UC–Santa Barbara.

So although I knew something about the gathering storm clouds of rebellion when I went off to Corvallis, I was still firmly sailing on my parents' calm course. I still wanted to be their "good girl." The rebelliousness of the Beats, which was quickly transforming into the hippie generation, was terra incognito. My freshman year in college would pass prosaically, much like my senior year in high school. Like my sister ten years before me, I donned sweater sets and pleated skirts and tried to make new friends. I was thankful when Mary Ann's sorority asked me to pledge. I had desperately wanted to be asked and to belong, and I created friendships with my fellow pledges that continue to this day. Of course, my friends knew nothing of my secret. It was assumed that we were all virgins.

Dating was awkward; I was confused by how to manage the pressure to have sex that seemed to follow me everywhere. I no longer believed it would be necessary to refrain from sex for seven years so that I would be "intact" again, but I was so afraid of pregnancy that I now had a new possible label to worry about—"cock tease." It was apparently very wrong to go just so far, but no further, and I was held responsible by a boy from Alpha Tau Omega for causing him to suffer from something as horrible as the dreaded "blue balls." How did men succeed in turning sexual frustration into a physical malady caused by uncooperative women? The "blue balls" incident occurred when I attended a fraternity party where couples would get on a long, slick slide and ride it down to the house's completely darkened basement that had been lined with mattresses. There, ear-splitting music drowned out all noise of passion or resistance.

My beautiful roommate, blond, willowy Mona, was brought home from that same party nearly unconscious from too much alcohol. The frat boy who delivered her to our dorm had me buzzed down to the lobby. I found her limp, abandoned on a sticky, vinyl couch. I helped her upstairs, put our metal wastebasket next to her bed, and listened through the night to her retching. The next morning, she woke me up in a panic and made a mind-blowing confession: she could not remember how many boys she had had sex with the night before, but she knew there had been a lot more than just her date. She had been way too drunk to tell anyone that this was not what she wanted over the blaring, incessant music. This revelation was astounding enough, but there was more: the tampon she had been wearing when she went to the party had been pushed up into her so far she couldn't get it out. Together we walked over to the student infirmary later that morning. A grim-looking nurse called Mona into an examining room where the tampon was removed.

Afterwards, I too was ushered into the room, and Mona and I listened meekly to the nurse's standard, admonitory lecture about the dangers of alcohol. No one said anything to Mona about the tampon. No one asked her, "How did this happen?" and we did not dare offer any more information than was necessary. Mona and I were still so socialized to take responsibility for all sexual experiences that it did not occur to us to accuse anyone else of anything. Today what happened to Mona would be called gang rape, but in 1966, she alone was held responsible for what happened in the mattress room, and she held herself to blame. After that night, she was marked as "easy"; she had earned herself a "reputation"; the phone rang relentlessly, always for her. She left college after that first quarter, overwhelmed by the rabid sexual attention her beauty and her ingenuousness had thrust upon her. I was sorry to say goodbye to her, but I understood all too well the need to flee from that ruinous beginning.

For the homecoming parade at OSU, all the fraternities and sororities decorated floats. The night before the big game, the floats were pushed through campus and down to a playing field where a huge bonfire was lit for a rowdy pep rally. A girl named Carly designed the float for our sorority. Although we were all sexually inexperienced (or so it was assumed), our float conveyed a surprisingly different message. Carly bought an old double bed with a corroded brass frame at a secondhand furniture store, along with an ancient box springs and a creepy stained mattress. She got her boyfriend to put sturdy wheels on the bed legs. The pledges, me included, then dyed old sheets and pillowcases, following Carly's strict instructions to leave the sheets in the dye for hours in order to achieve the university's colors of florid orange and ebony black. The float was complete after we made up our bed on wheels with the vibrant sheets and pillowcases and attached painted banners with huge peace signs and the slogans "Make Love Not War!" and "Let's Hear It for Beavers!" (OSU's team name, although the off-color pun was not lost on us).

The night of the parade, we drew straws to see who would get to ride on the float. My straw was a long one, so I got to ride on the bed with four other girls and Carly. We donned our girlish flannel pajamas and fluffy slippers, perched ourselves on the bed and began our journey, pushed by a large group of our "sisters" also clad in pajamas and slippers, waving our "Make Love Not War" banners high.

We were a tremendous hit. As we clattered down the streets, we threw chocolate kisses to the students lining them, and Carly screamed our slogans through a bullhorn to the onlookers. They roared their approval. I can still remember my elation that night. Being the center of attention left me feeling not just exhilarated but deliciously naughty. Boys shouted at us "Get it on!" and "Let's do it!" We were thrilled. The float was risqué, political, and subversive.

How clearly did we realize that we were championing a message that had nothing to do with football and everything to do with the budding sexual revolution and mounting sentiment against the war? I didn't feel like a war protestor, but I did feel mischievous. Ironically, my first foray into protest was made in my pajamas on a bed. Sex had been so disastrous for me, yet I was now ostensibly promoting it with girls who seemed so innocent to me—with a purity that had to be maintained.

So many messages were blowing in the wind that year, and indeed, some girls were having sex. Mona was not the only girl that the darkened mattress rooms were fashioned for. All the fraternity parties I would attend that year featured slides that led to pitch-black basements lined with mattresses. That spring, Carly would move out of the sorority, marry her boyfriend, and, five months later, give birth to a son. The next fall, I would babysit for her. When my friends would gossip about Carly, shaking their heads and sighing over her "huge mistake" that had "ruined her life," I kept very quiet. Carly looked happy to me. Her baby boy looked like the answer to my dreams.

Nonetheless, although we had been pushed gleefully through the streets on a bed shouting "Make Love Not War," I was certain I could never reveal my secret. The same divide stood firm. Some girls had sex— "fallen" girls like Mona and Carly—but most girls—good girls—did not. It was 1967; we were well into the sixties, but girls still had to pay dearly for sexual waywardness.

In my honors' English class that spring, we read European and Russian fiction. Kafka's "Metamorphosis" left me cringing. I felt quintessentially other than the squeaky-clean students around me. Like Gregor, I too had been shunned by my family, but I would never reveal the Gregor Samsa within me. No one would see the cracked, brittle layer beneath my smooth surfaces. We moved on to *Madame Bovary*, which I also read with trepidation. I would never be Emma! I had no sympathy for her, especially when she failed to care lovingly for her daughter. Emma's desperate way-wardness and her horrific death resolidified the necessity that I not only keep my secret but that I continually seek forgiveness. In fact, *Madame Bovary* led me into another brief but intense religious phase.

I was enormously attracted to the Catholicism of Mona's replacement, my new roommate Jo Anne. The nuns at Jo Anne's high school had made the rules so clear for the girls: no French kissing, definitely no petting—both were venal sins that could lead to mortal sins and eventual damna-tion. Such exactness was appealing. Maybe I should become a Catholic, I thought. Then I would know all the rules; all I would have to do would be to follow them. If I strayed, I could go to confession and a wise priest would set me back on the right track by way of the mysterious rosary. The structure seemed a protective wall against complicated decisions and ever-insistent boys.

At the close of that first year of college, my English professor offered extra credit to anyone who would independently tackle *Anna Karenina*. I dove into the novel, skipping all the parts about Levin and Kitty, focusing exclusively on Count Vronsky and Anna, poor Anna. I could not sym-pathize with Emma Bovary, but I identified with Anna's terrible plight for I had loved Alec, my own Count Vronsky, and he too had betrayed me. Kafka, Flaubert, Tolstoy—so much to absorb. I took Gregor's horrible transformation, Emma's fall from grace, and Anna's hopeless capitulation to passion to heart. These novels stood as dire warnings: my reading for that first year at college left me more convinced than ever that I must not fall prey to temptation.

After a benign summer as a camp counselor, I returned to OSU for my second year of college, moved into my sorority, and made friends with Mimi, a restless sorority sister. Mimi didn't like the house rules. We were supposed to wear skirts to class, but Mimi insisted on wearing her jeans and cords. To me she looked like Joan Baez, and I thought she was incredibly lucky to have the name "Mimi," just like Joan's sister Mimi

Farina. She had long dark hair; she wore black turtleneck sweaters; she went to candlelight peace vigils with her poetry professor. Mimi encouraged me to take a poetry class from him that winter and I eagerly took her up on it. I wanted to be like Mimi. Mr. Richards, the professor, invited us to his house to read our work. Mimi loaned me a turtleneck to wear with my jeans. I practiced French inhaling with her and bought some black eye liner.

On the first night, Mr. Richards told us to call him Josh. He offered us red wine as we sat around the crackling fireplace in his funky bungalow. I was nineteen; to call my professor by his first name, to be offered wine—all this seemed incredibly hip. We drank, smoked, read our poems, and listened to Simon and Garfunkel's *The Sounds of Silence*. I was enchanted. My friendship with Jo Anne and my flirtation with Catholicism fell quickly away. The lyrics of Simon and Garfunkel became my new religion, as I whispered knowingly "Hello darkness, my old friend." Josh invited us to his house again, and at that next meeting, he passed around a joint. It was the first time I had seen or smoked marijuana. I liked it and I liked Josh, but he liked Mimi best. When it was time for us to go home, she was the one he asked to stay.

Soon Mimi was getting demerits for not getting back to the sorority before curfew, but she didn't care. Then she checked out for the weekend, writing down that she was going home to Medford, but, in fact, she spent the weekend with Josh. How did the rest of us in the poetry class respond? We knew nothing about sexual harassment. Now, as an English professor myself, I am amazed by how completely inappropriate this man's relationship with his students was—he gave us alcohol; he gave us marijuana; he slept with Mimi. But in 1968, we were charmed by him and in awe of Mimi. She was the chosen one. All we felt was envy.

Martha's Vineyard, 2004

I don't know what happened to Mimi. That spring I left Corvallis to study in London and Paris. By the time I returned from Europe, Mimi had left the sorority, and I transferred to the University of Oregon, leaving all vestiges of sorority life behind. Nonetheless, I still think of Mimi with admiration, my female equivalent of the "free wheelin'" Bob Dylan. I hope Josh did not hurt her. I hope she knew how to transgress and to flourish. So many did not. I hope she took from Josh what he had to teach her and then moved on into her future. I hope she's not a corporate banker or an executive at Halliburton.

I picture her living in a comfortable cottage on the Oregon coast, surrounded by a rambunctious garden of unruly vegetables and blowsy, unkempt flowers. She's there with her dogs, her crystals, her patchouli, her poetry, and her potter's wheel. She lives on, my symbol of the unconventional artist I could never quite become. Her allure has never tarnished. Even now as I conjure her up, she beckons to me from her candle-lit window, holding some answers for what I still might become.

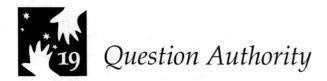

19 Question Authority

Europe, 1968

I LEFT CORVALLIS for Europe and six months of plucky travel, radical-
izing dislocation, and an autonomy that permitted me to finally cast off
my "good girl" facade. The eager sorority pledge with the pixie hair cut
and the tidy shirtwaists was revamped. I still wanted very little to do
with men and nothing to do with sex, but living in London during the
appalling spring that saw the assassinations of both Martin Luther King
Jr. and Bobby Kennedy finally ignited a political fire in me. The progressive Islington couple I lived with for those first three months regarded
America as violent and vulgar, but they liked me and we loved sitting
late over the dinner table talking about Vietnam protests, draft resisters,
Civil Rights, civil unrest, violence, drugs—topics that had always been
verboten in my parents' home. Seeing "home" through their eyes made
LBJ's America look ugly.

Far away from parental and institutional authority, I dove headfirst
into different waters: I drank and smoked; I hitchhiked all over the UK
with my girlfriends—to Dover, Devon, and Cornwall. On one foray, five
of us, sitting on the back of a flatbed truck, watched in wonder as Stone-
henge loomed in the foggy distance. We took an all-night bus to Aberdeen
and then hitched as far as Inverness, Loch Ness, Loch Lomand and then
back to Edinburgh in time to catch the night train back to London, leaving
just enough time to get to our Monday-morning classes. We took incredible risks and sometimes found ourselves in dangerous circumstances,

like the time a friend and I accepted a ride to Canterbury in a lorry only to find ourselves locked in the back with no way to know if we were actually headed for our destination. When the back of the lorry was finally unlocked and we climbed out to find ourselves in front of the Canterbury Cathedral, we quickly forgot what had been legitimate fear and continued accepting rides from whomever would stop for us.

We scoured London, walking for hours and hours from Regents Park to Westminster. We took our classes seriously, reading and then seeing performances of Anouilh's *Antigone,* Beckett's *Waiting for Godot,* and Tom Stoppard's new play *Rosencrantz and Guildenstern Are Dead* (1967). We left behind the high school canon of Shakespeare, moving on to *King Lear, Othello,* and *Henry V,* which we then saw performed at Stratford-upon-Avon. We studied British colonialism; were appalled by the Elgin Marbles, stolen from Athens by Lord Elgin in 1806; shuddered as we read *Heart of Darkness* and imagined Marlow out on the Thames, retelling his tale of colonial horror. I bought my first pair of bell-bottoms and a brown suede jacket at the Beatles' Apple Boutique on Baker Street. Trading in my sneakers for leather boots was a concrete gesture of moving from the fifties to the sixties, from my hermetic home to the changing larger world.

In late June, just one month after the Paris student riots, the occupation of the Sorbonne, and the French workers' strike, our group moved to Paris for the summer. I lived in a small pension off the Boulevard St. Michelle, which put me front row center for all kinds of turbulence in Paris that summer of 1968. The *gendarmes* patrolled relentlessly, breaking up small groups whenever more than four or five gathered on the street. Nonetheless, one night I felt the nauseating sting of tear gas as I was swept along the boulevard with a crowd of protestors. I loved the turmoil, the excitement; Paris was a powder keg of thrilling unrest; all authority was under interrogation, all tradition was suspect and the "old road [was] rapidly aging" (Bob Dylan, "The Times They Are A-Changin'," 1964).

Free of my parents' control, I took on the seductively tantalizing guise of a sixties radical wannabe, yet I still could not liberate myself from an ongoing sense of shame and an enduring loneliness. As I explored the Latin Quarter, the Louvre, the *Jeu de Paume,* the Rodin Museum, Notre Dame, Versailles, Fontainbleu, as I immersed myself in *Le Rouge et le Noir,*

Swan's Way, Un Coeur Simple, and *L'Étranger,* I could not put a stop to my despondent longing for Alec and for my baby girl. Annoyed with myself, I took up muttering, "Put it behind you" and "Let it go" to myself, trying to squelch my old mantra, "My Sorrow; my Sorrow." I hated feeling like an impostor; I wanted to belong to a movement, yet I often felt I was living the wrong life—that I was not supposed to be in Europe at all. Even in the epicenter of Paris's heady nonconformity, the conflicting divisions of my selfhood would not coalesce. Paris was seething with energy; mischievous fun and serious politics were everywhere, yet I would helplessly descend into melancholy, fantasizing incessantly about Sorrow and Alec even as I walked beneath the Eiffel Tower or gazed at Monet's "Waterlilies" series in the *Orangerie.*

I did make good friends. We all wanted to take the same giddy risks, but I was stymied, often silenced by my difference. My friends thought me pensive, deep. I appreciated their dramatic interpretations of my moodiness but continued to harbor my secret. No one could ever know me—not all of me, not the real me. While my friends threw themselves headlong into the rowdy, frenzied streets, I usually watched from the sidelines, estranged and forlorn.

Eugene, 1969

When I returned to Oregon from Europe, I was still that pensive girl, but I knew better what I wanted. I knew I could not go back to sorority life, the strictures of which I now found confining and petty. I wanted to be part of a more liberal student body; I wanted to live in a more freethinking town. Although Eugene wasn't Paris, it was exciting nonetheless. Hippies were ubiquitous, and I set out to be one of them. My well-worn Apple Boutique clothes were perfect. I joined sit-ins, candlelight vigils, marches. I road my old bike everywhere, bought pot, tried mescaline, was spellbound by *Midnight Cowboy* and *Easy Rider,* zoned out listening to "In-A-Gadda-Da-Vida" (Iron Butterfly, 1968) and "Light My Fire" (Doors, 1967).

I loved Eugene. My parents did not. Although the sheer distance of Europe had given me six months of delicious autonomy, I was back within reach of their machinations again, and they were not going to let go, not yet. Their great concern about me still focused entirely on my sexuality. Where was I to live if not in a dorm or sorority where curfews were still steadfastly enforced? For my junior year, I agreed to live in a dorm for juniors and seniors that had minimal rules, but enough to please my parents. As my last year approached, a new friend, Elaine, asked me to share an apartment with her, and I was adamant that finally I had earned this adult right. They could trust me, I insisted. At first my parents agreed, that is, until I once again committed the unpardonable.

Home for summer vacation, I dated a man, David, who was in his twenties and had his own apartment. I was not allowed to visit him there because we would have no chaperone. Frustrated by the short leash my parents still kept me on, I did what so many teenagers do—I lied. Mind you, I was twenty-one now, but that did not matter to them. I could not go to David's apartment. Period. On the night that Neil Armstrong walked on the moon, they tried to find me. My cover story that I was staying with a girlfriend was quickly discovered when they called her house and found out from her father that she was out of town. My parents drove to David's apartment, found me in his darkened living room watching the moonwalk, and dragged me out the door.

Once again it was off to my mother's doctor the next day. It had been four years since the day that changed my life, the day Dr. Cook had informed me that I was pregnant. Although I told my mother that David and I had not had sex, she would not be dissuaded. I can still remember my mortification when she told Dr. Cook she thought that I had "hot pants." Did she believe I had some libidinous gene, passed down perhaps from my Uncle Richard, that damned me to sexual excess? My girlfriends and I had whispered about "nymphomaniacs," but surely that label could not be applied to me. I had had sex once, paid greatly for that misstep, and had been chaste for five years. This time, to my surprise and hers, Dr. Cook shook his head and replied to her "hot pants" query, "Don't we all?" Not the response she wanted.

Surely my parents could have trusted that I would be careful with my sexuality. In fact, I had taken on the unpopular task of reigning in many eager, ardent young men for quite a while, even when faced with mattress rooms, accusations of "cock tease," and "Make love, not war" slogans. But

I had never dared tell my parents of those escapades and my resistance. Their obsession with what they saw as my sexual vulnerability still seems overwrought to me. They were apparently convinced that I could not say "no" and that I would get pregnant again if they did not make sure I was living in a highly structured situation.

After the David fiasco, the apartment was forbidden. They made their ultimatum: if I did not move back into the campus dormitory, there would be no money for school and I could not return to Eugene. It was 1969: four hundred thousand people went to Woodstock; Lieutenant William Calley was tried for the My Lai massacre; Sirhan Sirhan was convicted of the assassination of Robert Kennedy; a giant oil slick contaminated the Santa Barbara coastline; the first draft lottery was held; Charles Manson's cult murdered Sharon Tate, her friends, and the LaBiancas; James Earl Ray was sentenced to ninety-nine years for killing Martin Luther King Jr. My parents' world seemed to be shattering around us, yet they were fixated on whether I had sex or not.

I was both fed up and determined. It was the end of the decade, but finally, finally the antiauthoritarian spirit of the sixties overtook me and obliterated my excessive need for parental approval. Not only would I "question authority," I would fly in its face. I borrowed $300 from Karen, packed up my old Ford Falcon, drove back to Eugene, moved into the forbidden apartment with Elaine, and got two jobs—one making submarine sandwiches and another keying data into a massive computer on campus. The jobs gave me just enough money to pay my rent and buy some food. I started my senior year in college with little security but with exhilarating independence.

On a brilliantly crisp day that fall, I pedaled to campus as thousands of maple and elm leaves drifted down. The tree-lined streets were blanketed with a new crunchy floor. As I waited for Elaine to get out of her class, I looked up into the limbs above me just in time to see a leaf leave its branch and fall directly down on me, brushing my forehead like a blessing. A favorite word at that time was "cosmic," and this blissful moment truly qualified. Elaine eventually emerged in her raggedy pea coat and jeans, and we pedaled our bicycles through campus, headed for the Student Health Center.

A classmate had told Elaine that if you were a full-time student, you could get a prescription for "the pill" there. Could this be? A doctor would just give us birth control even though we were single and had no parental approval whatsoever? It seemed impossible, but we were just daring enough to give it a try. Nervous, we egged each other on, giggling all the way there. In the lobby, our voices soft, our glances furtive, our whole demeanor sheepish, we told the intake nurse why we were there, fully expecting her to turn us away. Instead, she simply asked to see our student identification and told us to take a seat.

Elaine was called in first. Before she reappeared to tell me what had happened and provide some more encouragement, my name was called. It was my turn. I was weighed and measured and then ushered into an examination room but told I need not disrobe. The doctor came in, asked if my periods were regular, listened to my heart, took my pulse, and without further inquiry, hastily wrote me out a prescription. He ripped it off the little pad and handed it to me along with two small white plastic packets: two months of free birth control pills "to get started with," he said. It was that simple! I had been prepared to lie, to say that I was about to be married, but he didn't ask me one question—he just handed me freedom.

Elaine and I raced back to our apartment, took our first pill, turned on *Nashville Skyline* (1969), and lit a joint. Dylan and Cash twanged off key: "Please see for me if her hair hangs long / If it rolls and flows all down her breast." I listened to their doleful harmony over and over again, still pining, after five long years, for Alec, wishing I could be his "Girl of the North Country." Sorrow stayed secretly with me. Although I pressed her memory into the crevices of my consciousness, her unrelenting flicker continued to burn into my everyday life. Nonetheless, I finally could leave one fear behind.

Martha's Vineyard, 2004

Although we still hear politicians today who say things like "Just say no" and preach abstinence, my parents' obsession with sexuality seems so misbegotten and unbalanced. Did they not know that I could have been having lots of sex for years? Did they not know how afraid I too was of pregnancy?

Yet even after all we had been through, we could never talk over these matters. Instead, they foolishly convinced themselves that a dorm room and a curfew would keep me from having sex, whereas an apartment spelled outright promiscuity. I wish they had known me better.

The end of the sixties was such a tantalizing time; the music, the clothes, the political scene were so stimulating that to resist the call for change was for me impossible. I triumphantly reneged on my promises to my parents and entered a new world, and I still say, a better world, wholeheartedly committed to heady ideals like peace, justice, civil rights, and yes, to love. Maybe they did me a favor by setting up an ultimatum that would finally put an end to my patience with their demands and conditions. Instead of docilely conforming one more time, I leapt over the barrier they tried to raise and landed with a certain amount of grace and success on my own two feet. It felt so good to defy them. Ironically and without intent, they provided my first bid for self-reliance and my first taste of empowerment.

20 *Damaged Goods*

Eugene, 1970

A MILITARY HELICOPTER is roaring overhead as I pedal my bike to my job at the campus computer center. Despite the din above me on this dazzling May morning, the university is calm, recovering from a tumultuous week of living up to its nickname, the "Berkeley of the Northwest." On every corner a National Guardsman stands, his automatic rifle at his side. As I ride by, my book bag slung over my shoulder, it feels as if the university has been invaded, as if I'm riding through a war zone. Am I foolish to be so exposed? My insubstantial tie-dyed T-shirt and jeans contrast dramatically with the formidable, multilayered gear of the soldiers.

As in well over a hundred other colleges in the United States this week, the president of the University of Oregon has had to suspend classes after antiwar protestors set up flaming barricades and blocked access to the university. More protestors broke windows and set fires in the ROTC building. Then students took over the administration building. Daily I have joined the huge throng gathered in front of the building and listened to speaker after speaker shout passionately into a megaphone. Now that the Guardsmen are on campus, the crowds have disappeared and the administration building has been "retaken." All small gatherings are quickly dispersed.

This turmoil began when Nixon announced that he had ordered the invasion of Cambodia, sparking student protests nationwide. But the catalyst for the flaming barricades and violent confrontations in Eugene came four days later when we received the news that four students lay dead at Kent State, shot down by National Guardsmen not unlike the ones that now stand at every corner I pass. I stop my bike in front of the student union lawn, and linger for a moment beside four fresh graves, dug in memory of this outrage.

I have recently returned to Eugene after spending the winter in Astoria, Oregon. Not having forgotten the meaningful impact the Watts Riots had on my sequestered adolescence and the lessons I had learned about privilege, I, like so many at that time, wanted to use my own education to better the lives of the less fortunate. When I found a program that would allow me do my student teaching in a school for underprivileged young adults, I jumped at the opportunity. I spent the winter teaching at the Astoria Job Corps Training Center, living with a group of equally earnest young men and women in flimsy apartments that were part of huge military housing complex built in the wooded hills above Astoria during World War II. The series of fourplexes where we lived were at first glance drab and uninviting, but their setting in the dark winter woods was lovely, and in the evenings with the heat turned up and the windows glowing, they came to look welcoming, even homey.

Monday through Friday we drove "on base" to work with African American and Hispanic teenage girls from Portland, Tacoma, and Seattle, all of whom were struggling to learn how to read as they trained to be custodians, hospital attendants, and grocery clerks. Our students lived in large, dreary dormitories on the converted military base.

To me, the center felt more like a prison than a school. It was surrounded by tall barbed-wire fences and had an imposing gate at the entrance that was guarded twenty-four hours a day. There were huge differences between the lives of the Job Corps students and us, their student teachers. Our students were angry and raunchy. They had attitude. Most showed dramatic disdain for the authority figures that were shaping their futures: the police officers, judges, and social workers. Nor did they have much respect for the Job Corps administrators or the teachers that had immediate and usually indifferent control over their lives. The majority had been sent to the Job Corps Center rather than to juvenile detention centers or jail. They could not leave the grounds without written permission and an "official" escort. But the students did like us, their student teachers, probably because we worked with them one-on-one and could be easily distracted from the reading lesson at hand by their compelling stories of their lives at the center and at home. They readily captured our sympathies. We were not permitted to serve as escorts for them, which, looking back now, was probably a good thing, for although we were sincerely well-intentioned, we were also trusting, naïve, and easily manipulated.

As far as my fellow student teachers and me, we were not rich, but we had our own money and almost no constraints. We were all white, even our one international student, a polite and highly serious young man from what was then still Rhodesia. Like the rest of us, he was on a privileged path. This path, so different from that of our students, had taken each of us about twenty-one years to follow and had led almost directly and almost effortlessly to a college degree with few opportunities for straying. Safely on task, we breezed through the gate of the Job Corp Center every morning and evening in our funky cars, radios blaring. Our status as college seniors, soon to graduate with teaching credentials and a strong sense of social commitment and potential, gave us a carefree autonomy. Although we too, like our students, were angry at authority figures, our anger was, for the most part, not based on any actual, firsthand experiences with injustice. Our anger was directed almost exclusively toward racist and hawkish politicians who, in fact, had very little impact on our immediate lives. The young men who were part of our program all had student deferments, and when they graduated, if they took teaching jobs in inner cities and began graduate school, they would be able to avoid the draft.

Every night we would gather in one of the cozy, overheated apartments that had once housed lieutenants and captains. It seemed appropriate to us that now the apartments were decorated with lots of paisley fabrics, rock posters, candles, and incense galore. With no homework to keep us busy, we would light the incense, turn up the music's volume, get high on cheap pot or cheap wine, and blast Blood Sweat and Tears, *Hair*, Joni Mitchell, and Janis Joplin. We'd sing along with John and Yoko: "All we are saying is give peace a chance." My roommate taught me how to

cook huge pots of cabbage, tomatoes, and hamburger that we'd raven-
ously gobble up.

My student teaching was both constructive and fun. Unbelievably, this
was the first time the circumstances of my life had given me the chance
to get to know women of color, and I loved listening to my students' stories and learning about their complicated lives. Helping them learn the
mechanics of reading was valuable for them, but hearing them talk about
their lives was enlightening. Perhaps I was being voyeuristic, but their
stories—alternately funny and harsh and sometimes tragic—fascinated
me. I know I spent more time listening and learning about and from them
than teaching. It was here that my commitment to social reform, to equity,
to justice, and to pacifism all solidified. It is a commitment that can still
run hot today.

April found me back in Eugene for my last term as an undergraduate,
witnessing student unrest at its height. I had reconciled with my parents.
They had been irate when I had first refused their support and headed
back to Eugene on my own, but they had also been impressed that I had
managed my last year in college independently. They had actually offered
to pay not only my tuition but also the rent for my tiny attic apartment
where I would live alone for that last spring. I loved my little home. I
pushed my single bed into the narrow dormer and slept with my head
practically sticking out of the window that I kept wide open. Sometimes I
would awaken with my hair wet from the Eugene drizzle. And now I had
a boyfriend, Allen, who slept with me there sometimes.

Allen was a strange young man. Today he would probably be diag-
nosed with obsessive-compulsive disorder and have medication to relieve
his fixations. He was preoccupied with unaccountable eccentricities about
his food, his car, and his workspace. He had a consuming need for precision that mystified and challenged me. I wanted to be perfect too, at least I
thought I did, so I would readily overlook his peculiarities and try to meet
his requirements. To me, he was handsome and adventurous; he had a
circle of easygoing, fun-loving friends, and most of the time, he seemed to
want my company. He liked my athleticism. I was the first girl he had ever
met who could keep up with him when he went backpacking. Together
we joined the university's mountain climbing club and scaled Mt. Hood,

Mt. Jefferson, and Mt. St. Helens years before its summit would erupt and disappear forever. He was for the most part apolitical; I think he saw himself as a kind of hippie Grizzly Adams, but he respected my political zeal and my ambitions to teach in an inner city. Nonetheless, I annoyed him in a myriad of ways. He didn't like the smacking noise he said I made when I chewed my food or the odor of my breath. He didn't like the cluttered state of my tiny apartment and the spoiled food he would sometimes find in my refrigerator. Although I certainly wasn't fat, he would complain about my thighs and reprimanded me when he found a candy bar wrapper under my bed or the remains of fast food in my trash can.

We had sex, and as far as I knew, it was fine; I had so little experience with which to compare it. When he asked why I wasn't a virgin, I offered him a very brief explanation about the one boyfriend I'd had before him with whom I had had sex one time—that's all I said, and for a while that seemed enough for him. He had had sex with his high school girlfriend too. Incongruously, it troubled him that I was on the pill. He seemed to think that this would make me sexually available to other men and urged me to stop taking them even though he wanted to have sex with me. I might have complied just to satisfy him, but my fear of pregnancy was even greater than my oversized needs to please him. Our relationship was getting more and more serious, graduation was approaching, and friends were getting engaged and setting wedding dates. Allen had not proposed, but he would surprise me by talking casually about our lives together after we graduated. The time had come. I could not dissemble anymore. I had to tell him the truth about my pregnancy, my lost baby, and my ongoing sorrow.

Terrified of revealing my secret to anyone but especially to him, I got myself drunk one night and then, in the classic style of the countless novels I had read, announced, "There's something I have to tell you." As I continued on, blurting out some of the sad details, I descended into uncontrollable crying and had to stop. One might have thought he would offer comfort, but instead he had an instantaneously heartless reaction. He was shocked, incensed, and pitiless.

His response should have been an unmistakable warning for me. I should have ended our relationship right then, but those "shoulds" were unavailable to me, and I had no advisors. Instead, I found his wrath entirely deserved. What I had done, he maintained, was reprehensible, and I agreed. Not only had I had sex and gotten pregnant, to him it was unpardonable that I had given my baby away. He accused me of being unnatural and cold-hearted. Plagued by a consuming self-loathing, I granted him every word. None of this was new. I had condemned myself years ago.

For a reason I still cannot figure out, it became imperative to him that he tell his father, a Presbyterian minister, the truth about my past. He prepared me for bad news. He was sure that when he told his father, he would surely forbid our relationship. He was amazed that upon hearing the truth, his father and his mother admonished him for being condemning and unforgiving. He was stunned by their response: they not only forgave me, they felt sorry for me. They urged him to be compassionate. He said he would try, and I became a sort of "project" for him.

It was 1970, a year of dramatic social change, protest, upheaval, and progress. The first Earth Day was celebrated; millions protested pollution. It was not only the year that the twin towers of the World Trade Center were completed but also the year that the Weather Underground was formed after a Greenwich Village townhouse exploded and killed three Weathermen. Later that year, the Underground helped Timothy Leary escape from a California jail. It was the year that courtroom trials began for the Chicago Seven, the Charles Manson family, and the Black Panthers Bobby Seale and Huey Newton. It was the year that the Beatles broke up, and Jimi Hendrix and Janis Joplin died of drug overdoses. It was the year that Germaine Greer published *The Female Eunuch,* arguing that women had a right to sexual freedom and vaginal pleasure. It was also the year that the *Mary Tyler Moor Show* debuted, but even though Mary was a single "working girl," she did not experiment with sexual freedom.

It was 1970 and we were in the midst of an extraordinary social and sexual revolution, but individually, most of us felt the sexual mores of the 1950s still heavy upon us. Girls I knew might have sex with their fiancés, but in my circle, casual sex was still illicit; "one-night stands" were forbidden. I still saw my own sexual past as shameful; something that had to be hidden. Despite his parents' tolerance and sympathy, Allen could not forgo his initial condemnation of my early sins. Together we saw *me* as deeply flawed, maybe even ruined.

Allen proposed after graduation, and both his parents and mine urged us to marry. It was still unthinkable that we would live together. My parents may have discouraged the marriage had they known of Allen's mean-spirited reproach, but I concealed his sporadic animosities. For harmful, inscrutable reasons, I accepted his proposal. We had a small, pretty wedding in my parents' beautifully blooming, tiered garden. Allen's beaming father married us. My choice for our wedding song revealed more than I knew. A friend sang Simon and Garfunkel's "Bridge Over Troubled Waters," and I was certainly "troubled waters," believing foolishly that marrying Allen would "cure" me and that we would now live happily together. The *San Marino Tribune* reported the event in detail: "The bride wore white lace with flowers woven through her hair." The façade of propriety was still intact.

Our marriage was a fiasco: short, cruel, and sad. We immediately moved across country to Washington, D.C., where Alan went to work as a civil engineer, building tunnels for the subway system that had just begun construction. I doggedly submitted to his castigation for six months. He chastised me for leaving milk on the counter, for not shutting the kitchen cupboards, for not hanging up my clothes, for leaving the bathtub too scummy, for not lining up the towels neatly on their racks, for slamming the car door, for eating too much, too fast, too noisily, for letting my hair go frizzy, for enjoying a McDonald's milk shake, for flopping gracelessly into an easy chair. He alphabetized our spice rack, our record albums, our books. He stacked and restacked our plates and bowls. He aligned the place mats with the napkin holders and repositioned the salt and pepper shaker on our breakfast table. He fiddled with the venetian blinds until they hung perfectly parallel. His fastidiousness was beyond me. I was a constant irritant, an inevitable failure. I just couldn't get anything right.

Throughout those painful months, he kept insisting that when I had given birth, I had been stretched out inside, and therefore I was not giving him enough sexual pleasure. Allen had read about something like this in Mario Puzo's novel *The Godfather*. Sonny's girlfriend had to be "fixed" after Sonny was gunned down so that she could go on to have a "normal" sex life with a "normal" man. Taking Mario Puzo and Allen on faith, I humbly made a visit to a gynecologist.

Once again, another crucial moment of my life occurs in a gynecologist's office with me on the examining table: as the doctor is giving me the pelvic exam, I tell him about my husband's complaint and ask him if I can be repaired by an operation—stitched up tighter inside. He stops the exam and stands, looking at me intently over my propped-up legs. I am surprised to see that he is disturbed by my question. Slowly and earnestly he tells me that there is nothing wrong with the size or shape of my anatomy—interiorly or exteriorly; in fact, he says he would not have known I had had a baby had I not told him. He says several times, "This is your husband's problem, not yours." He explains carefully that he is not a psychologist, but to him my husband's complaint sounds like a psychological problem because, he reiterates, there is nothing abnormal about me. He urges me to see a marriage counselor.

I bounded out of that office, happier than I had been in months, unexpectedly and gloriously released from Allen's damning verdict that I was damaged goods.

Martha's Vineyard, 2004

My automatic capitulation to both Allen's puritanical version of my past and his insistence on my defective sexuality remains a mystery to me even today, for I had been warned.

The spring before Allen and I married, while I was still living in Eugene, my friend Karen and her new husband Bill had come to visit me and we had gone backpacking with Allen. After a tense weekend during which I had failed to chew quietly enough, speak softly enough, or defer categorically enough to Allen's expert mountaineering skills, Karen, Bill, and I dropped him off at his house. Together, we breathed a collective sigh of relief; finally we could relax. As we drove back to my apartment, Karen couldn't contain herself: "He's so mean to you, Janet. Don't marry him," she said. Bill quickly concurred.

But I could pay no heed to their well-meant warning. Allen was the first man with whom I had entrusted my secret, and his response had seemed completely warranted. He felt no differently about me than I felt about myself. Neither could I take a chance and refuse Allen, nor could I believe Karen when she said that I deserved better. Who would want me after I confessed the truth? Allen and I were poster children for neurotic codependency: he needed to "fix" me, I needed to be "fixed." We found what our respective psychological demons demanded and then we let ourselves drift into what now seems like lunacy. My D.C. gynecologist's calm reply, "There's nothing wrong with you," was a life-saving assertion, and I tried to take it to heart, but I would need it repeated again and again for years to come.

The irony is that the first man I told my secret to, Allen, has turned out to be the only one who has ever been anything but sympathetic when hearing the story. But how could I know his response was aberrant? I was so trapped by the need to keep the secret that I had isolated myself from friends who would have immediately counseled me to get out of Dodge. Instead, I lacked all common sense, and the secret kept me confined in a sadistic little web. Until I lived with Allen, I never knew enough to have sympathy for the wife in that odd nursery rhyme "Peter, Peter, Pumpkin Eater." Only then did I come to identify with her plight, for I too became an easy target for a man who wanted to keep me in his own pumpkin shell. The secrecy that I thought protected me actually kept me gullible and pliable. The only lock Allen needed was my own self-loathing, and my only avenue for redemption seemed to be Allen—that is, until I told the doctor.

Under the intoxicating influence of that news, I opted next for something dramatic. Throwing propriety and social expectations to the four winds, I ran away to New York with the man I thought was my rescuing knight, my Lancelot—a seemingly wondrous Latino man who was managing the restaurant where I had gotten a temporary job as a waitress. I had known him for only three weeks. Although Allen was already making good money as an engineer in D.C., I had gotten this job because I was so bored, sad, and desperate to get out from under Allen's thumb. We had a large garden apartment in Chevy Chase, Maryland. It was packed with new furniture, new clothes, and state-of-the-art camping equipment; two new cars were parked in front. Yet one evening before Allen came home from work, I packed a suitcase, wrote a note, and took off penniless into the night with a stranger who had more allure and more promise of safety than the reformatory my marriage had become.

Before my decision to run, I had confided in my rescuer, Ricardo, that I had a baby, sensing the revelation would be the litmus test for whether he would help me. When I said, "I have a daughter," he instantaneously won me over by replying, "That's wonderful; let's go get her! Where is she?" When I explained, weeping bitterly, that I had lost her, that she was far beyond me, somewhere out in the world where we couldn't find her, he got tears in his eyes too. I read his sympathy as sincere. His calm acceptance of what had heretofore always been my ugly secret seemed to promise unconditional love, even though we hardly knew each other. The secret was still shameful for me, and I asked him to keep it for me. His kindness was novel and deeply comforting.

Now I can see that Ricardo's response to my story was not unusual, but at the time it sounded unbelievable. His kindness made him seem like Jesus, Gandhi, and Mother Teresa to me. Shame and guilt, which had been intensified by my parents' need for secrecy and discretion and then even more by Allen's condemnation, had skewed my perceptions of my past and myself. So feeling I needed to be saved twice over—from the cruel "laboratory" Allen had constructed for me in order to be "remade" and from my own annihilating sense of damnation—Ricardo seemed to be my only option.

My flight from Allen, six months after promising "to love and obey" him for the rest of my life, still surprises me. But perhaps it wasn't so out of character. It was already in my mind that in a crisis, flee. My parents had taught me that when they put me on that plane for Cleveland. And I was still the same girl who had taken "Cast Your Fate to the Wind" as her personal theme song. I wanted to be daring; I was adventurous. Once again I took Dylan's words to heart; I set out to "strike another match, go start anew." I desperately wanted Allen's chapter in my life to be "all over now, Baby Blue."

I was running away from a man who could barely tolerate me, even though he claimed to love the "me" he was in the process of creating. I was running away from a man who made me feel like I ate greedily, looked sloppy, and dressed unattractively. I was running away from a man who thought that I was so spoiled internally that I had to be redesigned. It isn't surprising that Ricardo, who told me exuberantly and repeatedly that he found me beautiful and sexy, won my heart. No one had ever whispered such sweet things to me, and they rolled off his tongue so smoothly. I was willing to go anywhere just to hear him tell me that I was perfect. When he said, "Let's head for New York City—I have an aunt in Queens," I did not hesitate.

I had also confided in Ricardo that I had desperately wanted to have a baby, but that Allen had forbidden children until I was capable of being a good mother. Ricardo responded with the perfect answer, declaring simply, "I would love to have a baby with you, the sooner the better." With these words, the die was cast. I packed my bag and ran away into the night, naïvely believing that now that I had found my handsome prince, I was finally on the right road to happily ever after. I would never see Allen again.

21 *The Life I Was Meant For*

Los Angeles, 1971

THE FIRST PERSON Allen called that night after he found my note was my father, who was more than alarmed by my impulsive flight and fearful of what I might do next. Testimony to his love for me, he went right into action to get me back. His first move was to hire a Chevy Chase lawyer to find me. His words to the lawyer were simple: "Try and talk some sense into her."

Ricardo and I had run away to New York City and had "hidden out" at his aunt's in Queens for a few days. However, we had little money, and it had soon come time to return to the D.C. area and find out if Ricardo still had his job. He didn't. I don't know how the lawyer found us, but the day after our return, he knocked on our door at the motel in Bethesda, Maryland, where we thought we were hiding.

The lawyer urged me to return to Southern California. My parents, he explained, were frantic and had hired him to "rescue" me from this crazy Panamanian who had spirited me off in the middle of the night from my deeply worried husband. Part of their panic had been caused by Allen, who, rather than accepting the hard-to-take fact that I had left him, described my disappearance as a kind of kidnapping. The police didn't buy the kidnapping theory. After all, I was twenty-two and not the first fed-up wife to run away with another man. But my parents thought I just might have been forced to go against my will.

Despite my repeated assertions that I was fine—better than ever, in fact—no one would believe me—except Ricardo, that is. Apparently I truly was acting completely out of character. My parents and their lawyer were adamant that I return to California, and finally, true to character, I caved into their insistence and reluctantly agreed to fly home. By now the lawyer was so uncertain of my reliability that when it came time to go, he flew to LA with me.

My father was unwilling to let his wayward, irrational daughter out of his clutches again, and his motives were understandable. He wanted to stop me, to reel me back in, to reason with me, to set me back on the path that I had so dramatically stepped off. Somehow he had to get me back under control—not necessarily his control, but certainly under the control of the value system in which he put so much stock.

He did not anticipate my loyalty to my new love—Ricardo. I found I could be as adamant as my father could, and although my parents and the Chevy Chase lawyer tried to reason with me, I insisted that I would not stay in LA unless Ricardo joined me. "Either Ricardo comes to LA or I return to him in D.C."; those were my unbending conditions. Unbelievably, in a bid to keep me safe at home, my father bought Ricardo a plane ticket to LA, and he agreed to come. But they were not open to the idea of Ricardo staying at their house, and I certainly didn't want to live with my parents. Once again, my friend Karen stepped in to help me. She was so relieved that I had finally gotten up the gumption to leave Allen and so impressed by the dramatic turn my life had taken that she offered to let us stay in her cool bohemian cottage in the Hollywood hills while she and Bill vacationed in Alaska. Within days, I weathered my parents' disapproval, packed my bag, met my new lover at LAX, and moved into our temporary home together in Hollywood.

My parents tried hard to talk me out of my live-in relationship with Ricardo. My mother even got me to spend an hour with her psychiatrist, who insisted that Ricardo and I would eventually find we were culturally at odds and unsuited for one another. I would hear none of it. Ricardo went to work managing a Hamburger Hamlet; I got a job selling china at Bullock's department store. We set up housekeeping together in a tiny apartment over a massage parlor in Sherman Oaks. We were happy. Compared to my marriage to Allen, this was Eden. Released from the demands of Allen's perfectionism and my unavoidable propensity to disappoint him, I delighted in my new, unexpected, undemanding life and my new man.

Ricardo was both happy and frustrated. He could not find a way to erase the blue moods to which I would sometimes unaccountably succumb or cure the insomnia that continued to plague me. He was surprised that I didn't want to stay out late and explore the LA club scene with him, drinking and dancing. He wanted that first girl he met—the lighthearted, sexy California girl who had spontaneously decided to pack her bag, leave her husband, and embark on a life of high adventure. But that was only part of me. The more pressing part of me wanted a baby—needed a baby—to soothe those blue moods and fill the emptiness that had nothing to do with Ricardo. I had been waiting for six years. When I became pregnant only two months after our "escape," I was ecstatic and immersed myself in my pregnancy.

Ricardo explored the LA club scene on his own and with my blessing. I had a much more important task to attend to, carrying a healthy baby. My parents were appalled by all of this and refused to see me once I told them I was pregnant and unmarried—again! This time, I paid them no mind, reveling in my pregnancy, cherishing each baby kick as the months passed. Yet when my perfect son was born, I wept for three days. How could this be? I was shocked that his birth had not "cured" me; I loved my new baby with a startling passion, but there was something in me that kept pining for that first baby—my baby girl.

Shortly after Todd's birth, my divorce from Allen was final. Ignoring my mother's psychiatrist's warnings and our own growing suspicions that we might indeed be unsuited for each other, Ricardo and I married immediately. Only now did my parents agree to see their new grandson and meet their new son-in-law. Unpredictably, they liked Ricardo as did my sisters, their husbands; even my grandmother liked him. Ricardo had a way of charming the women of my family just as he had charmed me. We were not used to such effusive flattery, and it was irresistible. My family must have been dubious about his ethnicity, clearly mirrored in their new grandson's ruddy skin and brown-black eyes. But they kept such thoughts to themselves. Ricardo's work ethic and intelligence impressed them. He left Hamburger Hamlet and, with my father's help, got a position as an insurance adjuster, which he was so good at that he was quickly promoted to litigator. His English was flawless, his manners impeccable; in short, despite a questionable start, my family found him acceptable. My parents helped us buy our first home, and I got to begin the career I had prepared for. I went to work teaching third grade in an inner-city elementary school in Pacoima. I loved my work, I loved my baby boy, and I was ardently committed to loving my husband. Finally I had achieved my dreams—this was the life I was meant for.

Martha's Vineyard, 2004

How quickly and easily I left behind my sixties radical spirit! I did somehow make time to campaign for McGovern with Todd in a backpack, and I watched with fascination as Agnew resigned and Watergate unfolded. But for the most part, I burrowed down comfortably into my new lifestyle. Todd's babyhood was a delight. Each of his new accomplishments pleased us to no end. I made friends with my fellow schoolteachers who were also having babies. Life revolved around baby showers, family barbecues, pool parties, and birthday celebrations. I planted flowerbeds and a vegetable garden in our backyard. I baked bread, crafted homemade Christmas gifts, and took up needlepoint. I didn't drink, and I even stopped saying "damn" just as soon as Todd began to talk.

My music choices reflected my new world. I'd blast my stereo as I cleaned our little California bungalow; now it was Carly Simon singing "I Haven't Got Time for the Pain" or Billy Joel crooning "Just the Way You Are."

The San Fernando Valley, 1972–75

Ricardo and I had an understanding. He had Friday nights to himself: "Boys' night out." I didn't ask what he did; I didn't really care. But odd things began to happen. One night while he was still working for Hamburger Hamlet, I called him at work, surprised when his boss told me he was not working that night. I waited up for him, concerned, mystified. When he came in the door and I asked where he had been, he said he had been asked to work at another restaurant that night. Okay. It seemed plausible.

Another night, after he became an insurance adjuster, he came home late, smelling of perfume. I asked where the perfume came from and he told me he had to get a statement from a gay man who pranced around him and spritzed him with cologne. Definitely a dubious story, but—okay—I bought that one too.

Another night he didn't come home until dawn. I frantically awaited his return, and when he finally got there, he made up an elaborate excuse about police who harassed him as he came out of a bar, declaring to me dramatically that he was lucky to be home at all. I ingenuously took the bait and even felt sorry for him rather than suspicious. I was so determined that we would have a good marriage, that we would have a stable family, that I would not allow myself to consider other possibilities. I would make our lives work by being patient, self-reliant, and thankful for the attention Ricardo did show me. I eventually came to learn that Ricardo began a secret life shortly after we arrived in LA. But I avoided that truth for as long as I possibly could.

And I had my own "other" life too. It wasn't a secret life, but it had nothing to do with Ricardo, and that troubled him. I had returned to university. When I began teaching for the Los Angeles School District, I was given a temporary teaching credential because California required a fifth year in college. I needed to go back to school for that fifth year, but ironically, I didn't need courses in education. I had met all those requirements at the University of Oregon with my BS. Instead, I needed the equivalent of a bachelor of arts, and since my minor had been English, it was logical that I complete my requirements in that subject.

I enrolled at California State University at Northridge, which was only blocks from our house, delighted to be taking upper-division English courses like "The Romantic Poets" and "The Victorian Age" instead of "Methods of Teaching Social Studies." I loved the courses' reading and writing assignments, but most of all I loved the spirited, thought-provoking class discussions. All week I was surrounded by eight-year-olds at my job. On breaks in the teachers' lunchroom I got to interact with other adults, but our talk was always about our students and our own children.

When I got home, it was just Todd and I, since Ricardo rarely made it home early. Don't get me wrong; my afternoons and evenings with Todd were wonderful. I made sure I had "quality time" with my son, but it wasn't intellectually stimulating. When Ricardo was home, he watched TV shows in which I had little interest. So my night classes became an invigorating break; the reading was captivating and my writing earned me good grades.

As I approached my last semester, with just one more class needed to complete my requirements for the school district, I regretted that it was all soon to come to an end. I came to campus late one afternoon with Todd perched on my hip, dressed in his bright yellow overalls. I was there to turn in my term paper and I found my professor in his office. I was so proud of Todd, my greatest accomplishment, and my professor made appropriate cooing sounds. But then he asked me to sit down. My face flushed.

"Had I done poorly on my final exam?" I asked.

"Quite the contrary," he replied.

In fact, I had written the best exam he had read in years, he said. He gave me several specific compliments, using words like "inventive" and "vital." Flustered and self-conscious, I thanked him and rose to go, but he was not done. I sat back down, giving Todd my car keys as a distraction. He went on to ask me to think seriously about applying to graduate school, that he would recommend me, that I had a fine mind, and that I should continue my education.

Astounding! I had always done well in school, but never before had a professor taken such an interest, sitting me down and stating confidently, "You can do this. You should do this." I said I would think about it, thanked him, and stumbled out into a smoggy but resplendent California sunset.

Could I earn a master's degree? I had never imagined myself as a graduate student. My life blueprint almost duplicated the one my parents' culture had projected for me: it was a Dick-and-Jane life in the suburbs with children, a dog, a cat, and a loving husband. I was breaking the mold enough by teaching school. But mine was a "second income," an avenue for my "do-gooder" instincts, insisted Ricardo. It brought in extra money for vacations, a shiny VW camper, a new leather jacket to replace my old tattered one from the Apple Boutique. Ricardo was doing the important work for the family. And I desperately wanted another baby. Todd was two. Most of my fellow teachers had their babies two years apart. I was the only one with just one.

When Ricardo came home that night, I told him about my professor's suggestion. I was stunned by his crass response. He claimed that all my professor wanted was to "get in my pants." This seemed impossible. I was familiar with flirtatious professors and there had been none of that. Still, Ricardo's response befuddled me. It made me feel guilty for the attention I had just received even though I was positive it was legitimate. Ricardo went on to admit that he was relieved my schoolwork was almost over; he was tired of babysitting on the nights I had class. He was tired of watching me read and type papers. He had no interest in the Romantics or the Victorians or the Modernists. My focus, he said, was supposed to be on my family, on him.

For reasons that now seem immature and sad, I accepted his patriarchal version of my interests and ambitions and abandoned the notion of graduate school. Perhaps, I thought, focusing more on my family would finally bring me the emotional equipoise I longed for but that still eluded me. Perhaps domestic commitment was the key to finding a tranquil room filled with sunshine where I would feel complete.

Martha's Vineyard, 2004

I was so earnest. I desperately wanted to please, especially the men in my life. I wanted Ricardo's approval. I kept our house clean if not immaculate, did the grocery shopping, prepared all the meals. When Ricardo returned home in the evenings, I would rush to fix him a cocktail, just as my mother had done for my father. I kept his daily supply of clean shirts crisply starched and ironed. I took care of all the baby's needs except for those nights, once a week, when I had class. Then I would put Todd to bed early so Ricardo could relax undisturbed after his hard day at the office. I made all the arrangements for Todd's child care while I was teaching, dropping him off at his sitter's house each morning and rushing back to get him by 4:00 each afternoon.

It was easy to make Todd happy, but Ricardo was restless, in a constant search for something ineffable, for inner peace, he said. I was never sure. For weeks the Maharishi Mahesh Yogi's *Science of Being and Art of Living* lay, spine broken and dog-eared, on the back of the toilet, and he read and reread passages out loud to me from it while I gave Todd his bath or fixed dinner. Then he took up transcendental meditation, exhorting me to keep the baby quiet as he locked himself away in the extra bedroom. When those endeavors produced no significant enlightening effects for him, he enrolled in Silva Mind Control courses. My efforts to make him content in the role of husband and father—to feel that Todd and I were enough—fell short, and he seemed to mentally squirm under the structured predictability of our suburban lives.

Perhaps it was hard to be married to someone like me. Even though years had passed since I had run away from Allen and his obsessions, I could not quite give up the pursuit of perfection he had kindled in me, perfection in myself and inadvertently in others. Ricardo fell into the role of the flawed husband, always having to apologize for being late, forgetting to call, letting his cash disappear unaccountably, or spending too many hours behind a locked door meditating rather than joining me in the day-to-day responsibilities of parenthood and housekeeping. I was driven and a kind of dynamic energy field seemed to surround me that pressured him to do more and be more when all he wanted was to tune out.

Ricardo searched for peace from me and my frenetic pace, and I worked hard at home, at school, and at being a good daughter for my parents. I was again desperate for their approval, and I knew I could best win it by idealizing my home life. I never gave them a hint of Ricardo's recurring discontent. To them we seemed to be living "happily ever after." They still needed to be protected from my potential to upset their lives, to overturn all apple carts. I was determined to be just what they wanted me to be, whether that required baking homemade pies for all family gatherings or pretending my husband was the epitome of Ward Cleaver.

I was also obsessed with pleasing my professors, almost all of whom were male. I studied diligently, spending too many nights writing and rewriting term papers. I could not amass enough As. Each one was a validation of my worth. When I saw C+ on a returned linguistics midterm, I was devastated and ashamed. I slunk out of the classroom, more determined than ever to master the subject, even if it took memorizing the entire text-book. To compensate, my professor allowed me to write an extra paper on the futuristic slang in Burgess's *A Clockwork Orange*. I came out of the course relieved and grateful: my professor had restored my fragile self-esteem by giving me a sympathetic A-.

The principal at Pacoima Elementary School, a demanding and sur-prisingly hot-tempered, ambitious man, was also someone I wanted to please. My fellow teachers would complain bitterly about his autocratic methods, but I had left all attempts at questioning authority behind. It became imperative that my classroom have the most colorfully decorated bulletin boards and that my students always be orderly and disciplined in case he might walk through my classroom on one of his unannounced "checks." When a student was unruly or defiant, I would never refer him or her to the school administration since that would be an admission that I could not manage my responsibilities with poise and authority.

I had left Allen far behind, but I could not shed a neurotic need for perfection and acceptance. I could not relax my standards or lower the hurdles I set up for myself day after day. Looking back, I think my desire to please those "in charge" must have begun even before Allen, who hap-pened to play right into my emerging compulsions. Perhaps it was when I left for Ohio to have Sorrow. Despite my egregious failings, it was then that I started to believe that I could scramble back into favor if I never made another mistake. However, the psychological cul-de-sac of being a perfec-tionist is that it is impossible. I could get very good grades, but I could not ace every test I took or every paper I turned in. I could work hard to keep my home tidy, but my two-year-old could turn it topsy-turvy in minutes. My third-graders were inevitably squirrelly and sometimes disobedient. Indeed, no one can manage the performance of perfect student, perfect teacher, perfect daughter, or perfect wife and mother. And my husband's dissatisfaction was mounting day by day. I stayed ferociously busy, trying to keep "on top" of my multifaceted life, but I actually had very little con-trol over the people and circumstances that filled my days.

When I agreed to forego graduate school because of Ricardo's jeal-ous reservations, I did gain some leverage in another of our ongoing disagreements—whether or not to have another child. Before I brought home the news of my professor's enthusiastic recommendation for higher education, Ricardo had been adamantly against having another child. Now, as a kind of tradeoff, he agreed to another baby: "You can't go to graduate school, but you can have another baby," he proffered. Ricardo's insecurities, my own dedication to family as my first priority, and my inextinguishable longing for another baby eclipsed the desire for graduate school. Like so many women, then and now, who must choose between a demanding career and a demanding family, I chose family. "You can't have both," I told myself.

 *Flying Solo*

THE NIGHT AFTER my second daughter's birth, I was triumphant. Giddy and sleepless, I held her hour after hour as she slept deeply. Every time she stirred, I would help her nurse. Finally, I thought, she has arrived, my Helen Marie, named after both her grandmothers. Yet even this—my exquisite baby girl—was not entirely restorative. There still remained a deep yearning, an inextinguishable desire that unnerved me. Sorrow would not be quelled.

Nor did this angelic baby strengthen our marriage, as I had delusionally imagined. Instead, the stark realities of Ricardo's infidelities were finally revealed. I could no longer deny them, so either I had to forgive them or he had to change. The cultural divide my parents had predicted now loomed. I did not want my allegiance to him to waiver, so I tried to extract new promises from him and to set aside what I had learned, to start over again with a new baby and a new commitment. Outwardly I may have appeared to be a loving, giving wife, but in my heart, I was growing to despise him. Still I persevered. I thought that if I just kept pretending to love him, he would change and I could forgive him. But Ricardo was tired of always being "the problem." Sensing that our life together was about to crumble, I secretly tried again for the one thing that had made me gloriously happy in our marriage—my babies. I was purposefully careless with birth control.

When I became pregnant with our third child, I pretended to be surprised, but Ricardo was genuinely surprised and frustrated with me for this "mistake." In an attempt to win him over, I packed up our VW bus and asked him to accompany Todd, Helen, and me on a kind of pilgrimage. We would go to the High Sierras and Yosemite Valley, the Edenic locale that had helped me mend my broken relationship with my parents years before. I was sure that as we walked up to Happy Isles and onto Vernal Falls, my dreams for this new baby would rub off on him, that we would be reunited, a family again. The same wild beauty that restored me at seventeen would work its magic on us all. In a picture I keep, I am perched on a granite boulder, my stomach just beginning to protrude, Helen at my side, Todd climbing the rock behind us. I smile brightly for Ricardo's camera, hopeful and inspired.

But this pilgrimage failed. Nothing would be restored. Ricardo soon made it clear that he had had enough, and our relationship, a crucial component to my sense of well-being, disintegrated. Separation and divorce followed. Inevitably, Sorrow haunted me throughout my pregnancy; my insomnia was worse than ever through those long months, but the birth of my third daughter, Kezia, did not disappoint. I found great solace in her coming.

For a while, I reveled in the tumultuous life of young motherhood, always with a baby on my hip—bottles, diapers, Cream of Wheat, the stroller, the park. Always they were there with me, and I did not regret that there was no man to interfere. When I was awakened by uneasy dreams of Sorrow in the middle of the night, I would go and watch them sleeping, breathing in deeply the soothing, sensual smell at the napes of their necks. Who needed a husband when I finally had all that I needed?

Ricardo's departure also made it possible for me to apply nervously to graduate school. When I was admitted, I was full of trepidation and began my first graduate seminar doubtful about my capability and the wisdom of this decision. I was, after all, a single parent with an infant, a two-year-old, and a six-year-old. My resources were stretched thin. My maternal obligations were powerful. Perhaps it would all be too much.

I was exceedingly busy with my children, my teaching, and my pursuit of an advanced degree, so busy that I remember those years after my divorce as often on the brink of either pandemonium or panic. It was as if I were being tossed around in a deeply complicated whirlpool

Janet with Todd and Helen in Yosemite Valley, 1977.
Photographer unknown. Courtesy of the author.

of responsibility, barely able to keep my head above water, grabbing at one task and then another. On weekdays I was in constant motion: everyone was up by 6:30; I made breakfast and we were all dressed, fed, in the car by 7:45; then the dash, first to the babysitter's, then on to Pacoima Elementary School, where I was ready to greet my third graders by 8:30; I held the lid on thirty eight-year-olds and managed some learning from 8:45 to 2:45; then back to the sitter's; drop Todd at soccer practice; get Helen to speech therapy; then the grocery store with Kezia; pick up

Helen; pick up Todd; home at 5:30; dinner, baths; 8:00 and everyone was in bed; story time until 8:30, then it was my time to study.

Unless I had class that night. If so, it was a scramble to find a babysitter on a school night—forever an ordeal. Prepare a quick dinner for the four of us; instructions for the sitter; class from 7:00 to 10:00. If one child got sick, my carefully orchestrated dance of responsibility slowed to a crawl. I received ten days of paid family leave a year, and I used every one of them and more. Weekends were a respite: my chance to wash and fold huge loads of laundry, clean house, mow the lawn. Saturdays revolved around Todd's soccer games, or if not soccer, then Little League. If there were no games, I would load the kids in my forest green Beetle and we would head for my parents' home in North San Diego County where they had recently retired and where they were always happy to greet us.

With all this activity, one would think I would be falling thankfully to sleep every night without fail. Yet when night came, the dull pain of Sorrow would return, invading my necessary steadiness with melancholy and anxiety. I studied for my graduate courses with an intensity that probably dismayed my fellow graduate students, but my diligence had as much to do with escape as it did wanting to succeed. Where was Sorrow? Was she well? Was she loved? She was twelve years old now. Was she happy? What if she wasn't? What if she needed me?

Despite everything I had done to compensate for losing her, she was irreplaceable. Now, when I needed sleep so badly, my insomnia, which had never completely subsided, returned with a vengeance. Alone in my own home with my children, my morsels of sleep were sporadic and fitful, haunted by recurring dreams whose inevitable outcomes my unconscious would not revise.

Dream One:

The baby has been left behind. She is back on the other side of the seared, rolling hills we traversed all afternoon to get to a green valley where we have come to live. I must have forgotten to put her in the car when we gathered the picnic supplies and clambered in. Like the infant Oedipus, she has no shelter from the elements, since I left her lying on her back on a blanket in the middle of a hot, sunny meadow where we stopped. She is not old enough to turn over or crawl away. I begin to panic as I picture her, her tiny fists flailing and her feet kicking the air. It is still warm, but evening will be coming on, and she will soon feel the chill and be easy prey for the gaunt fox that will come to gaze at her from the cover of the surrounding woods. Although many of us had come in the car, now I can find no one to drive me back to the meadow. The dust-laden gray car has disappeared. I start running up the first long hill, but I am immediately drained of energy. My legs are dream heavy; I can barely make any progress up the scorched road. I know there are many more hills between the meadow and me, between my baby and me. I try to walk fast, but my leaden legs only inch their way up the endless, steep incline.

Dream Two:
I put the baby down for her nap, and, seeing that she is sleeping peacefully, I start repairing the phantasmagoric disorder of the house. I have innumerable tasks. They take me hours and the other children need attention. Meals have to be prepared and other necessary errands lead me through a Dickensian maze of unknown, empty streets and shuttered shops. I suddenly realize days have passed, and I have not once returned to the room where I left her. Surely she has been wailing for someone to come and get her. How could I have not heard her crying? I fear she is dead. I have not returned to care for her. I approach the door that I closed days before. Everything is insufferably still. I stand in front of the door, paralyzed. I want to touch the doorknob but I simply cannot move.

Haunted by these nightmares and badly in need of real rest, I went to the counseling center at CSUN to talk with a therapist. I did not tell her about Sorrow, but I did admit that I was feeling overwhelmed by my responsibilities and frazzled by my inability to get a good night's sleep. She gave me helpful, practical advice—a trick that worked for me then and that I still put to use. She told me that when I felt I just couldn't accomplish what needed to be done, to imagine myself in a play. Whether it was a play in which my role was bathing the baby, frying the hamburger patties, managing my third-grade reading groups, making a well-articulated point in a graduate seminar, or falling asleep, I was an actor and this was my performance to complete. Grasping at straws, I took her advice. Remarkably these visualizations helped immensely. I still did not sleep well, but I managed to proceed through my appointed rounds with a healthier measure of composure and a sense of achievement.

One night in the midst of all this I watched a made-for-TV movie about an unhappy teenage girl desperately searching for her birthmother. In the movie, a compassionate social worker willing to bypass strict regulations helps the girl find her birthmother's address. The girl arrives at her mother's house during a party. Standing outside looking in through the lighted windows, she can see happy people warmly chatting and laughing. She hesitates but finally rings the doorbell. It is her birthmother who rushes to the door, thinking another guest has arrived. When she sees the girl, she knows instantly that she is looking at her daughter, just as I would know instantly if my daughter came to my door. I cannot recall how the movie ended, if it was a happy or troubled reunion, but watching the drama unfold opened a door of possibility for me. Maybe I could let Sorrow know where I was—give her my name and where she could find me if she needed me. And so I began my first search thirteen years after Sorrow's birth.

The hardest part was approaching my mother, but one afternoon while my father was safely out of their house, I gingerly asked, my heart racing, if she had any papers that had to do with my daughter's adoption. This was the first time I had said one word to her about the secrets of 1965. She looked worried and replied quickly and with finality that she had nothing—no records, no names, nothing. My aunt had taken care of all the "arrangements." If there were papers, Aunt Jo would have them.

It took me awhile to recover from that initial foray. I felt guilty for troubling my mother with my request, for bringing that painful year up again. Clearly she didn't want to discuss it. Her answer had been clipped and conclusive. Weeks passed, but slowly I built up the nerve to write to my Aunt Jo, asking her for any paperwork that she might have and the name of the adoption agency she had worked with. Her return letter was brief and admonishing. All documents were long ago destroyed. She couldn't remember the name of the adoption agency, and if she could have, she wouldn't have given it to me. She said I was making a mistake asking for this information. Frankly, she was surprised that the notion had even occurred to me. She had advised me years ago, and she still insisted that I should keep these secrets locked away in my memory, or better yet, forget them. I could sense not just admonition but also impatience, maybe even anger in her words. It was wrong of me to ask for any information; I had no right to try and find this girl. She was someone else's daughter, and they had been promised that their identity would never be revealed. Although my daughter would be told she was adopted, that was all she would be told. My part in this family drama was canceled, erased forever, as it should be. My aunt's closing words were blunt and emphatic: "Drop it!"

Her letter saddened me, but again my feelings of guilt were even greater. What had I been thinking, dredging up an embarrassing, upsetting past? Clearly, I had disconcerted my mother and now my aunt. I thought back to the day Aunt Jo had bustled out of the room to fill out Sorrow's birth certificate. What had she put on it? Had she given Sorrow another name? What about my name? Was I listed as Jan Mason or Janet Ellerby? What if I dared to call all the adoption agencies in Akron? According to my aunt, I had no right to make such calls. And if I did call, would I ask for the records of Jan Mason or Janet Ellerby? How could I find Sorrow when I didn't even know my own name? It was too overwhelming. Once more, I resigned myself to my fate, but I kept on dreaming that someday, somehow, she might knock on my door.

Looking back at those first years on my own, I am impressed by what now seems like dauntless energy and courage. At that time courage was not what I felt. I was barely getting by. Ricardo was an unhelpful ex-husband. Occasionally he would take Todd and Helen for the weekend, but the baby, Kezia, was too much for him. There was one Saturday night when he finally consented to take her too. Thankful for the relief, I went to dinner and a movie with a girlfriend. Home alone afterwards, I characteristically took a long time to fall asleep, but it mattered little since the next morning I could sleep in, or so I thought. I had just fallen into a sound sleep when the doorbell, ringing and ringing, awakened me. My alarm clock read 1:20. I rushed to the door, turned on the yellow porch light, and peered out the peephole. There was Ricardo with Todd and Helen, blinking sleepily in the bright light, standing behind him in their pajamas. I tore open the door. "Where is the baby? Where is the baby!" I gasped.

When Ricardo had put her down to sleep in her portable playpen at 9:00 P.M., Kezia began to cry. When she still had not stopped by midnight, Ricardo, thoroughly unhinged, had put her and the two older kids in his car and driven them all the way from his apartment in Marina del Rey to my house in the Valley. I rushed out to his car, which he had left idling in the driveway. Kezia was slumped over, strapped into her car seat, snoring loudly through her stuffy nose, deeply asleep. I unbuckled her and carried her gently to her crib. Ricardo left; Todd and Helen tumbled into their beds and fell asleep immediately. I watched Kezia sleep for a while, her only stirrings the tiny shudders that intermittently convulsed her body, sure signs that her crying had been long and hard. The next morning she called from her crib at her regular time, 6:30, delighted when I came to retrieve her and brought her back to my bed, unwilling to snooze for even an extra five minutes despite the traumatic night she had just weathered. My baby was as attached to me as I was to her, and it was clear that it was up to me alone to keep her safe. Ricardo continued to take Todd and sometimes Helen for weekends, but Kezia would not spend the night again with him until she was over three and Ricardo had moved in with his girlfriend, Linda. It would be up to Linda to coax Kezia to sleep without me.

Ricardo's monthly child-support payments ($300) were often late, and when he decided to go to India to study with the Maharishi, the payments stopped for a year. In 1972, when I started teaching for LA Schools, I made $13,000. While I was married, my salary was our second income, and it was wonderful to have my own money. I didn't feel like I had to ask Ricardo when I wanted to buy a new blouse or a bouquet of fresh flowers. By 1978, after our divorce, I was making $16,000, but now it was my primary income, and I could never stretch it far enough. My car was undependable; my children regularly needed clothes and shoes, and, of course, they wanted toys. My health insurance didn't cover all of the pediatrician's costs or the myriad bottles of Dimetapp and amoxicillin as each of them endured persistent ear infections and stubborn bouts of bronchitis. But we did manage to enjoy each other. I took great pleasure in my children. Most of the time.

Dating was dreadful. For example, a handsome friend of a friend, Bob, asked me out to dinner; I eagerly accepted and arranged for a babysitter, looking forward to a night out. We had a delicious dinner, but part way through I realized that I didn't like Bob at all. His jokes were crude. He bragged about himself with an arrogance that was undeserved. He drank a lot. When we arrived on my front porch, I turned coolly to say "thank you" and a firm "good night." He was shocked.

"That's it?" he said. "I can't come in?" he asked.

He had paid for my dinner, he declared, and now it was my turn. Apparently, payback was sex.

We wrestled there on my front porch for a moment, wedged awkwardly between the front and screen doors. It seemed he was not going to let me in the door without him. By now, I found him completely repulsive. Had I liked him just a little, I might have let him in out of guilt. He might have persuaded me that I owed him something. But I got through the door, alone but shaken. The babysitter and I peeped out the front window, watching as his car peeled away from the curb. Dating seemed to involve a kind of informal agreement that almost hinted of prostitution: if a date spent money on me, I should comply sexually. Unmoored by this event, I felt lost at sea.

I knew women who did have casual sex with multiple partners, but not many. A fellow teacher would tell us about her sexual adventures over the lunch table. One day, shortly after my terrible date with Bob, she told us that she had telephoned a man she had just met and asked him if he wanted to "fuck" her. That was the word she used—just like that! I was flabbergasted by her audacity, but the man was not. He replied, "Definitely," and they immediately arranged a rendezvous. No wonder Bob had found my response unreasonably cold and stingy. I wasn't even willing to kiss him.

Another time, when my dryer broke, I went over to a neighbor's house to use hers. As the dryer twirled, I sat in the family room, chatting with her and her husband as the kids played with their son in their backyard. Gradually the subject turned to sex, and they told me unabashedly that they were swingers. Would I join them in their hot tub some weekend soon? Panicky, I offered my apologies, gathered the kids, and fled, our clothes still damp and heavy in the basket.

Then, at my elementary school's Christmas party, I watched my beautiful student teacher, Leslie, flirt boldly with a handsome playground assistant who I had a secret crush on. Their scorching affair began that night, and I witnessed its progress until it slammed to a halt when he broke her heart on Valentine's Day by returning to his high school sweetheart. Leslie was devastated, cried pitifully, and came to work hung over, but the very next weekend, she eagerly started up with a new heartthrob from Manhattan Beach.

It was the close of the swinging seventies; I was thirty years old—at my sexual peak, so I was told; yet I was hopelessly unprepared to swing. I was still constrained by the conservative values of my parents; sex outside of marriage felt wrong—enticing perhaps, but ultimately wrong. I tried to rise above my inhibitions but could not escape the guilt and regret that inevitably followed all sexual forays. I still harbored fantasies that I was meant for my first love, Alec, and he for me. Fifteen years had passed, but I had not yet abandoned the romantic belief in the sacredness of that love: the first cut is the deepest.

I spoke to Alec for the last time at the close of that decade. He lived near my parents' new home with a woman, but he had not married. When I met him unexpectedly coming out of a coffee shop in exquisite Leucadia, the bougainvillea blooming profusely above us, how badly I wanted to impress him, to show off my children, to dazzle him with my new liberated state—I was in graduate school, I was a teacher, I was single! He showed no interest.

Desperate to say something that might ignite a spark of interest, I told him again about our daughter, that she was thirteen years old, that her name was Sorrow. He shrugged, but he knew I was telling the truth. I rushed on, spilling words about my unsuccessful try at finding her, that I wouldn't give up. What would he do if I found her? Could I tell her his name?

"Yeah, whatever," he mumbled indifferently.

He had to go. He had to help someone move.

"Bye," he muttered.

And he was gone, down the Pacific Coast Highway, clearly relieved to escape my presence.

I was ashamed. I had been holding my heart out to this man for fifteen years—half of my life. I would not do it again—and I have not. I have never seen or spoken with him since. Nonetheless, his last rejection was a harbinger of more bad luck. The next afternoon, on our return to the San Fernando Valley from my parents' home, an elderly woman ran a red light and smashed into my green VW Bug. The car crash sounded like a train wreck—an earsplitting boom as metal hit metal and glass shattered. Kezia's car seat saved her life, for it was her side of the car that took the brunt of the impact. Kind people came running, while I grabbed for diapers to stop the blood coming from Todd's face and Helen's forehead. A stranger I never had time to thank reached in through the crushed side window, unbuckled my screaming baby, and pulled her out of the car through broken glass and crumpled metal. She stopped crying as soon as he gave her to me. She was spotted with blood too, but it was my blood, not hers. The four of us sat down on the curb. Someone brought blankets and draped them around Helen and Todd and a towel for me to hold over my left eye, which kept filling up with blood. I looked at Todd and saw his left cheek hanging open. Helen's blond head was scarlet. So much bright red blood was lost on that curb.

We sat there in an uncanny stillness, stunned; no one was crying. We listened to sirens coming closer, and I vaguely comprehended they were coming for us. The ambulance pulled up. Two EMTs dashed out and quickly began ministering to Helen and Todd. They loaded us all into the same ambulance. Helen and Todd almost seemed to fall asleep on the way to the hospital and only stirred when they were gently lifted out.

Todd needed over forty stitches to put his cheek back together, Helen needed twenty to mend the cuts on her head, I needed ten over my eye. The nurses used a hair dryer to get the tiny shards of glass out of Kezia's fine baby hair—miraculously there was not a cut on her. My sister came and took us home. When we walked into the house, I looked at Todd and Helen, their swollen faces covered with purple bruises and black stitching, so transformed from the perfect shining faces they had had just hours ago. We all started crying.

I cried for weeks. Although I had not caused the accident, I felt responsible. I berated myself for having such a vulnerable car, for having overpacked it so that things went flying and cut the children, for not reacting fast enough when I saw that big car out of the corner of my eye, speeding inexplicably toward us. No one else witnessed the accident. I kept picturing my green light. It had been green, right? The elderly woman admitted that she had run the light, that her brakes had failed her as she tried to stop, but had they? I couldn't stop second-guessing that second before impact. Regardless, I had failed to protect these children; now they would carry scars for life. My self-loathing, which had abated over the last few years, came boiling to the surface.

Over the following weeks, I fell into the same moroseness that engulfed me after I lost Sorrow. I stopped eating, stopped sleeping, and I cried and smoked so much that I developed a serious cough. My guilt tormented me so intensely that I fell willingly into illness, becoming so sick, in fact, that I had to be hospitalized. Through nights of pneumonia's fever and sweat, I wallowed in self-pity at the Northridge Hospital. Ricardo came to stay with Helen and Todd. My parents took Kezia to their home in San Marcos. I had to drop the Blake seminar I had been looking forward to.

Slowly, I got well, went home: we all healed. But I was afraid. Much of my confidence exploded in that car crash. I could not make it as a single parent. I was failing in significant ways. I couldn't keep my children safe. I was always broke. I was always sad. I needed help.

 *Cougar Gulch*

San Fernando Valley, 1980

IN THE MID-SEVENTIES, my sister Anne and her husband had chosen to take a new course—a simpler, more natural path. Not unlike our parents' bid for a better life when they moved from Michigan to Southern California, Anne and Bill sold their home in Southern California and moved themselves and their son and daughter away from the noisy, congested pollution to the clarifying promises of rural North Idaho. Miles outside a small town, they raised their children in a home made from the timber of their own forest. They strove to live off the land; every year Anne planted a huge garden; they raised chickens, goats, and rabbits and fed the family with the meat and vegetables they grew. It seemed idyllic when I visited them that summer after the auto accident.

The kids and I had boarded a Greyhound bus for the thirty-five-hour trip to Coeur d'Alene. Anne's new world enchanted us. Her woods seemed pristine, her life style wholesome, even pure. She suggested that when I finished my MA, I move there too. Down the gravel road from her twenty acres was an ancient, tiny farmhouse for sale. Tall, singing pines surrounded it and stretching out behind it was a huge pasture. Why not change my life? One year of intense work, and I could flee the smog and congestion of the San Fernando Valley and the ongoing wrangling with Ricardo over money and the weird sense of propriety he felt he had over my dating habits.

The possibility of another escape to the Northwest was exhilarating. On the long bus trip back to LA, I read with a sense of wonder and promise the copy of *Walden* that I had purchased at the Coeur d'Alene bookstore. Like Thoreau, I would find a better place, removed from the hot and complicated world of Southern California, a cool place in a lovely valley. It would the place I was meant for. Like Thoreau, I would "come home to my solitary woodland walk as the homesick go home"; I would "dispose of the superfluous and see things as they are"; finally, I would "come to myself."

Our summer trip to Idaho provided temporary respite and a new dream, but upon my return to LA, I descended into the same depression that had plagued me after the car crash and my bout with pneumonia. Tellingly, I could not snap out of it until my good-looking neighbor Landon broke up with his girlfriend and started flirting with me over the fence that separated our backyards. Suddenly with a new man paying attention to me, my life looked promising again. He was cute, he drove a sports car, he made what seemed like lots of money as a meat cutter, he proposed on our second date.

How could I say no? I was deeply apprehensive of the dating scene, Alec was forever lost to me, my credit card was maxed out, the Datsun I had bought to replace my totaled VW was just as undependable as all my other cars had been, the roof of my house was a sieve. It doesn't rain much in Southern California, but I was drowning and Landon felt like a life buoy.

Although I told him I loved him and most of the time believed that I did, I found myself trying to expand his horizons or, to say it more bluntly, to make him more like me. He was frustratingly apolitical, not because he rejected dominant American values but simply because he was unconcerned and inattentive. One of the first things I insisted upon was that he register to vote. I wanted to make sure he would be a good liberal, so I showed him where NPR was on his radio dial and lectured him on the catastrophe that would surely unfold if Reagan defeated Carter in the upcoming November election. When I realized he rarely read anything, I urged him to take up reading the newspaper and provided him with a stack of novels. When he told me he couldn't get into *The World According to Garp* (1978) and admitted that he didn't know who Marshall McLuhan was after we saw *Annie Hall*, I was dismayed. Nonetheless, my emotional neediness and financial shakiness encouraged me to dismiss my misgivings and proceed with optimism.

After all, Landon was a meat cutter not a master's candidate. He made an impressive hourly wage and had health benefits that made my heart swell with affection. He made much more money than I did, even with the credits LA Unified School District was giving me for all the graduate courses I had completed. Sure he watched a lot of TV and his favorite movie was *Rocky II*, but his carefree attitude was incredibly attractive to me. For some bizarre reason, I was impressed by his ability to down shots of tequila and water ski on one foot. Furthermore, he easily passed my litmus test on Sorrow, displaying no qualms about her birth or her adoption. Most important, he wanted to have a baby with me. I was thirty-two and desperately wanted another baby. I was still trying to supplant Sorrow's memory and naïvely eager to cement this new relationship. The baby would do it.

I had taken Landon to see *Annie Hall* not only because it was my favorite movie of the time but also because I identified closely with Annie's zany confusion over relationships, with her frigidity, and with her quest for independence and intellectual credibility. I took Woody Allen's closing words in the movie to heart. Allen makes a joke about an uncle who thinks he's a chicken. The family doesn't tell him that he's not a chicken "because [they] need the eggs." Allen's joke seemed to be telling me something; at least this is how I interpreted it: even though love is irrational, based on fleeting affections, maybe even an illusion, we should keep pursuing it because, no matter what, we will always "need the eggs." We will always need the affirmation of another in order to feel whole, unbroken, sane. I needed crates and crates of eggs, layers and layers of affirmation. I couldn't resist what looked like a safety net that would catch us all at last. After knowing Landon for only three months, I married him, this time in my own backyard, but again with flowers in my braided hair, a guitar strumming, and gooey, rum-laced, homemade carrot cake for all. Afterwards, we honeymooned in Hawaii where we spent more money than Landon ever actually had.

I graduated that spring with my MA. Landon was as eager as I was to escape LA and live near beautiful Lake Coeur d'Alene where he could water ski all summer and snow ski all winter. With Joni Mitchell's lyrics urging us on, we took the steps we needed "to get ourselves back to the garden"

("Woodstock," 1970): we quit our jobs, sold our houses, and planned our own "stardust" escape to our northwest version of "Yasgur's farm."

I traded in my Datsun for an antique Bronco to pull Landon's ski boat on our trek north. Ricardo, who initially had not protested the move, changed his mind overnight and threatened to get a court order to keep me from taking the children out of the state. So once again, leaving town turned into a high-stakes getaway. In the dead of night, we packed a U-Haul with all our belongings, throwing the kids' Big Wheels on top of a maze of furniture and boxes, and we were off for the little brown farmhouse on the gravel road in an exotic spot called Cougar Gulch, seven miles outside of Coeur d'Alene. Under the thrall of Thoreau, I vowed to "dispose of the superfluous and see things as they are, grand and beautiful"!

Perhaps obviously, the marriage began to fail almost immediately. I quickly found two jobs I loved—teaching part time at the community college and selling books at the same bookstore where I had purchased my copy of *Walden* the summer before. Landon found some temporary work in Spokane when we first arrived, but no one would take him on full time after he was accused of stealing meat. He denied the theft vehemently, and for a while I believed his complicated narrative of being framed. Then his unhappy thirteen-year-old daughter, Ginny, decided she wanted to live with us rather than with her mother and brought with her all the problems she thought she would be leaving behind in California. Her arrival threw off the delicate balance we were all trying hard to maintain in our new family configuration.

One late afternoon after a lengthy argument about Ginny, who had been caught stealing at school (but claimed, coincidentally, that she had been framed), Landon grabbed her roughly by the arm, marched her out of the house, pushed her into our new Subaru, and left, wildly fishtailing the car down the dusty gravel road that had quickly lost its sense of enchantment. I looked at the muddle around me—an unemployed husband who resented the two jobs I had secured, a stepdaughter with deep-seated emotional problems I was only beginning to grasp, a tiny house with too many people in it, and three innocent children whose lives I had painfully complicated.

At my wit's end, I thought, "If he can just leave like that, so can I!" I screamed at Todd, who had just turned ten, "You're in charge!" and flew out the door, into the rickety Bronco, and down that same gravel road. This was unusual for me. I tried never to leave the children unattended, no matter how desperate I felt. But this evening, my hopelessness was so intense that I did leave them and sped into the dusk, almost daring the old Bronco to roll over on each upcoming curve of the country roads I followed.

My attention was not on the road, nor was it on the argument that precipitated my dash out the door, nor was it on the unworkable quagmire into which my new marriage had so quickly sunk. My thoughts were locked on Sorrow. Although I had come all this way to start a new life with a new man, every road inevitably led me back to her. As I careened down the bumpy, twisting highway, crying and muttering, my words were for her: "I have to find you, Sorrow. I have to find you, Sorrow!"

This crazy car ride was the closest I ever came to suicide. Today I am shocked by how easily I could have hurt others on that road after leaving my three children alone to face the approaching night. I put so many lives in jeopardy. The not-so-mysterious demons that propelled me would not abate, even though more than fifteen years had passed since Sorrow's birth. Finally my tears waned, twilight changed to dark, and I turned the car around. When I drove up the gravel road to our little house, all the lights were blazing. Still no Landon or Ginny, but my children came running out to greet me, clearly frightened by my uncharacteristic getaway. Hugging and crying, we stumbled into the warm kitchen where Todd had been preparing tomato soup for his little sisters. Overwhelmed by my jumble of conflicting emotions, by all that I had foolishly risked, I sat down at the round wooden table and let him serve us. Three faces sipped their soup and looked to me for so much. But, in fact, they gave me much more—the reason to live without Sorrow.

Landon and Ginny headed back to LA with his ski boat attached to our dependable car, the Subaru, leaving me with yet another unreliable one—the decrepit Bronco—and the brown farmhouse. I was not sorry to see him go; I was really only sorry there was no baby this time. I had tried to become pregnant and would try again, driven by my unappeasable need to replace Sorrow. But I never conceived again. I could ask myself

Todd, Helen, and Kezia with their pony in Cougar Gulch, 1982.
Photograph by the author.

how many babies would it have taken to restore what I had lost, but having studied Lacan's ideas on a desire that can never be quenched, I know the answer.

My children remember the four years we lived in Cougar Gulch as idyllic. They had a pony named Red Feather, ducks named Cheese and Quackers, chickens that actually did lay crates and crates of eggs, dogs, a cat, and three sweet bunnies. I had anticipated a Walden Pond existence, and I had a huge garden where I did, in fact, successfully grow beans. But I slowly became dismayed by the provincial closed-mindedness, the racism and sexism that often come with small-town life, especially in North Idaho, home of the Aryan Nations Church and meeting ground for several other white supremacist organizations. A fellow teacher and I started up a local chapter of NOW, and in the four years I lived there, we persuaded only five other women to become dues-paying members. In the meantime, there were two battered women's shelters for a town of 19,000, and they were always operating over capacity.

The proverbial last straws came when, to my horror, Todd asked for a rifle for his twelfth birthday. My son the hunter didn't fit with my "grand and beautiful" Thoreauvian dream. Then our male duck drowned all the darling newly hatched ducklings in the pond. On top of that someone shot and killed our family dog, the one we had brought all the way from California so that he could have a better life with no fences, no leashes, not even a collar. We came home to find him lying in front of our door, a sticky trail of blood behind him that let us know he had dragged himself home before dying. He probably had been after someone's chickens, but that made the death no less heartbreaking. Then our other dog broke into the rabbit house and literally scared the rabbits to death. I still cringe as I hear again Todd's anguished call for me and see in my mind's eye those limp, furry bodies, warm but imperturbably still. The dog hadn't bitten them, just terrorized them; there was no blood anywhere. Todd had gone to the barn to feed them and found the door open to their pen; they seemed to be asleep, but even though we gently shook them over and over again, we couldn't wake them up.

Poor kids—having to witness all of that; watching tearfully as I dug graves, first for our dog and then for their bunnies. What had I been thinking, bringing children into this benighted gulch where death came right to our doorstep? The San Fernando Valley had been balm and honey compared to this. If Thoreau had only filled in the complexities of nature for me, its beauties and its horrors. He probably did, but I had not been listening.

The very last straw came when my neighbor up the road accused me of corrupting his wife. I had invited June to go dancing at the North Shore with me one night while her husband, Mike, was gone, out in the national forest breaking new trail. That night, June decided to leave the bar with a man she had been dancing with all evening instead of coming back to Cougar Gulch with me. I was surprised when she cornered me in the bathroom to ask me to keep her kids, Shane and Shauna, for the night, but I wasn't shocked. I knew her marriage was rocky, so I readily agreed and headed home alone. June arrived around ten the next morning, gathered up Shane and Shauna, and left. She offered no explanations and I asked for none.

That was it, or would have been if June had let it alone, but for some reason, days after, June told Mike that she had gone home with a man that she had met one night when she and I had gone out dancing. That day Mike called me, sounding cheerful, and asked me to stop by their house. Ingenuously unsuspicious I complied, but this time I was shocked when June opened their front door. I couldn't take my eyes off her two blackened eyes. She led me out to their garage where Mike was up on a ladder, hammer in hand, repairing a rain gutter. He never came down from the ladder; he just yelled while brandishing his hammer at me: "Stay away from her, you crazy bitch!"

Clearly, we were neither in Eden nor on Walden Pond. It was time for another escape. Avoiding Mike and June, forbidding my kids to play with Shane and Shauna, downright fearful of life in Cougar Gulch, I applied to the PhD program at the University of Washington in Seattle, was accepted, and once again, we packed up a U-Haul truck and set off for yet another new start.

Martha's Vineyard, 2004

I had kept on the move, having left San Marino for Ohio, for Indiana, then for Oregon, for Washington, D.C., an escape to New York followed by a return to California and the San Fernando Valley, and then to Idaho. Now I landed in Seattle. So many escapes, so many disruptions. People sometimes marvel at all I have accomplished, and it is true, I have achieved a lot. But I needed to. Driving fast to evade Sorrow, venturing into the unknown, unrealistically trusting first this, and then that—whatever offered hope to mend the tear in my soul. My children served as the key to an abiding coherence, preserving my focus, compelling me to negotiate a way out of despair and isolation, furnishing ever-challenging household tasks to dissipate my dejection. I loved them with a fierceness that is by all accounts excessive. That they could never really heal me is beside the point. Having them was restorative; they saved me. Although I would marry yet again when we reached Seattle, this marriage too would be peripheral to the real relationship I was committed to, for it was only through these children that I could forget the lost baby, at least for a while.

The kids and I were a team, and the men that joined us at one stop or another were incidental to my real needs and desires. Along the way, my central secret multiplied into a profusion of secrets, the pebble tossed in the pond sending out incessant ripples of more and more subterfuge. I had to keep secret the real reasons why my husbands walked out, trying to make it look like Ricardo was a guilty philanderer and Landon a bumbling ne'er-do-well, when, in fact, they probably left because my commitment to them was shallow, incomplete, and finally unsatisfying. I had to keep all kinds of secrets from new friends about my first baby, about all those ex-husbands, about a sullied past that at first glance surely would make me look like a fickle libertine. So much shame; so much to hide.

Awash in the habit of family secrecy since childhood and more dramatically during and after my year of banishment, I was socialized to repudiate a critical part of myself. My most intense and demanding emotions were buried. Such fragmentation in early adolescence had left me unable to effectively negotiate relationships, especially with men. Famished for approval and highly vulnerable to demonstrations of kindness whether sincere or manipulative, I had no trustworthy foundation from which to measure other people, no objective criterion, no wariness, no perspective. Whether individuals merited my esteem or not, I wanted their admiration. Acquiring the approval of others worked at least superficially to mask a self I saw as essentially flawed.

My secrets became even more disgraceful to me when I made friends with women with young children. I could not fault them for their ardent involvement with their babies; I had felt that way too. Yet such devoted maternal intensity made it easy for me to imagine how quickly they would damn me: "How could you give your baby away? How could you?" they would demand if they knew the truth. The secrets continued to multiply. Shame surfaced when I imagined good friends discovering the truth— friends who thought they knew me well and who had unguardedly and courageously confided their own secrets in me. I had never told them; so guilt gave birth to culpability and even more shame for all my duplicity and dissembling.

Years after our divorce, Ricardo, angry with me for moving our children to the Northwest and in a vengeful mood, told them that I had given away a baby girl before they were born. He knew it would be the cruelest way to hurt me. Perhaps unconsciously, or not, he wanted to undermine my children's trust and love. Since I had abandoned one baby, he seemed to be saying, I might abandon them. It is testimony to their generous hearts that they came to me gently and lovingly, asking carefully about what had happened, understanding immediately my great loss. Since then, they have been my protectors, rarely my judges. Their love for me has been unconditional despite the many disruptions they have had to withstand: adjusting to new schools, new neighborhoods, new friends; the marriages; the stepfathers; the divorces and the good-byes to people they cared for and who cared for them.

And I was a girl of the fifties and sixties, filled with typical fairy tale imaginings: to marry her one true love; to have children with her loving, faithful husband who would in turn be a loving, devoted father; to do work that mattered, that could help make young lives better; to create a stable and welcoming home full of beauty and warmth—of course, that's what we all wanted; maybe we still do. But I am amazed by how easily I surrendered those dreams over and over again as soon as the fairy tale tarnished.

Of course, one reason is that in the 1970s and 1980s, the divorce rate skyrocketed, and I joined a rapidly escalating number of divorced women. Because there were so many of us, we didn't have to confront the divorcée stigma prevalent in the fifties. After all, *Kramer vs. Kramer* had swept the Academy Awards in 1979, and its protagonist, Meryl Streep, not only left her husband so that she could become "a whole person," she also left her six-year-old son. But popular movies and the rise in the divorce rate do not explain the number of times I dove optimistically, heedlessly into a new marriage, with little consideration of the dangers below. Nor does it explain the number of times I decided I had to extricate myself from bewildering marital unhappiness. Each time, as I stepped away from my promises, I found myself paradoxically scared and exhilarated by the unknown possibilities of independence. Rather than stay stranded on the woeful shores of discontented marriage, I kept opting for change. I wanted to find home, to finally come home, but everywhere I went, something was missing.

Repetition Without Redemption

OUR MOVE TO SEATTLE WAS, like most moves, sad and exciting. I hated to leave our beautiful Coeur d'Alene, to give up on the better life I thought I would build there, but I had been brought down to earth by the realities of Cougar Gulch. The chance to work toward my PhD was intimidating but enticing, and Seattle was an especially pleasant city to relocate to. So, in the summer of '85, we arrived in another new city and another new life.

As I began work for my PhD, I suffered severely from a sense of fraudulence, my own version of what is commonly known as the impostor syndrome. Throughout my first year of study, I was convinced that I had been admitted to the graduate program in error. As soon as I let my "capable scholar" mask slip, someone would check admissions records and find the administrative mistake that had allowed me to enroll.

I worked hard at constructing a persona for myself by imitating the intimidating graduate students around me whose intellectual verbosity dominated our seminars. The theory explosion had hit the graduate program at UW, and those in the know, or those self-confident enough to sound like they were in the know, loved to throw theorists' names and terms around. I sat through seminars in a cold sweat, horrified by the whiz kids that surrounded me. I had no idea how to pronounce Cixous or Derrida, let alone was I close to grasping what my fellow students meant when they spoke with such assurance about "phallologocentrism" or "aporia." Although I actually resented these geniuses, I practiced carefully in the art

Todd, Helen, and Kezia in the kitchen in Seattle, 1986.
Photograph by the author.

of mimicking them in order to hide my own painful ineptitude, the "real" mute stolidness that I felt at my core.

For the first three weeks of classes, I barely slept—not because of incessant studying but from unremitting anxiety. Finally, I stumbled zombie-like into the student health center where I was able to convince a doctor that I wasn't depressed and, therefore, not sleeping, but that I was not sleeping and, therefore, a wreck. Even though he insisted it was depression, he agreed to prescribe sleeping pills. I have never really been able to get by without them since. How I envy those for whom sleep is a lovely respite rather than a nightly battle with a restless enemy—my own churning mind.

Still feeling like a secret gatecrasher, I followed my peers and professors as we delved into the uncertainties of postmodernism, which ironically taught me that the dim-witted self I thought I was hiding was as constructed and contingent as the brainy mask I was assuming. Unfortunately, learning that I did not have an authentic, essential self to conceal did nothing to bolster my self-confidence as a scholar. My scholarly interests, however, were to become a telling example of my psychological struggles and the lasting effects of losing Sorrow. Because I was fixated on my past, I was fascinated by Freud. Because I had lived through my own primal scene on the night of Sorrow's birth, I started analyzing infamous primal scenes in literature: scenes like Jane Eyre's abandonment in the red room, Quentin Compson's peek at Caddie's muddy drawers, and the Ancient Mariner's slaying of the albatross.

I was fascinated by first-person narrators who harbored secret traumas that could not be healed unless they could tell the story that would assuage their pain. It is no wonder that four years of study would eventually lead me to write a dissertation entitled *Repetition and Redemption* where I would focus on narrators obsessed with their pasts and their offenses: confessors, like Rousseau and Augustine, and anguished malcontents like Conrad's Lord Jim, Faulkner's Quentin, and Proust's Marcel.

Not surprisingly, as a graduate student with three children living on a teaching assistant's salary and sporadic child support, I was once again in economic jeopardy. We had affordable housing—a tiny apartment smack in the middle of the university's family housing complex, a wonderful place to raise children. There were families of all nationalities. My daughters' best friends were Takumba, from Kenya, and Prezca, from Nigeria. Still, even with the cheap rent, I couldn't ever quite make all the ends meet at the end of the month.

A kind and gentle poet named Taylor had taken an interest in us. Taylor seemed to be just as emotionally wounded as I was. He wept easily when he heard a sad song or wrote a sad poem, and I found this sensitivity appealing—at first. Although he was often "down," Taylor insisted that I made him happy and he swore he enjoyed the pandemonium of a small apartment with two little girls, a teenage boy, and an insanely busy mother. I made it clear that I would put the children first, followed by my career. He would come third. Yet he still wanted to marry me. I tried for a while to resist the lure of restored financial security and sympathetic companionship. Although his emotional sensitivity seemed as if it should be a good thing, in reality his sadness made me sad, and I found his doleful eyes disheartening, his mournful poetry depressing. When our sad moods coincided, our despondency could be stifling.

But Taylor had a selling point that proved to be ultimately irresistible: he was attentive, kind, and gentle with the children. He took us all to his Montana mountain cabin and taught the kids how to catch fish. They loved him for that. Then he offered me a choice. Either we marry or we break up. He couldn't cope with the anxiety, the tentativeness of our relationship. Fearful of being on my own yet again, I acquiesced and began my fourth marriage on already-shaky ground. Ever the romantic optimist, I believed that the marriage would give both of us the security we needed to restore one another, that it would provide the firm emotional foundation we both badly needed. And I still wanted another baby.

The marriage ended after three years with no baby. But this time, surprisingly, I was the more psychologically healthy partner. My PhD was complete, and I had secured a tenure-track job at a time when such jobs were particularly difficult to get. Once again I had the opportunity to head off to new territory—this time to the coast of North Carolina. Taylor had fallen into a deep depression that my successes only seemed to aggravate. He did not want to leave the Northwest, but I was ready to start all over again. We agreed to a compatible divorce, and once again I was on my way, now with more secrets than ever. In my new life as a first-year professor in North Carolina, not only could no one know I had long ago given away my baby, but they also must never know I had now been married four times.

Martha's Vineyard, 2004

My acquiescence to Taylor's proposal was obviously not uncharacteristic. For my entire adulthood, I had been so emotionally needy that I would ingenuously and repeatedly consent to the desires of others. Alec, Allen, Ricardo, Landon, and Taylor had only to show me a modicum of attention, tenderness, approval, even disapproval, and I invited them wholeheartedly into my life without pausing to consider the price that could be exacted for their interest. I was never comfortable with dating, especially because the decisions about whether to have sex or not were always up to me. Men wanted to have sex regardless; it was always up to me to decide whether it was "right" or not.

The sexual revolution had blurred the lines between propriety and impropriety. From the late sixties when I met Allen until the mid eighties when I met Taylor, female sexual adventurousness, which had once been labeled as promiscuous, came to be seen as healthy and natural. Although Madonna was considered outrageous by many, her songs revealed the bold sexual temper of many women. In "Burning Up," she sings, "Unlike the others I'd do anything / I'm not the same, I have no shame" (*Madonna*, 1983). The sexual phobia of the fifties and early sixties had evaporated. Women had clearly acquired the right to act on passion rather than waiting for a man to make his moves.

Although I had lived through this sexual revolution, I simply could not free myself of my own sense of sexual impropriety. Outside of marriage, sex for me was never casual, always a risk. I had paid so dearly, had suffered such a loss that my sexuality became overly precious, a part of me that could not be light, relaxed, and freely given. I wasn't cold; I was afraid.

So understandably, I moved too quickly from getting to know my lovers to marrying them. Although outwardly I championed independence and autonomy—playing the part of the tireless, single, working soccer mom to the hilt—inwardly I craved the intimacy and security of marriage. My failure to attain either genuine intimacy or lasting security inevitably led me back to my familiar demons: guilt and shame, which now not only emanated from losing Sorrow but also from what seemed a flawed sexuality and too many divorces.

Four times I committed myself to different marriages that were so tenuous and fragile that they were doomed from the start. I needed a secure emotional safety zone where I could recover and reintegrate my hidden, secret self with the precarious "super self" that I worked so hard to maintain. What looked like achievements could also be interpreted as frantic attempts to bolster a wobbly ego with whatever was at hand: advanced degrees, new husbands, new babies, new jobs, new homes in new locales, new dogs, cats, rabbits, chickens, ducks, even a pony! I have read enough psychoanalytic theory to know that this quest to fill a void is not uncommon. Empty and lost at our deepest emotional core, we ceaselessly look for solace, for fulfillment, for peace—for more of something, although we can't say what. I have pursued that surcease with a tenacity that still surprises.

But always, beneath my ostensible effervescence, I was hiding secrets—not just the despondency surrounding Sorrow but increasingly an ever-widening complex of related secrets. Because I was so burdened with shame and a high-strung fearfulness, I could never relinquish myself to the truly intimate connection I craved with a partner. I simply had no faith in the unqualified acceptance that would permit such a connection. I remarried and remarried, each time ignoring my fear that my new husband would be deeply disappointed as soon as he figured out who I really was. To me, securing commitment depended on fakery, on trying my best to be someone I thought would be loveable. And when my charades failed, which, of course, was inevitable, separation and divorce followed. These ruptures were not necessarily painful for me because I was so exhausted by my dissembling that the chance to be truer to my own personality, history, and wants always came as blessed relief. Paradoxically, being alone again was satisfyingly restorative.

 **25** *Grace*

Wilmington, North Carolina, 1990–97

ANOTHER MOVE, another U-Haul standing in our driveway, loaded to the gills with our battered, much-moved belongings. But this time we were headed all the way across the country to a location and a culture that on first glance seemed so different from Southern California and the Northwest that I feared we would stand out as conspicuous aliens. What would the South of 1990 be like? Would it still be under the sway of Jim Crow traditions? What would it mean to live in the Bible Belt? Would it be like North Idaho, home to conservative supremacists, feminist bashers, and "bubbas"? Would I be able to understand my students' Southern drawl? Would the women I hoped would befriend me be saccharine and cunning Scarlett O'Haras? The only significant thing I knew about my new state was that its senator was the diehard conservative and segregationist Jesse Helms. How in the world would I fit in?

When we arrived in the densely humid heat of August and walked out on the deck of our new home, cicadas roared rhythmically all around us. We had never heard such a bizarre cacophony. It sounded as if I had moved my children to a jungle, as if an alligator might slither up from the swampy woods behind us at any time. We had moved from a large, liberal city that held the record for the most atheists per capita to a city with not only churches on almost every corner but churches whose parking lots were overflowing every Sunday morning. I was the only single working mother in our neighborhood, which made me feel more liberal than I really was and more out of my depth.

Nonetheless, despite my uneasiness, I had a home of my own, a great new job, and my little family. It would be just three of us—Helen, Kezia, and me. After helping me move, Todd returned almost immediately to Seattle to begin his freshman year in college. My daughters gamely started school only to find the teachers rigid, the lunchrooms segregated, the schoolwork unchallenging, and their peers standoffish. How could they possibly be happy here? They tried to appear so in order to please me, but their new life required huge adjustments. They missed their brother, Seattle, the "U" district, and their friends. And they missed Taylor. I had changed almost everything that represented security in their lives, and they were at incredibly vulnerable ages—fifteen and thirteen—perhaps the worst ages to ask children to move.

This could have all proved to be a recipe for disaster, but not for Helen and Kezia. They bravely put the best face on it all and settled in. With some tears, but not that many, they both managed to navigate a new neighborhood, new schools, new teachers, and new curriculums. They made new friends easily and became readily involved in school activities. I don't think I quite appreciated their willing flexibility, especially because I was consumed by my own new workplace and—this time—the quest for tenure.

My secrets endured. In any discussion with my new friends and colleagues about motherhood, childbirth, adoption, marriage, or divorce, my now-long-held secrets had to be kept. When subjects of honesty, authenticity, and truth became topics of discussion, my secretiveness tormented me, but paradoxically, I was a reliable dissembler.

For example, when an editor who was considering my dissertation for publication suggested that I take a few weeks to write an autobiographical introduction to the manuscript and then resubmit it, I froze. In the dissertation, I had taken three hundred pages to elucidate the difference between creative and compulsive repetitions. My abstract reads, "The heart of the dissertation is a series of readings of a variety of texts in which each autobiographer has lost a clear, sufficient sense of selfhood and undertakes the task of self-narration in the belief that a repetition of the past will serve the present more efficiently." The prescient editor wanted me to provide a personal account of my own creative repetition. Suddenly embarrassed by my manuscript, which apparently suggested my own turmoil and need for redemption, I tucked it away in a far corner of a bookcase hidden behind my large easy chair. I did not return the editor's subsequent considerate phone messages, and I never went back to the dissertation, not even after my mentor urged me to mine individual chapters for conference papers or journal articles.

Unknowingly, the editor had suggested a task that I was emotionally unprepared to tackle. To write what he wanted would have required that I reveal what I had kept hidden for most of my life. Although the event was fundamental to my sense of selfhood, it had been sealed in a secret place where no one could enter.

Seven years passed. I worked hard, wrote a lot, got published, and got tenure. My children grew up. By 1997, both Helen and Kezia had graduated from high school and were in college; Todd was on his own quest for adventure, enlightenment, and love. I had learned how to let them go, for they insisted, as they should have, on their own independence. My career was secure. It took seven years of relative peace and well-being for me to reach a point where I could finally disturb the placid surface and question the subterfuges I had been concocting for so long. In fact, life moved me to a place where self-examination could no long be denied.

I had been in a solid relationship for several of these years with a smart, good-looking, easygoing man, John, a fellow English professor. He enjoyed my company as a fellow intellectual, competent teacher, good mother, and good friend. This felt quite new. He was neither woefully needy nor unreasonably resentful of the time I gave to my children or my work. He was straightforward, truthful, and loyal, *but* he did not want to rush into marriage. His love for me was healthy and welcomed, but also unsettling. Given my lifelong insecurities, I lacked confidence in myself, in John, and in his commitment to me despite his ongoing regard and fidelity.

For the past twenty years, my most trustworthy bond had been socially acceptable (though most likely psychologically unhealthy); it was my thorough commitment to my children. They came first. But as they got older and insisted on their own autonomy, I realized I was losing my companions (and the crutches I leaned on to fend off the desolation that still encroached on me occasionally). John was a stable element in my life, but in order to handle the hours of isolation, insomnia, and depression when he wasn't around, I did what has now become a cliché: I built an intricate and intense friendship with an e-mail correspondent, another man thousands of miles away. While deeply in love with John, I felt compelled to keep another man secretly in the wings, for surely, eventually, John would recognize my irredeemable flaws and leave me on my own again. I needed a backup for an ending that seemed inevitable.

Perhaps unconsciously, I left my e-mail open one day and went off to run a list of errands. With no intention of prying, John simply sat down to use the computer and there before him was the secret correspondence. The results were cataclysmic. He was shocked and hurt, and I had to admit my duplicity. Yes, I had a secret relationship, albeit vicarious, with another man. Yes, I poured time, energy, and heart into this intangible yet necessary liaison. Yes, I had a secret life.

How mortifying it was, the day that he caught up with my dishonesty. Getting caught was misery. I had to admit my untrustworthiness. There was no one else to blame. Finally, I saw myself objectively, if such a thing exists: I had *never* presented myself honestly, even within my most intimate relationships. Apparently, my belief that I was unworthy of love cut much deeper than my ability to commit to intimacy based on truth. My fear of rejection would not let me stop undergirding my relationships, especially this one with John, with a deceitfulness that I knew was lethal but could not resist.

But this time was different. The pattern I had counted on, of falling back on someone else, unraveled. I could not fall back on my secret e-mail correspondent. I was angry and exasperated with this man whose clandestine presence had sabotaged my life. I could not fall back on my children; they were all away at college, busy with their own interesting lives. My women friends could offer no comfort, for I was so profoundly ashamed of myself, once again, that I could tell no one the strange narrative I had been secretly living. For the first time, I alone had to face my tired, desperate deceitfulness. Alcoholics call this place hitting bottom. I arrived there because of a craving for acceptance and a corresponding disbelief in its possibility. But I was indeed there, at the bottom.

Martha's Vineyard, 2004

I am not a particularly religious person, but I do believe in moments of grace. Perhaps it's similar to the epiphanies routinely discussed in literature classes or moments of enlightenment the faithful attest to after months of prayer and meditation. When moments of grace do strike, and I believe they do, they can wonderfully break through unconscious, habitual responses. Grace can overturn decades of customary, unexamined behavior. It can overturn long-held family dicta that secrecy and duplicity are more prudent than truth.

My moment of grace came on the day I realized that I could, that I must start telling the truth. Connection requires truth. Simple yet for so long inconceivable to me. Much like the crack of lightning that snapped me awake me one night when it ignited the intricate boughs of the magnolia tree outside my window, grace awakened me with a shock. It was so simple: tell the truth. With startling clarity, I began a whole new way of being in the world. There could be truth and there could be connection.

And John did not leave me in disillusionment and distrust. Instead, he compassionately heard me out, not just once but for agonizing weeks. Brimming with anguish, we followed the jagged narrative—all that had happened to me, the silent weight of the past that seeped into every interaction of the present. Together we analyzed the psychological compulsions that had kept me marooned on my island of secrecy. John saw through my masks, uncovered my hiding places, and watched me unravel the intricate complexities of my past. Those hidden stories had once felt indecent, degrading, and shameful. But John, clear-eyed critic that he is, helped me gather all my stories and recast them in ways that let me see how cultural and psychological winds had blown me here and there.

When I interpreted my stories for John, I was no longer the disgraceful, disobedient daughter or the unforgivably yielding girl at Florence Crittenton, no longer the wayward adolescent with "hot pants" or the capricious wife. John revised my stories with me, making them rich with social significance, windows through which I could more thoughtfully remember, interpret, and understand the unprecedented decades I had grown up in. Through his eyes, I could look compassionately back at everything I had been with new hope at who I could become. As we reinterpreted my stories, I realized this was just the first step. The time would come when I would have to tell my truths to others who cared for me and thought they knew me. Truthfulness could not exist between just John and me; it had to be pervasive.

Although I know that honesty is rarely a panacea, that it doesn't solve all problems, for me it had a direct result. On a typically beautiful San Diego morning, John and I stood together on my parents' patio, surrounded by their lovingly tended orchids. Our families stood by us, willing to suspend, at least for this important moment, their skepticism, their anxieties, and their memories of previously failed marriages. John and I pledged confidently to be husband and wife. The relationship, the longest I have shared with any one man, has remained secure and loving over the years that have followed that morning. I have found a partner who knows me as well as I know myself, maybe even better, and loves me. Such wholehearted devotion to the most authentic me I can muster still seems incredible, yet I know it to be true.

With a new way of being in the world and with a trusting companion to help me along the way, I could set off on a new journey, not one that would take me hightailing it across the country, not this time. There was no jam-packed U-Haul required; this was not an escape. It was, however, a leap, a plunge into new territory where all kinds of baggage awaited me, a narrative quest that would change everything.

THE $\mathscr{R}$ETURN

26 *Telling Secrets*

Wilmington, 1998–99

WHEN JOHN AND I began to talk about my past, I tried to tell him about the night of Sorrow's birth. It had been thirty-three years since Sorrow's birth, thirty-three years since I had whispered some of the details about that night to Tina while she sat next to me in the gray, gloomy room at Florence Crittenton. I had kept silent for a long time. It was time that I try to tell John my real story.

I say I "tried," but as I began to relate the event, I was stymied, unable to get to the foyer of the Florence Crittenton Home and all that happened there. On my first attempt to tell, John sat next to me, stroking my hand, murmuring encouraging words, but as I approached that moment in my narrative, pressure built in my chest, a lump formed in my throat, tears welled up in my eyes, and speech became impossible. John advised me to take some deep breaths. We walked around the block so I could gather myself, and then we sat down again. This time he put his arms around me, and I felt better, so once again, I tried to step into the story, but to no avail; the pressure built, I choked up, began to cry, couldn't continue. We realized that there was not only an emotional block but also a painful physical barrier that had kept me from turning the long repressed and intensely private images of that night into the spoken word. My unconscious simply gagged me.

Since I couldn't tell him the story out loud, John suggested I try writing it down. Surprisingly, this I could do. I didn't know it at the time, but I was practicing what is called scriptotherapy, a process that let me write through the trauma, finally integrating it into my life story rather than repressing that which would not be repressed. Scriptotherapy was a healing experience because I could bear witness to the trauma and at the same time fashion a more healing story.

When John read my first, sketchy account of the wait in the foyer, the taxi ride, the nurse's rough hands, the unbearable birth, and my last gray days at Florence Crittenton, he was flabbergasted. He told me gently that I should have told him about this, that he should have known this about me. In fact, he said, it seemed to him that I should have told someone long ago about that night. It couldn't have been healthy to keep that secret for so many years. He urged me to tell others about my ordeal in an effort to work through the traumatic memories that continued to disrupt my emotional harmony. Seven years had passed since the editor considering my dissertation had asked me to openly narrate a personal account of my own suffering. I couldn't conceive of telling the story then. Now different circumstances afforded me the emotional support and motivation to make the attempt. And so began the serious reading and writing that would eventually become my first book.

Having decided that narrating my secret could be salubrious, I looked for support and inspiration by reading memoirs by women whose experiences struck an intuitive emotional response in me. As I nurtured my writing by reading, I found that, like me, many memoirists were also struggling with the painful consequences of harboring family secrets. Lately our culture had encouraged many of us to lay our secrets down for public display. With dismay, I saw them sensationalized on daily talk shows. Nevertheless, I came to understand that telling my secret in the right forum could be an integral step to my recovery. When I began, I didn't know that I was writing a book, that my narration of the night of Sorrow's birth would evolve into a blend of autobiography, literary analysis, and cultural criticism. My first and most important purpose was to narrate the secret that had kept me psychologically isolated and emotionally fragile while also compromising my integrity. The first chapter told the story of bearing Sorrow.

When I shared that chapter first with John, then with close women friends, then with my sisters and children, I felt like I was taking huge risks. To open one's heart so completely is dangerous. But the kind and loving responses I received made it possible for me to keep writing and, in so doing, increase my self-understanding of the lingering symptoms that emanated from that long-ago night. I had a keen sense of compassion for all who are asked to hide an integral part of themselves out of shame and fear. I came to understand that in late-twentieth-century America, it was almost always a damaging and unnecessary mistake to hide behind the trappings of appearances. Finally, I could live my life out loud.

In the summer of 1999, as I was nearing the completion of the manuscript, I returned again to the High Sierras, this time for a week-long backpacking trip with John into the same high country I had hiked long ago when I was secretly carrying Sorrow. For this trip with John, my emotional health is better than I can ever recall; my insomnia persists, but it seems to be under control. Once again, I smile broadly for the picture. We have climbed very high to reach this campsite—over 10,000 feet above sea level. The pines that grow at this altitude are scrubby but indomitable; a stream of glacial melt crisscrosses the verdant alpine meadow that stretches out behind us. As we crouch for the photo, we are in high spirits, triumphant after our demanding climb.

Now, I think, I have found the key. I have told Sorrow's story and arrived at last at the chapter's end. The past will finally abate, and the possibility for a whole and pure happiness will be mine. But it is not to be. Sorrow is still with me, as always. On this wilderness pilgrimage, I wrap her all around me and carry her on.

Martha's Vineyard, 2004

By telling my secrets, I risked revealing a complicated, flawed selfhood, but I wanted to and could take that chance. Rather than continuing to live on the surface, avoiding exposure and self-knowledge, I wrote down the circumstances of Sorrow's conception, the anguish of her birth, and my helplessness at her adoption. I wanted a more complete self in my world and in my work. I wanted to exchange my carefully constructed counterlife for a more authentic life. I wanted to end my days on the run. I felt I was finally strong enough to take the chance that many people take

Janet with John in the High Sierras, 1999.
Photographer unknown. Courtesy of the author.

daily—living in the world forthrightly, drawing on their experience without fear of censure or rejection. With my own fragile interiority revealed, I dared to ask for acceptance.

Completing the book accomplished a great deal, but it did not end my sorrow. Friends asked, "Can you sleep now?" "Have your nightmares subsided?" Reluctantly, I acknowledged that neither had relented. Nonetheless, the book was restorative. It went far in mending my splintered past; it shored up my fractured self. But a book could not give me back my daughter.

The infant I had touched but was not allowed to hold would never be placed back in my arms. What was denied then was denied still. That which was lost was still irretrievable. I knew that throughout most of my life, I had been fortunate. Losing my daughter was the greatest loss I had suffered. But knowing that did not assuage my sorrow.

My first daughter and me. We had met for a moment on a frigid Ohio morning. Judged unfit for one another, we were placed on separate paths, but I never lost sight of her. We were two girls, traveling alone yet indelibly connected.

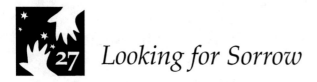

27 *Looking for Sorrow*

Wilmington, 2000

MY DAUGHTER HELEN has a friend Debbie who is adopted and has been trying unsuccessfully for years to find her birthmother. Shortly after I completed *Intimate Reading* while it was still in production, Helen asked me if she could tell Debbie about Sorrow. "Of course," I could now reply. A few days later, Debbie stopped by. Shyly she asked me, "Do you still think about Sorrow?"

"I never stop thinking about her. I think about her every day." I could tell she was moved by my answer, and so, to let Debbie see just how much Sorrow meant to me and how much she, Debbie, might mean to her birthmother, I gave her a copy of the first chapter, "Bearing Sorrow."

My own efforts at finding Sorrow had been sporadic, and like Debbie, I had only found dead ends. When John and I had married, I opted not to become Janet Clifford but to keep my maiden name, as I had done in the past. This was not for strong feminist principles but because I wanted my name to match any records that Sorrow might be able to obtain should she ever choose to look for me. I still was not sure what my Aunt Jo had put down on Sorrow's birth certificate, whether it was Jan Mason or Janet Ellerby, but I figured if I kept to Janet Mason Ellerby, both would be available to Sorrow.

A few years prior, I had obtained the yellow pages of the Akron telephone book with a list of all the adoption agencies, but none that I had called would verify they had handled Sorrow's adoption. Some of the voices I encountered during those nerve-wracking phone calls were kind and patient; others were clipped and hasty; some were dismissive. But the answers they gave me were consistent: all adoption records were sealed. Period. The only advice they could offer was that I register with the Ohio Department of Health to authorize the release of all identifying information about me—"the biological parent of an adopted person." This was my official identity.

In Ohio, not only are adoption records sealed, so are the birth records of adopted people born after January 1, 1964. Sorrow's original birth certificate with my name on it remains to this day locked away somewhere in the state of Ohio's catacombs. But I was able to learn the sequence of events that gave Sorrow a new name and new parents. After I had signed away all my rights to her on that dark, dreary day in Akron thirty-five years ago, the adoption was finalized, and Sorrow's adoptive parents had been issued a second birth certificate. This one listed their names as her parents and her new name, the name they had chosen for her. Nothing remained of me on that second birth certificate other than the date I gave birth to her and the county where she was born.

I did contact the Ohio Department of Health and register with the state's Adoption Reunion Registry, and in so doing, my name and address officially became available for release as follows: to "an adopted person 21 years of age or older . . . in accordance with Section 3107.41 of the Revised Code" if, the regulations state, "said adopted person files a petition in an Ohio probate court for the release of identifying information pertaining to the adopted person's biological parents." In other words, if Sorrow was looking for me, and if she filed a petition in an Ohio probate court, and if she had correct information regarding her place and date of birth, only then would my name, address, and telephone number be released to her and only if the Reunion Registry felt there was a match. It was the 1990s when I registered with the Reunion Registry, not the 1960s, but the stigma of giving up a child for adoption had not disappeared. According to the state of Ohio, Sorrow and I still had to be protected from one another. Filling out the paperwork gave me some hope, but even the people who ran the registry admitted that the procedure had not proven to be very effective in the past.

I had also registered with ISRR, the International Soundex Reunion Registry. This registry is a "passive reunion base," meaning its operators will not perform a search for you. They will, however, feed the information you provide into their database and notify both parties should there be a "match." Sorrow also had to have registered with ISRR if this approach was to have any chance of working. I tried to be optimistic, but I had so little information to give the registry. All I knew was the time and place of her birth and her birth weight—6 lbs. 4½ oz.—a tiny but astoundingly powerful bit of life forever etched in my memory. But the registry did not ask for birth weight. The crucial piece of information they wanted was the name of the adoption agency, which I had been unable to uncover. When I had pressed my aunt again for the name, she couldn't recall it, or at least that's what she said.

I felt I could go no further. I believed I had relinquished all my rights to Sorrow. Looking for her felt intrusive, clandestine; in short, it felt wrong. Who was I to think I could ask for information? I had no claim, no right to ask questions.

Whenever I did take a step in my uneasy search by making a phone call to an adoption agency, I would be so overwrought afterwards, my voice shaking, my body trembling, that I would take days to recover from just one brief, stilted conversation with an unknown bureaucrat. Yet, I knew how much Debbie wanted to find her birthmother, and I had made another friend, Donna, who was also paying an agency to find her birthmother. They both told me that they had dreamed of the day that their birthmothers might find them. Might Sorrow feel the same way?

At about the same time that Debbie and Donna were encouraging me to keep looking, I met Les, a graduate student at my university. Les was not a student of mine, but he sought me out after attending an informal reading I was asked to give from *Intimate Reading,* then still a work in progress. He met with me because he wanted to tell me his story, not an unusual outcome I have found since I began revealing my own. Les, who had been adopted as an infant, needed, he said, to tell me about his birthmother, and I was ready and eager to hear what he had to say.

She had recently made contact with him. Plagued by years of severe depression and alcoholism, she had used her troubled medical history to persuade a judge to open her baby's birth records so that she could warn him of possible health hazards. The judge agreed, the records were opened, and she eagerly made contact. She had never had another child, she was hopeful, she wanted to have a relationship with Les.

I was immediately sympathetic and before he could continue, confessed that I too dreamed of the day that I might find my daughter. My admission put Les on the offensive and the conversation turned in a way I had never anticipated: I needed, he declared emphatically, to be better informed about the "rights" of adopted children and their "real" parents!

It turned out that Les felt no compassion for his birthmother. In fact, he was angry that she had used what he saw as trumped-up grounds to open what were for him rightfully sealed records. After a couple of awkward telephone conversations with her and no face-to-face meeting, he informed her that he wanted no relationship with her, and he had insisted that she make no further attempts to contact him. I was stunned. Les finished his diatribe by telling me about the sacred relationship he had with his "real" parents.

Martha's Vineyard, 2004

Before Les had come to see me, I had been easily daunted by my own guilt, lack of entitlement, and insecurity, but after hearing his rant against his ill-fated birthmother and witnessing his complete lack of compassion, I not only felt unentitled, I felt real fear.

"What if I did find Sorrow someday and she was as bitter as Les?" I asked John.

Les's words left me even more certain that only Sorrow had the right to make the search that might someday bring us together again. It was she who was the innocent party; I was the bad mother, and by looking for her, I was the intrusive interloper, daring to encroach on the sacred territory of her "true" parents, those good people who chose her when no one else would. Given all that Les had told me, Debbie and Donna's hopes for finding their birthmothers now seemed the exception. I had taken some shaky, discouraging steps that the "law" grudgingly permitted, but Les's words rekindled my guilt; I could do nothing more but wait and hope.

 *OnAngelsWings.com*

Charlotte, 2000

HELEN AND I are in the car headed from Wilmington to Charlotte where Kezia, having just returned from New Zealand, now lives. It's Kezia's twenty-third birthday, and we are going to take her out to a fancy dinner to celebrate. Helen has a secret—something that she is not supposed to tell me until we get to Charlotte when both she and Kezia can tell me together. It has got to be good news because she is giggly, though nervous. I am curious, of course. Has one of them gotten a promotion? Is Kezia in love? Does Helen have a new boyfriend? What is this all about? We stop for milk shakes—my emotional nourishment and the food splurge I always make, ever since that Akron hospital, decades ago.

As we resume our drive, I tell Helen the little story of the forbidden milk shakes I drank after Sorrow's birth. I can talk about that time in my life now with a composure that surprises me. Today is a sunny, crisp November day in southeastern North Carolina. The heavy Southern humidity has finally evaporated, so we have the car windows down and the radio blasting as we try to harmonize with the Indigo Girls. Even though I am upset by the election debacle in Florida that will make George W. Bush our next president, I put that frustration aside. I am in a great mood, happy for this weekend getaway and the chance to spend time with my daughters.

I'm doing four things at once—singing "The Power of Two," eating a hamburger, sipping a milk shake, and driving—when Helen declares she cannot keep the secret any longer; she simply has to tell me. I smile, charmed by her girlishness, pleased that she doesn't want to keep anything from her mother, even for the hour it will still take us to reach Charlotte. I punch a button on the dash and the CD stops.

"Mom," she says, "we found your daughter. Mom, we found Sorrow."

. . .

Those words.
The ones I've been waiting for.

. . .

Helen stares at me, pale, concerned.
The blue of the sky, vivid, immense.
The glare of the sun, flashing in the side-view mirror.
The warmth in the car.
The food in my mouth.
I struggle to swallow.
My hands continue to turn the steering wheel, directing the car safely.
Somehow.
Slowly I pull onto the shoulder of the highway, caught in one of those liminal moments of slow motion, a moment like Sorrow's birth, a moment that lasts forever in my memory—its details, its momentousness.

Everything is lucid, hyperreal. I have been dreaming of this for thirty-five years, and now that it's here, I'm completely unprepared. I am frozen. I can't speak or react in any way. I don't laugh or cry. I lean back in the seat, close my eyes, try to keep breathing. Finally I get out two words:

"Tell me."

Helen is frightened. Later she will admit that she was sorry she had told me then, so merrily, so impulsively. "What have I done?" she thought. "Why didn't I wait?"

I am ashen and still.

My fingers tremble as I mechanically place the half-eaten hamburger back in the bag.

Once again I manage some words: "Please. Tell me."

"Mom, I should have waited until we got to Charlotte. Can you wait until we get to Kezia's? We agreed to tell you together."

"I can't wait. Tell me. What have you found?"

"Debbie found her, Mom."

"Debbie?" I am incredulous.

"Yes, Debbie. She called me the night of the election. I was watching the returns, like everyone else in the country."

"Her first words were, 'I know who your sister is, Helen.' I was annoyed that she was calling me right then, so I just made a joke of it, trying to get off the phone. 'Yeah, right,' I said. 'So you know Kezia. Big deal.'

"'No, Helen. I know who your *half* sister is.'"

I interrupt: "How could Debbie find out such a thing?" But Helen ignores this question.

"Mom, it may not be Sorrow. But we're pretty sure it is. Her name is Merideth, Mom. Her name is Merideth Mae. She's married and she has two children: Michaela and Drew. Kezia and I found her married name."

Now all the emotions that had not immediately surfaced emerge. I start to cry, but not hard like when Sorrow was born. No, this time I cry softly. I can feel the adrenaline racing up and down my legs and into the small of my back; goose bumps stand up on my bare arms. I shiver and reach into the back seat for my sweater, despite the warmth of the car. We sit silently for a minute, staring ahead. The noonday sun shines down on us; cars whiz by. The pressure that used to well up in my chest and throat whenever I would talk about Sorrow returns, making it impossible to talk. I keep breathing.

"Are you all right, Mom? Are you okay?" Helen asks.

"Merideth?" I manage.

"Yes, Mom. Merideth Mae. A woman in Mississippi named Cathy says that she is 99.9 percent certain that Merideth is your daughter."

"A woman in Mississippi? But how?" I cannot begin to make sense of the information Helen is giving me.

Helen explains as best she can: "Debbie got the date and place of Sorrow's birth from reading the chapter of your book that we gave her. Debbie's been looking for her birthmother. She has e-mail links with lots of online groups that help people with searches like hers. On the morning of the election, she went online and asked for help in finding Sorrow and a lady in Mississippi e-mailed her back—a lady named Cathy. She said she could help. Debbie told her to go ahead and in a just a few hours, she wrote back. She had the information. She gave Debbie Sorrow's name: Merideth."

We still had a long drive ahead of us, so we switched places and, with Helen driving, I tried to collect myself and pry more information from her.

That night, after Debbie's revelation sank in, Helen had been angry with her for broadcasting our family's secret over the Internet. How dearly we hold onto to a concept like privacy even when we no longer really want it! But here was Debbie, with unsought information that could not be ignored. Helen called Kezia, who was also initially angry with Debbie for putting out such a request for help without asking Helen first if she should do so. The two of them were immediately protective of me.

Anxious and confused, they realized they could not turn a blind eye to what Debbie had discovered even though they were highly skeptical. How could Sorrow's name be made available to Debbie so effortlessly and so quickly after thirty-five years of locked records and law-enforced secrecy? They decided that they would not tell me anything until they had proof that Merideth was, in fact, Sorrow. But then they realized they could not wait. They had to let me know about this mind-boggling possibility and agreed to tell me together—after Helen and I had arrived in Charlotte.

When we pulled up in front of Kezia's apartment, she walked out to greet us, took one look at me, and said, "She told you!"

I could only babble, "Yes! Yes! Yes! She did! I know!" It didn't matter to me how I was told or by whom; I was ecstatic. Nor was I the least bit annoyed that Debbie had initiated the search. I was thankful that she had done so. None of Helen and Kezia's initial concerns were my concerns. All I wanted was to hear the story over and over again, and they complied. Although they still had serious doubts that Merideth was Sorrow, I was irrepressibly hopeful. This was the first real possibility that I might find her. That alone was enough to make me euphoric.

Kezia gave me the exchange of e-mails between Debbie and Cathy so that I could follow the path that Debbie had taken to find Merideth. As I reread them now, I can sense a change in Debbie's responses as she processes Helen and Kezia's cautious reactions, their initial anger and on-going concerns:

From: Deborah
To: OnAngelsWings@egroups.com
Date: Tuesday, Nov. 7, 2000 9:42 A.M.
Subject: An Ohio search
Somebody please help me help my best friend find her half-sister. Her mother Janet Ellerby was forced by her parents to give a baby girl up for adoption when she was 16. I believe the baby was born in November of 63, 64 or 65. She was staying in the Florence Crittenton Home in Akron Ohio. But actually was from California. If anyone can find any info please let me know. PPPLLLLEEEAASSEE!!!! Thanks Debbie.

Cathy C. replied:

I can help you if no one else has offered.

From: Deborah
To: Cathy C.
Tuesday, Nov. 7, 2000 3:22 P.M.
Subject: Re: An Ohio search
Please do. I have not gotten any other responses. I talked to my best friend and I was wrong about her being born in November. It was actually March 20th but still not sure of the year 63, 64, or 65. Thanks a lot. Debbie

Cathy C. replied:

Merideth M. —— was her adoptive maiden name.

From: Deborah
To: Cathy C.
Date: Tuesday, Nov. 7, 2000 4:42 P.M.
Oh my God! How did you find that out? Thank you so much. Do you know how I might find out where she may be living now? Thanks so much. Debbie.

All this information comes to Debbie in one day—Election Day. That evening she calls Helen and tells her she knows who her half-sister is.

Helen calls Kezia and they are both taken aback. They don't know whether to be grateful or put upon. When such stunning news arrives unbidden, it takes time to process, time to figure out how one should even begin to receive it. Their responses that night to Debbie's forays were mixed. They felt as if she had trespassed on our family's privacy, yet her discovery was so significant that they couldn't dismiss it. Still, they must have spoken strongly to Debbie by phone, given Debbie's backpedaling in her exchange with Cathy the next day.

Cathy C. replied:

Have you had any luck?

From: Deborah
To: Cathy C.
Date: Wednesday, Nov. 8, 2000 7:48 A.M.
Subject: Re: An Ohio search
Not really. I wanted to ask you how sure you are that the name you gave me is the right person. I talked to my best friend [Helen] and her sister [Kezia] last night and they want to make sure 100% that this is the name of their half sister before going to their mother and turning her world upside down. They do not want anything getting out about their mom because she has considered this a private issue throughout most of her life and even didn't tell her other children for a long time. I did not inform them that I actually asked someone to look up this info. I basically just told them that a message came through on my email giving the adopted names and birth dates of a lot of adoptees born in Ohio and that this one matched their half sister. They are excited but they do not know much about the search process and are not sure whether to believe in all of this. I promised my best friend's sister [Kezia] that I would forward your email to her with the sister's name but if she writes you asking how you are sure, I would appreciate it if you would not tell her that I gave you her mom's name or even asked for the info. They are just kinda funny on that stuff without being a real part of the adoption community themselves. They don't understand about all these people who help others. Can you tell me how sure you are of this being the right person? Like on the info that you have, does it say that this adoptee was from the Florence Crittenton home or mention the hospital or birth mom's name and if so what is that name? Thanks so

much for helping out. I think having the name is a really good thing. They just need some convincing that it is for real. Debbie

Cathy C. replied:

Merideth Mae —— is the name of the only child listed as being born in Akron and on that day and adopted.

    Birth certificate number: ——

    You can call and order this birth certificate and compare the information. There are only 2 more possibilities. They are not listed as being born in Akron. They are county 9000. Which means they could have been born in one county and adopted out of another or that they were born in OH and adopted out of state. I would start out with Merideth from Akron.

    I will see if I can work on this a little tonight or tomorrow if you would like my help. I have 10 open cases in front of me right now; let me know if you need anything else.

    Cathy C.

From: Deborah
To: Kezia and Helen
Subject: FW: Ohio adoptees born 3-20-65
Date: Wednesday, November 8, 2000 3:25 P.M.
Hey guys. Here is the info that Cathy emailed me. Basically she is saying that this Merideth person is the only child born in Akron on 3-20-65 that was adopted. There are two others in Ohio that were born the same day and adopted but they were not born in Akron. I told her that I was forwarding this message to you all so if you have any questions you can write to her if you want. Talk to you all later. Debbie

Kezia then e-mailed Cathy who told her that she was 99.9 percent sure that Merideth was my daughter. She also gave Kezia other Web sites she might try in order to find Merideth's current name since it was likely that she would have married. Following Cathy's leads, Kezia found Merideth's married name and the name of her husband, Michael Joseph —— at Ancestry.com. The site also told her that Merideth and Michael had two children, Michaela and Drew. The next step was to find Merideth and Michael's address.

But first, back to the warm November afternoon after Helen and I had arrived in Charlotte: I had to process Helen and Kezia's revelations. First, I called John. He remembers me as being less ecstatic than he would have anticipated, although I remember myself as being in raptures. To him, over the phone, I seemed to be in shock. He advised caution. Like Helen and Kezia, he didn't want me to be disappointed. It seemed too much. Meanwhile, I was like someone who had just won the lottery and needed to go back and check the number on the ticket over and over and over again. John was happy, amazed that such information could be recovered so readily. Still, like my daughters, he was protective and unconvinced. Nobody wanted this to be wrong.

The world felt changed. I was like Dorothy after the tornado, stepping out of her fallen, black-and-white house from Kansas to find the technicolor world of Oz. The day and its planned activities were still to unfold, so I welcomed them with my heightened sensitivity—everything looked lovely, everything held promise. Helen, Kezia, and I carried on with our plans and went to the mall, which felt strangely sacred to me. Calmly I paced its long, huge halls, feeling blessed. We bought Kezia some birthday clothes, Helen and Kezia got some food, we shopped for bargains, then it was time to go. As we walked out to our car, twilight was upon us, and again I felt as if I were in a holy place—though all around me nothing but cars stretched out. The air was soft, caressing, and above me the evening star, the first star, greeted me. As had been my habit for the last thirty-five years, I again made my customary wish: "Let me find Sorrow."

Then, I turned to gaze at my two lovely daughters who, today, had tenderly given me such fresh hope. While they characteristically quibbled over who was going to drive, I was overwhelmed by my love for them and awed by their love for me. They had taken an emotional risk in telling me about this other lost daughter; maybe she would take away some of the devotion I had always shown them. But that possibility had never even occurred to them. They wanted to protect me from further pain, but they knew we had to see this out. Finally, they agreed upon a driver, and as we moved on, into an evening full of promise, I told them about all my years of wishing on stars, wishing that someday, somehow I would find Sorrow. She had always felt as far beyond my reach as the star, but now, maybe she was closer. Merideth Mae. Could it be?

When I got back to Wilmington, I requested a copy of Merideth's "official" birth certificate from the state of Ohio. I was hoping that I would find the confirmation I needed, that her birth weight and time of birth would match what I remembered so well. Prior to this, I had not known that anyone can request a copy of anybody's birth certificate, but there was Merideth's birth certificate in our mailbox just days later, bearing the seal of Summit County, Ohio.

What a blow! Her weight and time of birth were not recorded on the certificate. Only her name, birth date, her adoptive parents' names, and the date the birth certificate was filed, April 2, 1965, appeared. That would have been the day or the day after the adoption was finalized, the day I left the Florence Crittenton Home.

What to do next? My only option was to approach Merideth and ask her if what she knew about the circumstances of her adoption fit the information I had. But how to find her? We went to WhitePages.com. Nothing for a Merideth Mae, but sure enough, there was a Michael J. —— in Niagara Falls, NY. Scared, so scared I could not place the call, Kezia called for me. Her heart was pounding, but the only answer she received was the phone company's recorded message saying, "The number you have dialed has been disconnected."

From there we went to Peoplefind.com. I had Merideth's name and birth date—the vital information Peoplefind.com needs. I put my request in on a Friday. On Monday, the results were in my e-mail. There was only one match nationwide. There was the answer to my quest: her address, her birth date, her telephone number, even her alias, which was just her name misspelled. The results gave me the name of others living at that address, and there was more confirmation: Michael J. Everything matched the information from Ancestry.com. The Niagara Falls address had been a wrong turn, the wrong Michael J. Bizarrely, Peoplefind.com gave me the names and address of all of Merideth and Michael's neighbors. Eighty-four adults live on their New Jersey cul-de-sac, and now I had all their names too.

I was still wary; it all seemed too simple, so I e-mailed Cathy in Mississippi, asking her to explain to me just how it was that she could come up with Merideth's name so easily. She replied that she did not like to discuss her methods by e-mail, but if I would call her, she would explain.

Had she done something illegal? I wondered. If so, would that make a difference in my decision to try to contact Merideth? I called and called, but Cathy was hard to reach. She was online a lot and all I could get was a busy signal. I e-mailed her back, asking when was a good time to get her. She replied promptly with a time, but still I could not reach her. Now it was time for us to leave for California where we would be celebrating Thanksgiving with my parents and my son and daughter-in-law who were expecting their baby, my first grandchild—or so we thought.

There was only one thing to do: temporarily close the door that Cathy, Debbie, Helen, Kezia, Ancestry.com, and Peoplefind.com had opened. My parents and I had never discussed Sorrow's adoption, never in thirty-five years. I had only broached the subject that one awkward time when I had asked my mother for any records she might have. When I was in Pepper Pike and at Florence Crittenton, my aunt had always told me that my parents needed to be protected from the details of my pregnancy. I had been obedient. I had done everything I could to protect them, never telling them about the night of Sorrow's birth and hiding as best I could the consequent emotional demons. Although I had to let them know that my marriages had failed again and again, I had never talked about the complicated problems that had led to the divorces or the lonely anguish that had shadowed me for decades. Because I needed their approval so badly, I had always made it my duty to assure them that I was fine, that nothing was ever wrong, that nothing I took on was ever too much. Although they knew I was writing a book about contemporary memoirs, they had no idea that I was also telling the story of losing Sorrow. Like most people in my life, they did not know me very well at all.

I knew I could not tell them anything about this latest possibility, but one night after dark, my sister Anne and I took a long walk on the golf cart paths that fanned out behind my parents' home. I told her all that we had found so far. Her response was confirming. She was excited, hopeful, and she told me for the first time how sorry she was that she was unable to help me so long ago.

My parents had kept the real reason for my sudden departure for Ohio a secret from her too. She had not known the truth about my exile, that I had a daughter somewhere in Ohio, until I told her myself a year after my return as we sat together in a grassy patch of sunlight, playing with her newborn son. She had been stunned by my condensed confession, no more words than "I had a baby girl while I was gone; I had to give her away." That night, decades later, as we wound our way around the darkened golf course, she told me how guilty she had felt on that long-ago day, guilty for the great joy she was able to take in her baby boy, crawling through the soft grass in front of us. She had never been able to find the way to talk about my loss with me again. But now she could tell me. Now she could tell me that I was not the only one who thought of my daughter out there in the world somewhere. She thought about her too; she always regretted that she had not been able to intervene in some way so that we could have kept her. I was so surprised, so moved. I had always thought I had been the only one who wanted her.

When I told my son and daughter-in-law about our discoveries, the possibility of finding Sorrow added to their anticipation as they approached the birth of their own baby. With blessings from Anne, Todd, and Maria, I felt even more committed to follow through with my findings when we returned to North Carolina.

One afternoon on this California visit, we took a walk on my favorite shoreline at La Jolla, snapping pictures of the seals that have opportunistically taken over the Children's Beach. I had John take one just of me, hoping it would turn out well, and I could include it in the letter I was going to write to Merideth. Another day, I spent an hour combing through stacks of beautiful writing paper at an upscale stationary store in the Gaslamp Quarter. Slowly I eliminated pale ivories and light blues. Finally I made my purchase: thick, butter-yellow sheets of handmade paper, perfect for my letter.

Martha's Vineyard, 2004

So much had changed since Sorrow's conception and birth—in technology and in our culture. In 1965, parents were adamant that their daughters not have sex outside of marriage. When I did and, on top of that, became pregnant, I had to be hidden away. All lasting evidence of my fall had to be erased. Virginity was still a necessary symbol of value. Although it would be only one year later that Jacqueline Susann would publish her novel *Valley of the Dolls* and break social taboos by creating three female characters who have sex outside of marriage, each of these characters pays dearly for letting go of that vital signifier—her virginity. Both in life and in fiction, virginity was not something to relinquish without great cost.

But now, in the first decade of a new century, sex before marriage is routine—the traditional reasons for waiting quickly dissolving before our eyes. When my daughter found out her girlfriend was dating a man who was saving himself for marriage, she advised her to break it off with him—he sounded abnormal. At the university where I teach, consensual sex is not considered a problem. The problems are alcohol, drugs, and nonconsensual sex. At Take Back the Night marches, we chant through megaphones as we trek through campus: *"Yes* means *yes! No* means *no!"* When to have sex and with whom is still confusing for many young single women, but the consequences for having consensual sex are no longer life-altering and severe. Today, the fact that I had sex at sixteen seems unremarkable, hardly a cause for secrecy, shame, and exile.

There is also a new openness about adoption. Although many birthmothers still want original birth certificates kept under lock and key, the shame for being an unwed mother has dissipated considerably. More and more research is showing that closed adoptions are rarely good for those involved. In the 1960s, the theory that nurture could always trump nature was sacrosanct, but that theory has been revised. Now we know that biology plays a significant role. Birth records like Les's are being opened for medical reasons. We need to know the illnesses of our parents and grandparents whether the records warn us that we are prone to diabetes, schizophrenia, or alcoholism. We need to know where we can find a sibling if we need bone marrow to save the life of a child. Closed adoptions are a rarity. Even my friend who recently adopted a baby girl from Guatemala has the name and picture of her daughter's birthmother, should her daughter want or need to find her someday.

And, of course, the Internet continues to play a significant role in all our cultural and social exchanges. The connections it allows seem miraculous. Within a matter of hours, Debbie could make contact with a total stranger in Mississippi by way of OnAngelsWings.com. A grouping of like-minded people allowed her to find a kind stranger, Cathy, who was willing to give her a name from records that were thirty-five years old. Within minutes, Kezia could go to Ancestry.com and match a maiden name with a married name. Over the course of a weekend, with only a name and birth date, Peoplefind.com could locate precisely one woman out of millions in the United States. Suddenly information that had been inaccessible for so long fell effortlessly out of the sky and into our hearts, or rather it came flying through wires, connectors, and codes that few of us can conceptualize. It is not too difficult to imagine that dizzy transport of information as being directed by a mysterious hand. Suddenly a benevolent force stepped in, took charge, and began the process that could return what had been lost so long ago.

"Hello Janet . . .
It's Me, Merideth"

Wilmington, December 2000

UPON MY RETURN from California, I telephoned Cathy in Mississippi again, and this time she answered on the first ring. I explained my concerns about contacting Merideth. Cathy was kind and understanding and assured me she had not broken any laws in finding Merideth's name, nor had Kezia in finding her married name, nor had I in finding her address and phone number.

Cathy got into the business of helping adoptees find their birth parents and vice versa after she helped her husband, who was adopted in Ohio in the 1960s, find his birthmother. That reunion was so healing for both her husband and his birthmother that Cathy decided she would continue to help others reunite with their birth parents or their children. Out of almost one hundred reunions she has made possible, only two have not been positive.

When Cathy saw Debbie's request for assistance from the e-group OnAngelsWings, she e-mailed her immediately, offering her help. With the date and place of birth that Debbie provided, Cathy consulted the Ohio Birth Index, which provides minimal information about all babies born in the state of Ohio. Cathy had obtained copies of the Ohio Birth Indexes for the 1960s while helping her husband. All states have such indexes, but Ohio's are public record, thus available to the public on microfilm from the Bureau of Vital Statistics. The index showed Cathy that on March 20, 1965, there was only one baby girl born in Summit County (which includes the city of Akron) that was left unnamed on her birth certificate. Babies without names are an immediate indication of adoption since birthmothers often do not officially name their babies, although almost all do so privately in their hearts. In an effort to safeguard me, Aunt Jo had intervened and kept me from putting Sorrow's name on her birth certificate. It was the one lucky coincidence to come out of those terrible days, for she had actually provided Cathy with her first clue that this unnamed baby girl might be my daughter.

Cathy then turned to the Birth Supplemental Index, which lists amended or adoptive names and amended birth certificate numbers. This index gave a name change for the baby girl that had been born in Summit County on March 20, 1965. By cross-referencing the two indexes, Cathy could draw a definite connection between the baby girl born on that date and in that county and the baby who had been given the name Merideth Mae on April 2, 1965. My case was easy. Merideth Mae was the only previously unnamed baby girl born in Summit County on that date whose birth name and certificate number had been amended. So despite the fact that Merideth's original birth certificate was (and still is) sealed by law, other official records that Cathy had legally obtained told her that without a doubt, this was my daughter.

I was relieved to learn that no laws had been broken in locating Merideth; had Cathy found an unlawful way to open sealed records to find her, I probably would have still tried to contact her, but I felt better knowing that Cathy's methods were aboveboard and that she had reunited other birth parents and children successfully. With that part of the puzzle solved, I began to draft what I think will remain the most important letter of my life, the letter to Merideth.

I had quickly vetoed the idea of simply telephoning her, mostly because I didn't have the courage to make such a call, but also because I wanted her to get a letter from me, a letter that she could mull over for as long as she needed until she decided how she wanted to respond. I spent days on it. I showed a draft to John, who has been known to edit my writing heavily, but this time he had no suggestions. He liked it as it was. I knew it was not perfect, but I realized I had to send it off to her, hoping that my words would somehow serve as the first foundations of a bridge we might build. I painstakingly copied it over on the special handmade paper I had purchased in San Diego, starting over several times in an effort to get my handwriting just right—no smudges, no crossing out. I put the picture that John had taken of me in La Jolla with the tumultuous Pacific behind me in a separate, sealed envelope inside the letter. I wanted her to have the option of opening it or not. I wanted to give her lots of options. After all, I knew how angry Les had felt when his birthmother contacted him. Actually, although meeting and talking to Les had been discouraging and depressing, at least his response prepared me for a negative reply. If Merideth reacted to my gesture toward reunion as Les had to his birth-mother, well, I tried to be ready for that, to expect the absolute worst.

Here is what I wrote:

December 2000

Dear Merideth,

This is such a difficult letter to write. How to begin? First, please ex-cuse the formality of a certified letter. I want very much to know that you do receive this letter, so that is why I have used what feels like an overly dramatic process.

Through a series of somewhat miraculous coincidences, my daugh-ters gave me your name while I was visiting my youngest daughter on her 23rd birthday. They feel very sure that you are the child I had to give up for adoption thirty-five years ago. There—now I've said that . . . maybe this will get easier.

Merideth, that is a very long story, a very sad one for me, though I pray not for you, about a time in my life that I've never really recov-ered from. If all the following information that I have coincides with your knowledge of your birth and adoption, and if you would like to know that story, of course, I want to tell it to you someday.

But first, what I need to know from you is if you are adopted. If so, were you born on March 20, 1965 very, very early in the morning (be-tween 6 and 7 A.M.) in Akron to a young girl (only 16) who was living in the Florence Crittenton Home for Unwed Mothers? Did you weigh 6 pounds, 4½ ounces? Were you adopted by a couple who were in the medical profession?

If all of that information coincides with the information that you have about the circumstances of your birth and adoption, then it seems quite certain that I am your birthmother.

It's very important to me that you know that I do not want to intrude on your life in any way. If, in fact, I am your birthmother and you would like to know more about me, my family, my life, and if you feel you could tell me about your own, well that would be an answer to thousands of prayers. But if you feel that you in no way want any kind of communication with me, I will respect that completely. The one thing that I do ask is for some kind of response. It may be that you are not adopted; it may be that you have already been reunited with your birthmother; it may be that I am your birthmother but you do not wish to know me; it may be that I am your birthmother and that you have been waiting for a letter like this.

Whichever of those seems closest to the truth, I only ask that you give me some kind of an answer. If you are not the child I lost, I want to keep searching.

I have enclosed in this letter in a separate envelope a recent picture of me taken while I was visiting my parents in Southern California. It is yours to open if you would like or simply to send back to me unopened. I am easy to find. My address is ——; my phone number is ——; my email address is ——.

Know that I will try my best to accept any response from you with grace and understanding.

I send all my best wishes and hope,

Janet Ellerby

I took the letter to the post office, and with my heart pounding, I arranged with the mail clerk to send it by certified mail. And then, before I was really ready to part with it, he nonchalantly stamped it and tossed it in a bin well out of my reach. I stared at the bin.

"Should I ask for it back?" I asked myself. Frozen there for a few seconds, my eyes remained locked on the mail bin that held the letter that might break or mend my heart. Then the clerk's impatient words, "Next! Next in line, please!" penetrated my fog and I moved toward the exit. It was already on its way.

That was Wednesday, December 14. I figured it would take at least one week, probably more, for Merideth to receive the certified letter, think it over, and decide what she wanted to do. I had promised myself that I wouldn't even begin thinking about a possible response until Wednesday the twenty-first. The holidays were upon us, and there was plenty to keep me preoccupied as I prepared for our family Christmas. I had been keeping myself successfully busy for thirty-five years, so rather than dwell incessantly on my letter, it was not hard to allow the same energy that had kept me distracted for so long to propel me through those days after it had left my hands.

On Monday afternoon, the nineteenth of December, I rushed into the house, laden with Christmas gifts, hustled them upstairs and hid them under my bed, and then headed back out to the car to haul in several bags of groceries. As I passed the answering machine, I saw its little red light blinking cheerfully. I casually pressed the "play" button, and then I heard a voice—not the voice of a stranger exactly, but a new voice just the same.

> "Hello Janet . . . It's me, Merideth. I got your letter and I'd really like to talk to you. I'm home today, so if you can call me back, I should be here. My number is ——. I'll look forward to talking to you. Bye."

The rush of emotion as I listened to Merideth's voice was the equivalent of a freight train. There was nothing to do but let it barrel through me, wave upon wave of thrill, panic, joy, anticipation, dread, exuberance, and sorrow. What I couldn't do was pick up the phone and call her right back. I had been waiting for this for so long. What would I say? What if I made a bad first impression?

Upon first meeting me, people usually like me, but this call meant introducing myself to one of the most important people of my life. Usually when we meet someone who is going to affect us in life-altering ways, we are not aware at that first moment of their future role. I'm embarrassed to admit that I don't even recall meeting John for the first time when I came to interview for my job at UNCW, yet he came to be the love of my life. But today I was hyperaware of the impact my first conversation with Merideth would have on the rest of my life. I was standing on the brink of something so profound that I couldn't take the next step. If I blundered, the consequences would shatter me.

I needed help, and this time I had friends I could immediately reach out for, friends who could and would support me as I crossed this all-important threshold. First, I called John—he was not in his office. Then

I called my friend Amy who knew all about Sorrow, the search, and the letter—she was home. Quickly I told her that Merideth had called, but that I couldn't bring myself to call her back. As I held the phone to the answering machine, she listened intently to Merideth's voice. She told me that this was the voice of a girl who grew up in New Jersey, not the Midwest, but most importantly, she said Merideth's voice sounded kind and warm, and that I couldn't let my fears prevent me from calling her. We hung up. I appreciated Amy's encouragement, but I still couldn't make the call. Again I called John; this time, I reached him. He said he would be right home, to wait for him.

Methodically I put the groceries away. A half-hour later, when John walked through the door, I was sweeping the floor, trying desperately to keep my panic at bay. We sat down together in our living room. Slowly and carefully he reassured me: I would say the right things, I would make a good impression, I just needed to say what was in my heart, I just needed to be myself. All those clichés helped, and somewhat composed, I punched in Merideth's phone number, only to get the recording on her answering machine. Now I left my own message, saying simply, "It's Janet, returning your call. I'll try you a little later. Thank you so much for calling me. I'm looking forward to talking to you too. Bye."

Phone tag can be frustrating, but the messages we exchanged helped me get ready for our first conversation. I hadn't expected Merideth to call me. I thought that she would write. I was ecstatic but also unhinged. John suggested we take our dog for a walk, a daily ritual that always helped us relax while recounting the events of our day. I could call again when we returned. Sure enough, while we were gone, Merideth returned my call. This time she gave me a little bit more information, saying that she had a baby who was sick; she had unexpectedly had to take her to the doctor. She hoped I would call back. Now, finally, I was ready. The preliminaries were over; I wanted very much to talk to Merideth. I dialed and a man answered. I identified myself, and he kindly replied that Merideth was eager to talk to me, and then suddenly she was there on the phone with me.

She seemed so brave, much more courageous than I. She began by assuring me that all the details that I had mentioned in my letter matched up with everything she knew about her adoption. She had been born in Akron on March 20, 1965. Her parents were in the medical profession: her father was a doctor, her mother a nurse. She had been told that her birth-mother had lived at the Florence Crittenton Home during her pregnancy. She said that she had looked at the picture I had sent with my letter and that it was amazing how much we looked alike. She was sure I was her birthmother. I had found her.

Martha's Vineyard, 2004

As I look back to that afternoon, I feel a bit embarrassed by my timidity. I had been imagining scenarios of Sorrow's return for so long, yet I had never anticipated the gravity of this day. Like the night of her birth and the afternoon when Helen told me Sorrow had been found, this day stands out in my memory clear and whole. I could tell you how the Christmas tree was decorated that I sat next to as I made those calls, heart in mouth. I could tell you that it was an unusually warm December day, that as John and I walked the dog through our neighborhood, the sun was shining and the bells on the old church chimed with a ringing clarity. I could even describe the little pile of dirt I was sweeping up in my kitchen when John had walked in our front door.

I have a good memory, yet so much of my past is lost, so many Christmases blur one into the other, so many unseasonably warm days in Wilmington, the countless times I have swept my kitchen. The only way I can account for the lucid descriptions I can give of these days in my life is that they were momentous. They were the days that radically changed my life, first in a disastrously traumatic way; now, in a nerve-wracking but potentially joyful way.

As Merideth talked to me, her composure was helpful. She seemed like the adult; I was the child—exposed, unsure, and vulnerable. The trauma of the night I lost Sorrow wouldn't leave me. I could not relax. I still needed to heal, and she held the key to my cure. Even though I remembered the example Les had taught me about a bitter, unwelcome reunion, I had not really put up my guard. There was no possibility for self-protection in this. No matter what the consequences, I had jumped into unfamiliar territory, and held out my heart to my daughter.

30 Merideth's Story

OF COURSE I DIDN'T learn Merideth's life story in one telephone call, but slowly I would come to know some of the details. For decades I had worried about Sorrow. I had imagined a vulnerable youth, a precarious adolescence, an unpredictable young adulthood. I feared the price she might have to pay for an unhappy adoption, for not belonging, for not fitting in, for always feeling different. My anxieties were legitimate—such consequences can be the result of a mismatched adoption, but they were not for Merideth. She grew up in a family where she was greatly loved, where she fit in seamlessly, where she grew up secure and happy.

Merideth's life choices were different from mine. She was not buffeted by the winds of cultural turmoil as I was. She didn't feel the need to follow the tambourine man, endlessly escaping, always on the run. No, she's very different, very settled, very steady. And yet, there are connections to be drawn, especially between her and Todd, Helen, and Kezia. Although the details of Merideth's youth are, of course, different from the life I provided for her half-siblings, there are uncanny correspondences, similar challenges that all four children have had to face growing up.

Merideth's parents adopted her when her father, a radiologist, was thirty and her mother, a nurse, twenty-eight. Merideth was named after her mother's beloved sister, Helen Mae. Her parents went on to adopt two more children from the Akron Florence Crittenton Home: Scott and Drew. Then, when Merideth was seven, her parents divorced and her mother, Anne, took Merideth and her brothers back to southern New Jersey, where Anne had grown up and where her parents and sister still lived. Anne was going to have to raise three children on her own, and she knew she would need her family nearby for support. The divorce was not amicable, and the lasting bitterness kept Merideth from having a close relationship with her father.

Like Helen, Todd, and Kezia, Merideth and her brothers had to cope with their parents' divorce when they were very young. Correspondingly, Merideth, Scott, and Drew moved to a different state, away from their father. Anne's move to New Jersey, like mine to Idaho, gave us both a fresh start with caring family close by. Merideth, her brothers, and her half-siblings had to negotiate a separation from their fathers, an estrangement imposed by geographical distance and because of their fathers' subsequent marriages, an inevitable emotional distance. Both Merideth's father and Ricardo would remarry twice.

But for all these children, these separations and changes did not bring about extraordinary sorrow or insecurity. Merideth and her brothers grew up happily with Anne on one of New Jersey's scenic barrier islands, the vacation destination for thousands and only about ten miles from where she lives now.

Merideth's brothers tell me she was never one to get into trouble of any kind. She was an excellent swimmer and student, the president of the National Honors Society chapter at her high school. The family lived in an upstairs apartment close to the beach. They weren't poor, but money was often tight. Merideth started working at summer jobs as soon as she was old enough so that she could have her own spending money, and, like most teenage girls, she wanted to buy clothes.

Like Merideth, Todd, Helen, and Kezia grew up feeling the pinch of our limited resources. We too were never poor, but for much of their childhood we were on a careful budget. My kids still recall receiving one of Idaho's forms of subsistence: huge chunks of free cheese and butter. Like Merideth, all three of them started weekend and summer jobs just as soon as they could find someone to hire them.

Merideth's happiest childhood memories come from family adventures at a cabin her mother and Aunt Helen Mae would rent on a lake about an hour north of their home. There Anne, Helen Mae, Merideth, her brothers, and her cousins would hike and fish on the lake, make s'mores, and sing camp songs. Every year they would take a canoeing trip down a nearby river. Merideth remembers her mother and Helen Mae capsizing their canoe and laughing so hard Merideth thought they would never be able to right it and resume paddling. Merideth and her brothers had their own canoe, her cousins another, and they relished the race to see who would finish first.

Merideth loved the beach, especially "The Cove," a private beach along the inlet on the southernmost tip of their island. The only way to get to the Cove was to hike along trail through the marsh and maritime forest. The family would pack a lunch and start their hike in the morning. The Cove had huge sand dunes where Merideth and her brothers could run and hide. They would spend the day there, hiking back in the late afternoon, deliciously tired and sunburned.

These stories mirror the childhood memories that Todd, Helen, and Kezia still cherish. Fishing trips to Montana and long days on sunny beaches, first in Malibu, then on Lake Coeur d'Alene, then on Seattle's Lake Washington, and finally on the beaches of southeastern North Carolina. All four of my children seem to have been born with a need for the restorative balm of the ocean and an innate appreciation for unspoiled forests, clear lakes, and rugged mountains.

Merideth says simply, "I had a happy life and was loved." I like to think Todd, Helen, and Kezia would also describe their early lives in such straightforward terms. After graduating from high school, Merideth went to Douglass College at Rutgers University, where she majored in journalism. She enjoyed college but felt a bit lost in such a large university. After college she spent several months in London, which she remembers as one of the best times of her life.

Likewise, Todd, Helen, and Kezia all made their way through large universities. Even their majors in English, social work, and journalism corresponded to Merideth's. And like her, they too sought out and enjoyed world travel: Todd to Central America, Helen to Italy, Kezia to New Zealand.

When Merideth started on her career, she decided to stay close to home. She returned to the barrier islands of southern New Jersey to begin work in public relations. Remarkably, whether by fate or coincidence, at about that time I came east to live in my coastal setting—only twenty minutes from a barrier island rich with estuaries and abundant bird life—an environment that parallels Merideth's closely even though it is four hundred miles to the south. Our destinies could have taken us to distant lands, but somehow we both came to live in resort communities on the Atlantic coast only a day's drive from one another.

In 1992, Merideth married Michael when she was twenty-seven. She always speaks of him as her best friend. When I met Merideth, they had three children, Michaela, Drew, and Emma. Merideth says of them, "They are the light of my life." Together, she and Michael have made a home for their family with colorful flower beds on the outside and loving comfort within. Merideth likes to get her hands in the dirt. In this she is like her half-brother, Todd, who makes his living as a landscaper and seems to be able to make anything grow in profusion even in the dry, harsh climate of Denver. They are both like my parents, their grandparents, who have always surrounded themselves with gorgeous, award-winning gardens. Together they have inherited the proverbial green thumb.

Merideth's adoptive mother, Anne, died three years before I found Merideth. Her death was a terrible blow to Merideth; her mother had been quite ill but seemed to be on the road to recovery when she passed away unexpectedly. Merideth always speaks lovingly of Anne, whose greatest gift, she says, was her constant belief in her. Anne always told Merideth she could be anything she wanted to be, that she could accomplish anything she set her mind to. Merideth grew up believing that there were no limits to her mother's love, support, and encouragement. After her mother's death, Merideth felt an aching void in her life, so Emma's conception was a blessing. Nonetheless, Merideth knows, as do I, that there is no "getting over" losing someone so dear, even though we may somehow learn to live without their immediate presence.

So Merideth has lived through what I have not yet had to face—the death of a parent. She has preceded me in that painful loss. She has already felt what it means to be the one left alone, on her own to go on in the world without a parent's constancy, that reassuring sense of unshakable love. Maybe this is why she often seems to me to be more mature than I am. She seems more capable, more collected, more adult, perhaps for having weathered something so momentous. Or perhaps she just is a more levelheaded woman than I will ever be. I admire her equanimity and poise.

When I found Merideth, she had not been looking for me. Anne, she felt, was the only mother she ever needed, so she had never seriously considered looking for her birthmother. She says of her mom, "My mother was just the most wonderful mother you could ever want. She fulfilled all my needs." This admission does not bother me, and I hope Todd, Helen, and Kezia would say something similar. They too have all the mother they need. I am endlessly grateful that Merideth had Anne, who loved her unconditionally. This was, of course, exactly what I wanted most for my lost daughter.

The fact that Merideth and her brothers had been adopted from the Florence Crittenton Home was openly discussed in their family. In fact, that part of her life history never bothered her—that is until she had Michaela. After she had carried her baby for nine months and given birth to a daughter that she loved instantly and completely, Merideth realized that behind her adoption was a secret, sad story.

What she didn't realize, of course, was that throughout her whole life, I was always there, also her mother, desperately missing her, dreaming of the day that we would find each other.

Martha's Vineyard, 2004

As I learned the details of Merideth's happy life, I was overcome with relief. I had imagined numerous scenarios for Sorrow's life, the worst that she had been adopted by cruel, cold people who turned her into a drudge—like Cinderella. To find out that she had been raised in a secure and loving home by a devoted mother, two caring brothers, and an involved extended family assuaged an anxiety that had never abated. I am sorry that there were times in her youth when money was short and sorry that she had to endure her adoptive father's distance. I was also sorry for the pain of her parents' difficult divorce, but I also knew that had she been with me all those years, money would have been as dear and divorce as distressful.

There will be those who will want to say that Anne gave Merideth a more secure structure on which to build her life than I could have provided. Maybe. But I know that had I been allowed to keep Sorrow, I would not have been a neglectful or unloving mother. I know I would have loved her with the same steadiness and unconditional commitment that I have given to Todd, Helen, and Kezia. They have always been sure of my enduring love, even though the circumstances of our lives have been bumpy. Living her life separate from us, Merideth fared well. I wish I could have thanked Anne before she died for being such a loving and wise mother.

One of the warnings I have read concerning reunions between birth-mothers and their biological children is that if the adopted child's life has been difficult, if the child has felt like an outsider in the adoptive family, then the reunion is less likely to go well. The child, now presumably an adult, may be glad to have been found, but he or she will bring feelings of betrayal and anger to the new relationship. Because Anne had been such a caring and supportive mother, my reunion with Merideth was much less problematic. Despite her parents' divorce and the subsequent move to New Jersey, Merideth's relationship with her primary parent was never uncertain. When Anne died, Merideth told me that she was devastated. But by then, it seems that Merideth had such a sound family network that although her mother's loss will be forever painful, it was not hugely destabilizing. In fact, after our protracted and diverse journeys, when we finally met, Merideth's mental health was probably much steadier than mine. The consequences of her adoption had always been sad and often debilitating for me, but fortunately for her, they were happy and affirming.

Welcome Janet and John

This is really something
People will be envious
But our roles aren't clear
So we mustn't rush
Still, we are burning brightly
Clinging like fire to fuel
I'm grinning like a fool
Stay in touch
We should stay in touch
Oh! Stay in touch.
   —Joni Mitchell, "Stay in Touch," *Taming the Tiger*, 1998

Southern New Jersey, December 2001

HAVING FILLED IN THE GAP of the first thirty-five years of Merideth's life, I can return to the day that she received my first, all-important letter.

It was the Monday before Christmas, and Merideth had sent Michaela and Drew off to school but had not gone to work herself because her baby, Emma, was sick. A little yellow slip had been placed in their mailbox the Friday before, alerting them that they had a certified letter waiting for them at the post office. That Monday morning, Michael stopped to pick it up on his way to work. He called Merideth from his cell phone as he drove on to work, noting that it had a return address in Wilmington, North Carolina. Although they had vacationed on the Outer Banks of North Carolina, Merideth didn't know anyone in the state, but since she was the executor of her mother's will, she assumed the letter must have something to do with her mother's estate. She told Michael to go ahead and open it. He scanned the beginning of the letter.

"Oh my God!" he exclaimed.

Merideth immediately recognized the shock in his voice and thought it must be bad news.

"What? What is it?" she asked.

"Let me pull over. I need to read it to you word for word," he answered.

Michael pulled his truck onto the road's shoulder and began to read my letter to Merideth, but he had a hard time getting through it. He was very moved, so much so that his voice cracked, and the tears in his eyes surprised him. On the other end of the phone line, Merideth also started to get tearful. When he finished reading the letter to her, he asked, "Do you want me to come home?"

Merideth replied simply, "Yes."

Michael turned his truck around and started home. Merideth put down the phone. Emma was asleep in the other room. Slowly, Merideth sank to the floor, overcome by emotions she did not even realize she had. She began to cry, as she recalls, "with those deep sobs. It was a profound cry, the gut-wrenching kind, the kind that you have only a few times in your life." She cried hard for a few minutes, amazed by this unexpected outpouring of sorrow over a loss she had never even recognized that she carried inside. Then Emma awoke and came running to her mother. Merideth embraced her warmly, her tears still falling, but now she was laughing too, surprised again by a sudden feeling of joy that she again could not completely account for. When Michael walked in the door, he found her still on the floor, laughing and crying as she cuddled Emma. The significance of our long separation, Merideth's and mine, had been made clear.

Merideth and Michael sat in their living room, trying to absorb my words and what they meant. Together they decided to turn to her mother's sister, Helen Mae, for advice. Merideth called and read her the letter. Helen Mae did not hesitate. Her advice was immediate and certain:

"Merideth, call her right up and tell her she has found you," she declared.

Bravely, only hours after receiving my letter, Merideth placed the call that would lead to our first conversation.

Despite all my fears, that initial exchange went wonderfully for both of us. We had so much to tell each other that there was no chance for any awkward silence. Merideth was eager to tell me about her children, her husband, and herself. I was eager to tell her about her half-brother and his wife and the baby that they were expecting, about her half-sisters, about my husband, and briefly, how I had found her. I admitted that I was usually shy on the phone; she replied that she was too. Sweetly she said she found me very easy to talk to. In due course, I could hear Emma, unhappy in the background. Merideth admitted that although she didn't want to get off the phone and Michael was doing his best to keep Emma preoccupied, the baby had reached the point when only the unhindered attention of her mother would do. I understood that completely; it was time to go. We agreed that we would exchange pictures and that we both looked forward to talking to one another again soon.

Wilmington, December 2001

As I gently lay the phone down in its cradle, I was not yet completely aware of the shift my life had taken. Losing Sorrow had done much to define me for most of my life, and now that had been corrected—or if not corrected, modified. Had I actually gotten back to the baby that I had left behind again and again in my dreams? Would the baby that cried on and on in my delivery room memory fall quiet? Would the flashbacks that had been playing over and over again finally begin to fade?

It would take months to answer these questions. Gradually I would come to know my new self: a woman with four children—not three; a woman who had lost her first daughter—and found her; an instantaneous grandmother; a woman who had born Sorrow in secret and in shame; a woman who could now proclaim her returned daughter with the pride and joy of a new parent.

Shortly before I had found Merideth, Joni Mitchell had been reunited with her own daughter and written a song about it. Once again, as her song about losing "Little Green" had done, Mitchell's lyrics gave me words to articulate my own desperate wish that Merideth and I "stay in touch."

The day after that life-changing call, I went through boxes of old pictures and chose some to send to Merideth with another letter, which I again labored over intensely, trying to find the perfect words that would let me into her heart:

December 21, 2000

The Winter Solstice

Dear Merideth,

I went through some stacks of photos and came up with these that I enclose that will give you a better sense of me, my children, my husband, my sisters, my parents, and your biological father. I hope this isn't too much for you. I know how fast it all happened, even for me and I had longer to process this incredible discovery than you did. So, I understand completely if you need time to think everything through. I want you to know that you have always been a big part of my life. I've dreamed of you, worried about you, imagined you, imagined you imagining me—in short, I've always had a relationship with you. But now that we are in actual touch with one another, I want to respect your boundaries. I can't tell you how glad I am to know that you've had a good life. It sounds like you have strong family ties with your brothers, and I hope with your mother and father, and with Michael's family. And that's so wonderful! For me, there's nothing more important than family. They come first, no matter what.

I wrote on the back of the pictures a little bit of explanation for each. The recent ones are pretty self-explanatory. John suggested I put in a picture of me when I was your age, and when I found one of me at 35, I was a bit dismayed by all that permed hair! But that was 1983 and I guess it was not unusual for that time.

Your biological father's name is ——. The pictures I found and copied are from 1964, when we were high school sweethearts. Although he didn't learn of my pregnancy and your birth until a long time after you were born, I did eventually tell him about you. I haven't talked with him for about twenty-five years, but the last time I did speak with him, he was living near San Diego. He is a scientist. At that time, he was doing cancer research.

There's so much to tell you about how you came to be conceived in California and how I ended up at the Florence Crittenton Home in Akron. But I'll leave that for later.

I've told Todd and Maria, Helen, and Kezia about you and they are all very excited and so glad that you are you. One of my sisters is traveling, so I haven't been able to tell her yet, but my other sister is overjoyed that we found you and that you were so happy to be found!

We will be leaving Wilmington after Christmas for Brooklyn and will be staying with John's mother until Jan. 5th. Again, I don't want to push at all, but I do want to give you her phone number, in case it might be possible for us to actually meet.

If you're not ready to meet or if it's not possible, I understand completely. People always compliment me that I am a very patient person, and I think that is true about me. We really don't live that far apart and there is plenty of time now for us to meet.

I hope these pictures are fun for you and that your Christmas is full of love and warmth. Mine will be one of the happiest I can remember because of your phone call and because finally, finally one part of my life is over and a new one, full of promise, begins. Thank you, Merideth, so much for that.

With much love

Once again, with trepidation, I mailed this next letter off to New Jersey, daring to hope it might receive openhearted reception my first had won.

But that wasn't enough. Now that I'd found Merideth, I was insatiably hungry for more contact. Extremely nervous but praying she would not mind if I called, I telephoned her on Christmas Eve, ostensibly to wish her Merry Christmas but really to hear her voice again, to try to gauge from her tone whether she was glad to hear from me or if I was an annoying interruption during a hectic time with her real family. When she answered, she was in the middle of preparations for a birthday celebration for her Aunt Helen Mae; in fact, she was peeling shrimp. But she insisted she was delighted to hear from me, so we began to exchange more information.

I learned that her mother had passed away and that she was not close to her father. I told her that Todd, Helen, and Kezia had grown up in different states than their father and that they too were not on great terms with him. It seemed an interesting coincidence that she and her half-siblings had similar feelings about their distant, extraneous fathers. Most importantly, in this conversation Merideth and I established that we wanted to meet in person. I asked her if it would be possible to meet on January 3, since we would be in Brooklyn, which was not far from the Jersey shore. She asked if John and I would mind driving to southern New Jersey so that we could visit with Michael and her and their children in their home, apologizing that it would mean about a two-and-a-half-hour drive for us each way.

"Would you mind driving that far?" she asked timorously.

"Are you serious? How do we get there?" I replied.

Martha's Vineyard, 2004

I felt no resentment that Merideth had never considered looking for me, but I felt great relief that she did not resent that I had found her. In her first letter to me, she made it clear that I had not intruded and that it meant a great deal to her that I had never forgotten about her. She writes:

December 23, 2000

Dear Janet,

Hi: There is so much I want to ask you, and so much I want to tell you, I don't know where to begin. I never thought I would know you. And now that I do, I hope you might let me know about your life and family.

My two younger brothers, both of whom are also adopted, are very happy that you have found me—and I you. Thank you for seeking me out. It means so much to know that you remembered me and cared enough to look for me. I know it took courage to reach out to me, not knowing how I might respond.

I feel very blessed. I have had a good life. I grew up in a loving family; I have a kind and caring husband and three precious children. And now I know you never forgot me.

I'm not sure where we go from here, but I can hope that one day we may be good friends. I've enclosed a few pictures for you—I'll send more soon. Michaela and Drew are very curious about you and would like to see you. Please let me know if there is an opportunity for us to meet, I would like that very much.

Please feel comfortable calling me any time. Christmas will have passed by the time you receive this letter, but I hope it was a very happy one. Best wishes for a New Year full of new beginnings!

Merideth

These initial letters to one another are full of mutual reassurances that we can and do care about one another a lot, but I can also hear our apprehensiveness. Neither of us really knew how much we could ask from one another.

Here's how I felt: it was as if I needed to woo her, to demonstrate to her that I was worthy of being known. Again, my lifelong insecurities challenged me. I began my relationship with Merideth with almost no self-assurance. I wanted dearly for her to approve of me, yet at the same time, I still felt in many ways unworthy of that approval. Although her letter assured me that I could call her anytime, every time I went to dial the phone, it was a struggle. Nothing was casual; every step felt like a significant risk. I thought about Todd, Helen, and Kezia and how completely natural it was to call them, to ask them to come home, to ask anything of them. They might say "no," but the bottom line was they were in my life forever. Our relationships might stumble at times, we might have to weather disagreements and physical distance, but we knew we would always be closely interconnected.

Talking to Merideth was not like this—not at first. She was easy to talk to and she said I was too; our two initial conversations were not stilted. Yet behind my apparent ease, I was tense, fearful, trying for perfection. I had so many hopes and fears riding on these early contacts. We both wanted to meet, to get to know each other and our families. No matter how afraid of rejection I might be, I had to move forward, to reach out for my daughter, hoping that this time I would finally be able to hold her.

Southern New Jersey, January 3, 2001

Merideth and I decided together that John and I would visit her home for the day. With directions in hand, we started our drive through freshly fallen snow down the Garden State Parkway and the Jersey coastline. Though she had seen the initial picture of me that I had sent in my first letter and subsequent pictures that I had mailed her directly after our first conversation, the first letter that she wrote to me on December 23 had not reached me before we left Wilmington. In other words, I still did not know what Merideth looked like.

The drive down was beautiful but torturous for me. If possible, I was even more nervous than I had been when I had had to work up my courage to call Merideth back on that first day she left her phone message. I can usually calm myself for anxious events by being overprepared. When I took my PhD orals and when I interviewed for my teaching position at UNCW, I was so organized and primed with knowledge about my subjects that nothing could have gone wrong. But there was nothing to prepare here, no knowledge to cram into my head, no books to read or handouts to create. I was gong to be judged on the impression I would make as me alone—not as a professor, student, colleague. My fear of this ultimate test was almost overwhelming. The entire way down I sat stiffly and quietly next to John. He patiently stopped at several rest stops so I could use the bathroom over and over again. And then suddenly we were there, driving up her street, and then in front of her house. I thought I would freeze, that John would have to pry me out of the car, but as we pulled into the driveway, my eyes caught sight of a sign on the front door. It read "Welcome Janet and John," and on it Michaela had carefully drawn a picture of John and me arriving at this very house with a family of five waiting to greet us.

The welcome sign didn't make my fear disappear; it was definitely still there, but now I could not wait to knock on that door. Hardly before the car had come to a full stop, I flung myself into uncertainty.

Where did this sudden valor come from? I don't know, but I was moving fast, heading for the doorbell. John hurried along behind me. I rang the bell, and then there she was.

We looked at one another and saw ourselves reflected.

Merideth's resemblance to me is uncanny. I am a tall woman, as is she. Our builds and weight are close to the same. On that day, our hair length and hair color were almost identical. If you look closely, you will see that while her eyes are large and blue, mine are smaller and hazel, and her nose is straighter than mine, her mouth a bit wider, her hair thicker. Although I can see her birth father in her immediately, I have also seen

Janet and Merideth, first meeting, 2001.
Photograph by John Clifford. Courtesy of the author.

others gasp when they see us together. On that day, as we greeted one another shyly but warmly, we could not stop staring at each other. We kept
catching each other's eye, so we would quickly glance away, embarrassed
and self-conscious but unable to give up our lingering gazes.

Now any doubts that we might have had as to whether we really
were biological mother and daughter evaporated. Our physical likeness
was ample proof. That day we continued to build emotional connections,
though I'm not sure we really knew what we were doing. For what should
those connections be? We could not be mother and daughter, not in the
way she had been with Anne and I was with my daughters. That is a relationship that develops over years between an adult and a growing child.
And we could not be like sisters, even though many mistake us for sisters.
Sibling relationships are precious, but they too form over years and years
of sharing, love, and rivalry, of course. Nor could it be just a friendship.
There was more involved here. We had just met, yet the relationship was
already important to Merideth and absolutely essential to me. Somehow

what we would create would have to draw from all of those relationships. We would have to create a hybrid, something entirely new.

That day unfolded too quickly. We talked and talked, all four of us easily and sensitively. Merideth and I both benefited from having our spouses with us on that day. Her attachment to Michael is as vital as mine is to John, so both of us knew intuitively that having our partners there would ease the dramatic intensity of being together for the first time. It was too momentous an event to experience alone. Michael and John felt comfortable with one another from the start and unassumingly added the familiar to such an unfamiliar situation. I am sure two trained therapists could not have facilitated this meeting better. Once again I experienced the value of devoted support.

We toured Merideth and Michael's comfortable home. On this day it was surrounded by pristine snow, so markedly a contrast to the dangerous blizzard that howled on the night of Merideth's birth. The interior of their house reminded me of my own; there was a similar inviting warmth, a cozy comfort that she and I had both been able to bequeath on our living spaces. Each of us had spent hours perched on ladders doing intricate stenciling to decorate our walls. With Italian opera playing softly in the background, we sat down to an inviting lunch that Michael and Merideth had prepared—sandwiches, salad, shrimp to peel and dip—though none of us ate much given our level of excitement.

As I hesitantly related some of the details of Merideth's birth, she reached for my hand and held it firmly as I faltered during the hardest parts. Then it was time for the children to arrive home. John and Michael left to pick up Emma at her daycare, and the school bus pulled up to deposit Michaela, seven, and Drew, five. They came barreling through the door with exuberance, eager to meet John and me. I had brought the children and Merideth each a gift, and Michaela and Drew tore into theirs. Shortly after they arrived, Emma, who would turn two the next day, toddled through the door, followed by Michael and John. She came trotting up to me, just for a second mistaking me for her mother. When she realized she'd approached the wrong person, she hollered in frustration, kicking at the wrapping paper that was entangling her feet. Emma's single-mindedness was evident straight away. In an instant Merideth swept her up, and, having found the right mother, she burrowed into Merideth's lap, a safe perch from which to cautiously observe John and me. We took pictures and marveled at the children's beauty and energy.

Michaela, who had a friend at school who had been adopted, understood that I was Merideth's birthmother and had an appreciation of what that meant. But Drew was still trying to figure it out. Innocently he asked Merideth, "Did you come out of this mommy's tummy?" When she replied "Yes, I did," he went on to ask, "So if Janet is your real mommy, was Grandma Anne was your fake mommy?" Merideth answered sweetly and straightforwardly, "I am lucky, Drew; I got to have two real mommies. You only have one mommy, me, but I have two mommies." Drew readily accepted her explanation and ran off to get his Godzilla video to show me as I glowed with the pleasure that Merideth had granted me by acknowledging so unselfconsciously that I was, indeed, one of her mothers.

And then it was 4:00 and time for us to start back to Brooklyn. Almost five hours had passed. How could our time have gone by so quickly? It had been a joyous day, a perfect day, the kind of day a fiction writer might allow herself to create for the best possible ending. Would a book critic complain that the day's perfection was implausible? Probably. I have learned since that although reunions like Merideth's and mine can be joyful, they can also be strained and sometimes even grimly disappointing.

But today, for our second meeting in thirty-five years, the fates reversed themselves, recasting a dark, harrowing night of pain and loss with blue skies, benign snow, encouraging, empathetic spouses, and our own eager open hearts. In this fortuitous second act, we both took our first precarious steps back toward one another, cautiously and tentatively, but also with a trustworthy sincerity. What was lost had been returned.

 *Lifting the Veil*

January 2001

EXHAUSTED BUT EBULLIENT, John and I returned from Merideth's to his mother's house in Brooklyn that evening. Despite my fatigue, I got very little sleep that night, not because of anxiety but because of elation. My euphoria reminded me of how I felt after giving birth to Todd, Helen, and Kezia: simultaneously drained and energized by the wonder of my achievement. The next morning we took our film to a one-hour photo service, eager to see our snapshots and to show them to John's mother and siblings, all of whom were coming into Brooklyn for a family dinner that evening. I was nervous about how John's family would react. Would they be uncomfortable? Discomfited that their brother had married a "fallen woman"? Would they see my reunion with Merideth as a happy occasion or for the raising of eyebrows? I was still unsure about how people would interpret both the past and the recent events of my life.

John's mother had, in fact, been quite nervous about our trip to South Jersey. She loves intrigue, and as she has gotten older, she has become more and more dubious of the motives of others. She was worried that perhaps Merideth and Michael had invited us to their home as part of a nefarious scam that she had heard about on daytime TV. Her fears are telling of how suspicious our culture is of long-lost relatives suddenly reappearing in our lives.

"Why are Michael and Merideth asking you to come all the way to South Jersey?" she asked several times.

"Why aren't you meeting them in a neutral public place, like a restaurant?" she suggested.

"They want something," she surmised grimly.

Indeed, all of us wanted something—Merideth, Michael, John, and especially me—but our motivations were not material. We wanted to establish new connections, ones based on openness, understanding, and trust. That first meeting could have either launched an opening for our families or squelched it.

On the morning we had left for Merideth's, even though my mother-in-law's qualms seemed far-fetched, John had assured her that we would not, under any circumstances, give them money. When we arrived home that night, she was relieved. She wanted to hear every detail of the day's events, which we related carefully, and she was somewhat reassured. But it wasn't until the next day, when she saw the pictures of Merideth and me, of Merideth and Michael, of their ample home and their vivacious children, that she could finally put her fears to rest. From the pictures, it was more than clear that this was truly my daughter and the reunion had been authentic and happy.

I need not have worried about the responses of John's family to Merideth. We shared the pictures with them, and all were amazed by the extraordinary resemblance between Merideth and me. John's brother teased, "I knew you had a daughter in Jersey, but I didn't know you had a clone!" They were fascinated by the story, delighted that we had found her, and eager to meet her themselves. It turned out to be an unproblematic transition: when they first met me, I had had three children; now I had four.

When John and I returned to Wilmington, I still had an intimidating task ahead of me. Telling my sisters about my visit with Merideth was easy; they and their husbands were pleased. Even though they had felt uneasy about my sudden disappearance from their lives so long ago and wished that they could have done more, the secret had been airtight even from them.

Now they were relieved to learn that Merideth had had a happy life in a loving family and were eager to see pictures of her. We didn't have a digital camera then, but Kezia was able to scan one of the pictures of Merideth and me standing together and send it over the Internet. My sister Katie was at her desk at work when she opened the attachment; she gasped, pressed "Print," and rushed to the laser printer in the office workroom to receive a copy. As it came out of the machine, she burst into tears.

"What's wrong?" a colleague, also waiting for copies, asked.

Katie didn't try to explain; she just showed her the picture.

"Oh my, she looks just like you!" the coworker commented. She was pointing at Merideth, not at me.

Katie, who is not given to demonstrative affection, gave her colleague a hug and replied joyfully, "She's my niece!"

Now I had to tell my parents. Not only had I not told them anything of the evolving discoveries that had been consuming me since early November, I had never told them about the most crucial part of the book they knew I had been working on and that was soon to be published. Although *Intimate Reading* was an analysis of memoirs and included my own detailed narrative, I had been keeping this a secret from them, still trying not to disturb their tranquil lives by bringing up my shadowy past. I had described the book to them as a study of contemporary memoirs by women—a half-truth—but definitely not the whole story.

After *Intimate Reading* was published, many readers told me that they were incensed with my parents for sending me off to Ohio to be shamefully hidden away. They expressed surprise that I did not harbor a lifetime of anger for them. At first, I was taken aback by this response. Any anger I might have had for my mother and father had been extinguished many years ago. I had come to understand that they had gone to great expense and effort to try to protect me, not to punish me.

I have learned from years of reading and critiquing literature that it is rarely wise to judge characters in novels from the past by the ethical standards of the present. My parents came of age in a certain historical moment and were faithful to the mores of that time. In coping with my pregnancy, their intentions were good even though the outcome was painful and enduring. By refraining from ever discussing my months in Ohio and Sorrow's birth, they believed they were setting the best possible course for me. Relegating the memory of my Uncle Richard to their subconscious had offered them surcease. By analogy, they believed locking the memory of Sorrow away would also work for me. We had established a respectable cautiousness over the years, always avoiding any discussion of topics with emotional baggage. Now I was upsetting that judicious equilibrium and asking them to revisit my painful past.

Telling them over the phone about the truer content of the book and how it had led to finding Merideth was not an option. They were in their late eighties, and I knew it would be impossible for them to process the complicated story and its dramatic outcome immediately. They would need time to reflect on all that I had to reveal. I would not be visiting them again for several months, and this news could not wait. So I sat down to write yet another crucial letter. The following is the letter I mailed to them five days after Merideth and I had met for first time.

January 8, 2001

Dear Mom and Dad,

I have the most wonderful news. I didn't want to tell you over the phone on Sunday because it just seemed so much, so I decided to wait and write it all down so you can get the whole story from start to finish.

If you've looked yet at the pictures I've enclosed, you'll see they are of a young woman who looks a lot like me. And in fact, she is my daughter. Her name is Merideth Mae and she's 35 years old. She lives in New Jersey, with her husband, Michael, and her 3 children: Michaela (7), Drew (5), and Emma (2). Now for the story:

The book I have written is about contemporary memoirs by women and in it, I interweave my own memoir about my teenage pregnancy, going to Akron, and giving up my daughter for ahdoption. It's a sad story and one that I didn't really want you to read, but I was going to face that bridge when I came to it when the book actually came out. But I did let Todd, Helen, and Kezia read it. They've known about Merideth forever (though, of course, they didn't know her name was Merideth), but they knew they had a half-sister that I gave up before they were born.

Helen asked me if she could give a chapter of the book to her friend Debbie, who is adopted and who has been searching for her birthmother. I said of course, and hoped that it would give Debbie some comfort to know that her birthmother most likely thought about her often. In searching for her birthmother, Debbie has been in touch with a sort of adoption search group called "On Angels Wings." She decided to ask this group if they might have information about a baby girl born on March 20, 1965 in Akron, Ohio. A woman in Mississippi got back to Debbie right away with information about Merideth—the only baby born on that date in Akron who was given up for adoption. Debbie called Helen with the information, and Helen called Kezia. They had Merideth's maiden name—Merideth Mae ——. They then found by way of "Ancestry.com" her married name, and then they came to me with the information. I was overjoyed. We then went to "peoplefind.com" with Merideth's birth date and full name. And, that's how we found out that she lived in New Jersey. We were given her address and phone number.

The next step was to write the most carefully composed letter of my life. I gave her lots of options, making it clear that she need not establish a relationship with me, but to please just let me know if it was possible that she was my first daughter. The day she received the letter, she both cried and laughed, and then she called me right up on the phone. We had a wonderful first talk, and I can't tell you how happy I was to learn that she has had a good life, a very happy life, and that she had always wanted to be able to tell me that.

We talked again and I sent her pictures, and when she found out we were going to be in New York City for part of the holidays, she asked if we could meet. And we did. We traveled down to Southern New Jersey last Wednesday and were greeted by Michaela's "Welcome Janet and John" sign. When I saw that, all my nervousness melted away. Then all Merideth and I could do really was to stare at each other. She is so beautiful, so accomplished, so smart. She is happily married to Michael, who is a wonderful husband and father, and the mother of 3 precious children. Her parents adopted two more children after her, so she has two brothers. When she was 7, her parents divorced and her mother moved with her 3 children from Ohio to New Jersey to be near her sister, Helen. So Merideth and her brothers were raised there. She graduated from Douglass College at Rutgers—in journalism—and has worked in sales and marketing for 12 years. Sadly, she lost her mother three years ago. When she had Emma, she decided she wanted to stay home with her for awhile, but her employers just wouldn't let her go and let her cut her hours back to just two days a week on site and one day at home if she would stay with them. Michael is in the motel business and they have a beautiful home—cozy, warm, and welcoming.

We had a wonderful visit. I can't tell you how good I felt just seeing her. It was simply one of the best days of my life. As you can see from the pictures, she is tall, like me, and unfortunately I gave her my penchant for ear infections, and she also has a hearing loss. There's still so much we want to learn about each other, and we have decided that we will keep in touch, visit, and have a relationship. I'm not sure what it will be like. Probably more like sisters than mother and daughter, but we definitely are not going to lose touch with each other again. She can't wait to meet Todd and Maria (and Isla), Helen, and Kezia. In turn, they can't wait to meet her and Michael and their children.

So I have this wonderful news and I wanted to be able to share it with you. I know you will understand how much this reunion means to me. Although I never spoke of how hard it was to lose her, I know you knew that I was at a loss for years as to how to make an emotionally complete life. But I did learn how, and I have John and my own 3 precious children to show for it.

So, life just gave me this huge gift by bringing Merideth back after 35 years. I hope you can share in our joy and take comfort in knowing that she had a good life, that she made her mother the happiest of women, and that she is now happy to be found and eager to know us. I told her we were a family of huge hearts, a family where love has no limits.

I hope this news will give you the same kind of peace that it gives me, knowing that one chapter in my life closes happily and a new one opens, full of promise. I am sure you thought this was a chapter of the past and that you probably wouldn't choose to open it now, but I hope you can share in this wonderful discovery with me, John, and your grandchildren. Everybody I have told the story to is amazed and overjoyed. To me, it still seems unreal, but it is real, wonderfully so. I hope you can share my excitement and my joy.

I love you both so very much.

My mother and father surprised me. They immediately responded to my letter with pleasure. Like Merideth, they too called right away, just as soon as they had reread my letter and poured over the pictures I had sent of Merideth and me, and of Merideth, Michael, and their three new great-grandchildren. They were elated, and I was greatly relieved. The distress I assumed my book's revelations would cause dropped away. They wanted to write Merideth a letter themselves, so I gave them her address, unsure of what they might say but trusting them all the same.

Merideth had been uneasy about my parents' response but not out of concern for her own acceptance. She was worried about me. She knew I was nervous about telling them, and she readily understood that my fears had to do with breaking decades of silence, not from any shame about her. So she shared my relief when I told her my parents had called me to say how good it was that she had been found.

Since my parents and I had never talked about Sorrow, it had been impossible for me to conceptualize in what ways they had thought about her over the years or, for that matter, if they had even done so. The following is the letter they sent to Merideth:

Dear Merideth,

It is hard to describe the pleasure we felt when we received Janet's letter telling us how you were found, your meeting with Janet, your family, and history. The pictures are unbelievable.

There are some experiences in life wherein decisions are made that you are never sure are correct, so you draw a veil over the event. The memory never goes away, but the veil helps you live with it. You and Janet have lifted the veil and we are more grateful than we can express.

The above part of this letter was written by your grandfather. He also says, "Isn't it great this happened while we are still here?" I agree. We are both so delighted to hear all about you. He can pull the veil over things much better than I can. I wondered about you most of the time and didn't like to bring up the subject, so I tried not to. I agree it is wonderful that they found you while we are still here. My prayers have been answered.

I am enclosing pictures of us. They are old pictures—one at our 50th anniversary and another of about the same vintage. We'll get some new ones to send later. We are now going to celebrate our 67th in August. This makes us sort of reluctant to pose.

You have suddenly acquired a couple of aunts, a few uncles, a lot of cousins and even a couple of great aunts and even a great uncle. It will take you a long time to get to know us all, but it should be fun. We are glad you are going to Wilmington at spring break to meet Kezia and

Helen. We think you will like all of us, we really think we have a very fun family. However, we will admit that there is a possibility that we may be prejudiced.

Our grandchildren all call us "Mase" and "Pop." My maiden name was Mason so my college nickname was short for Mason. It will be 70 years this September since I sat down next to Pop in a Political Science class and that did it.

I'll write again, but in the meantime don't be scared of all these strange people that are going to love you. We have been hoping to be able to do that for a lot of years.

Lots of love to you and your family,

Mase & Pop

Martha's Vineyard, 2004

My mother and father's letter to Merideth was not only extraordinarily moving for me but also illuminating. In writing it, they broke through the veil that had separated us since Sorrow's birth. Now, my father's words helped me to understand how they had managed through the years to keep Sorrow's existence unspoken. It was simply their way of living with a difficult decision. What amazed me most was my father's implicit acknowledgment that they had never been completely sure that they had done the right thing. I had never suspected my parents worried over that decision. They always seemed so entrenched in the correctness of all the choices they had made in life, and I assumed they felt sure that this decision had been right as well. I was also astonished by my mother's pronouncement that she had always wondered about Sorrow. I had supposed that my mother and father had felt unrelated to that baby, that she was someone else's child for whom they bore no responsibility and felt no concern. She had been given away and that was the end of it, or so I thought. Now I learned that she had always been on their minds and even in my mother's prayers.

Finding Merideth was not just psychologically and emotionally good for me but for our entire family. It turns out that none of us had ever forgotten her. We had all been worried about her over the years. We had all had doubts about the seemingly incontrovertible decisions that had been made in 1965. And amazingly, we were all so glad that somehow those decisions had been overcome, that we could have a chance to know her, her husband, and her children. She had been erased from our daily lives but never from our dreams. Now we all could celebrate her return and in so doing heal those disabling silences that had haunted us for too long.

I would like to write here that all that I had lost was now returned, that all my pain had been vanquished. But I cannot. I realize now that I will always be drawn back to that shattered girl—Jan Mason—always returning to the gray room at Florence Crittenton, so sadly emptied, my depleted body, my sore breasts, overwhelmed by an unquenchable longing to hold a baby. In my memory, I still pace that dreary room at night, sleepless and sorrowful. Looking back now, I have to conclude that I was a bit crazy for a while there—like some madwoman in the attic walking up and down the length of that noiseless, stuffy room, or rocking back and forth on my musty bed, clutching a lifeless pillow. During those long nights, I would stuff the pillow under my nightgown and curl my body around it to try to feel the baby's weight again. Or I would cradle it in my arms, or press it against my breasts. I can understand all too well why women unhinged by the loss of a baby will sometimes latch onto a doll as a kind of mad replacement.

Even knowing what I do now—that Sorrow went on to become Merideth, that she brought joy and love to her mother, her father, and brothers' lives, that she became a contributing member of a community of coworkers, friends, and neighbors, that she grew up to be a loving and responsible wife and mother in her own right—it still feels cruel that I was left alone in that deserted room. Without my baby, without comfort, I was abandoned with nothing to hold onto and no one to hold onto me. Beyond logic, beyond decades of reflection on that room and that time, beyond Merideth's very real presence in my life, still an unappeasable and irrevocable loss lives on, so that even as I write these words, I weep once again for Sorrow.

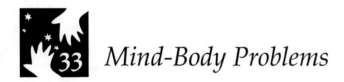 # Mind-Body Problems

THE DAY WE RETURNED to North Carolina, I immediately and again, painstakingly, composed my next letter to Merideth, thanking her for welcoming us into her home and into her life. I also extended an invitation to her and her family to come to Wilmington for Easter. We had talked about the possibility of them visiting North Carolina, but I wanted to make it official, and I made it a point to tell her that they could stay with us. My friends and family were surprised that I had asked them to stay with us rather than reserving rooms in the B and B across the street. Wasn't it risky, inviting an entire family that we had only met for a few hours to stay in our home for five days? It didn't feel risky to me. I was eager to spend as much time as possible with Merideth and her husband and children.

My letter had gone off to Merideth just as she was sending a letter that underscored the success of our first meeting. She wrote:

> Dear Janet,
>
> Michael and I really appreciated you making the long trek down to see us and our home. I hope that seeing me here gave you a better understanding of me and my life.
>
> Your candid recounts of experiences you've had throughout your life certainly helped me to know you better. I can't express my sorrow for all that you endured while carrying and delivering me. I hope the fact that I am no longer lost to you can help to ease the sadness of that time.

The day after your visit I had what seemed like an endless stream of phone calls from excited family members all waiting to hear about you. As I told you, my family has been so supportive and happy for me. And they are all so eager to meet you!

Besides my family, I've shared our story with several close friends, who went on to share it with practically everyone I know. This was made clear to me today when I finally made it into my office. I haven't been in to work since receiving your first letter. I was overwhelmed by the compassionate and joyful response of my friends and coworkers. Needless to say I accomplished very little actual "work." Everyone wanted to see the pictures you had sent, to hear the story again of how you found me, and to ask questions, and more questions. It's a pretty tight knit group of people that I work with, and I've been there forever, so many of us are very close. Everyone who has seen your pictures has said what a beautiful family you have.

Michael and I have been talking about a trip to see you, John and the rest of your family. I am so looking forward to meeting Todd, Maria, Helen and Kezia. We are trying to figure out a way to come down at Easter. This visit, of course, is completely up to you. If that time frame isn't convenient for you we can surely plan for another time.

Since you left I've thought of so many questions, like—what's your favorite color, your favorite author, your favorite time of the day, why did you become a teacher, how did you receive a doctorate while raising three children alone, what kind of music do you like, what did my father say when you told him about me, what was your proudest moment, what's your favorite flavor of ice cream, what are some of your happiest childhood memories, how did John propose, what's your favorite holiday. The list could go on and on! What an intimate connection we have and yet we know so little about one another.

I believe that God has granted me a wonderful gift. Most people in this world are fortunate to have one mother, and I have been given two. The wonderful, loving woman who raised me and the gentle, kind and gracious woman I have found in you.

I'll try to write often. Please call whenever you'd like. Take care.

With love,

Merideth

Plans were clearly underway for a family reunion at Easter, and I was overjoyed. Nonetheless, finding Merideth, meeting Merideth, and informing my parents, all these changes took an unforeseen toll on me. The new semester had just begun at the university and after holding my second day of classes, I returned to my office to find that I could not bend over to pick up my book bag. My back had locked up; I simply could not make it bend. This was a first for me. I had had minor backaches before, but they were never disabling and always disappeared after a few days' rest.

The cause of this rebelling back was elusive: I had not lifted anything heavy, I had not taken a fall, I had not been spending long hours at the computer or in my garden, I had not taken on any overly ambitious tasks. Yet here I was, frozen in a standing position that I could not explain. It was as if some diabolical wizard had touched me with his wand and turned me into stone. I finally figured a way to retrieve my book bag by squatting down and grabbing it, and I managed to get home by flinging myself into my car and behind the steering wheel and dragging myself out of the low-slung seat by my arms once I reached our house. By the time John got home later that evening, I was flattened out on our couch, feeling like a beached whale. It was as if I was paralyzed. I could wiggle my toes, my feet, and my legs, but when I tried to sit up or turn over, my lower back simply would not respond. I could barely move.

John had to help me get up, turn over, change my clothes—it was humiliating. I had turned into the baby that my own Nurse Ratched had accused me of being long ago in that wretched taxi cab on the night of Merideth's birth. This time, like then, all I could do was whimper.

I like to think of myself as being very physically fit—even tough. Oh, I suffered broken bones as a child; I have had my share of sore muscles from riding horses, climbing mountains, snow skiing, running 5 Ks; I have given birth four times. But now, after years and years of trustworthy resiliency, my body was failing me.

I am not one to put much credence in psychosomatic illness, yet clearly my locked-up back must have had much more to do with emotional tension than with my vertebrae. A friend who had recently suffered through similar incapacitating back pain told me bluntly, "You need drugs." The next day, I canceled my classes—something I'm loath to do—and hobbled into my doctor's office. Somehow I managed to perch on the examining table as unwanted tears dripped off my chin. I still couldn't quite accept that I wasn't going to be able to just tough it out.

The superefficient nurse practitioner breezed in and after a cursory examination, prescribed pain relief, muscle relaxants, and bed rest and gave me a worn photocopy of special exercises for the lower back. Clearly I wasn't the first person this has happened to, but it was new to me and disconcerting. Sheer will couldn't see me through this! Then again, was it new to me? Was it not once again a repetition of the original trauma? As I drifted into the warm stupor brought on by a Vicodin and a muscle relaxer, I couldn't help but remember the night of Sorrow's birth, the night that it took a tranquilizer to numb the pain and put me under. For two more days I lay in a cloudy, medicated drowsiness, interrupted now and then when John kindly brought me milk shakes and helped me to the bathroom. And then, seemingly overnight, my back was better—much better. I got out of bed and resumed my life. But the problem would occasionally return, and its return was always connected to contact with Merideth.

Was I getting so tense for these encounters that the anxiety would cause muscle spasms? Why, after all those years of being in excellent health despite my battle with insomnia, would I now, having found Merideth, suffer this setback? I eagerly anticipated our conversations and looked forward to her visit, yet I was incapacitated by frustrating pain and immobility. And then there is the weird repetitiousness of my cure, even the number of days it took me to heal and the food I craved. Surely there is a lesson here about the symbiosis of mind and body, of the deep rivers of unconscious fears and anxiety that flow through all the muscles of the body.

My reunion with Merideth continued in its positive manner. We had started out well and the new bond grew. Everything that could have gone wrong didn't. She was kind, warm, and eager to plan for our next meeting. My back "breakdown" is testimony to the immensity of our coming together. My well-being seemed to hinge on this new relationship. To find the all-important, singular person in my life who could put right what had been so wrong was staggering. Over the years of our separation, I had learned to live without her, not always well, but well enough. Now I could lose her all over again and this time, it would not be because of powerful adults who decided my fate, but because of something I did wrong, because I was not someone she would want to know. That pressure left me with an "Achilles' heel" that can still be exacerbated by emotional tension. Even though I thought I had always wanted to be the carefree vagabond, taking life as a lark, in fact I have always taken things much too seriously.

By the time Easter approached, Merideth and I had exchanged long letters. When she asked, "What did my birth father say when you told him about me?" I needed the breathing space that writing allows to relate that problematic moment:

January 27, 2001

When I told your father about you, well it's kind of amazing because at first, he didn't believe me. That's how secret you had been kept. He just couldn't accept that I had had you without him ever knowing you were even conceived. After talking for awhile and lots of tears on my part, he did come to believe me. I wish I could tell you that he was really sorry that you had been given away. I certainly wanted him to share in my sorrow. But instead he said there would have been nothing he could have done. When I asked him if he would have married me so we could have kept you, he simply said "no." I have to admit that that hurt a lot, and I still have some resentment that he could be so emotionally removed from it all. In the book that I've written, I refer to him as "Alec," and I'm afraid my resentment is even more tangible. I hope that won't be difficult for you to read. It was strange to see that you resemble him. He had so little to do with the creation of you, except there he is, indubitably, in your eyes and the shape of your nose. But, I want you to know that I am sure he is a kind, generous, and loving man. Remember that I was deeply in love with him, and for good reasons, but it was painful that he didn't love me in return with the same emotional intensity, and I felt betrayed for many years. Someday, you may decide to contact him and I would be supportive of that, but protective of you as well. I don't want you to feel rejection, so I would want you to go into it without any expectations. Of course, I find you so absolutely wonderful that it seems unfair in a way that he not know you are here in this world. I think he would be just amazed at your beauty, intelligence, poise, accomplishments, and your gorgeous children! And I know he would be thankful that you have had a good, complete and happy life. But I just don't really know him—it's been so long that I think I've probably made him into an imaginary man rather than the real man he is today.

Your conception was such a mystery and so miraculous really. But I know you were meant to be conceived and born for special reasons, that you have a purpose for being here. I've always known that and I'm glad I was able to bring you here.

Martha's Vineyard, 2004

Merideth did eventually contact Alec. My oldest friend, Karen, had "googled" him, and there he was, picture and all. How difficult it is to hide these days. Merideth sent him a kind letter with pictures of her and her family, and he e-mailed her back, a brief note wishing her well but also making it clear that no further contact would be desirable. I was appalled by his dismissal. His rebuff still seems unnaturally cold-hearted. His response to her makes me realize how different I am from the sixteen-year-old girl I have re-created for these pages, how far I have moved away from loving "him," whoever he was, with that unhealthy, idealized adoration of adolescence.

Looking back from this viewpoint of my life, I can recognize his unfeeling, unexplained rejections of me as heartless. I once interpreted the sporadic crumbs of his affection as positive signs that he would finally find his way back to me. Now I see them plainly as the signs of a fickle young man who, when he was without a girlfriend or some other consuming passion, would seek me out and then just as quickly cast me off. He never felt that inextricable link between us that I was so certain was there, yet he played with it, knowing my heartstrings were innocently tied to him. While I championed him for years and years, I was, in fact, simply one of many inconsequential memories.

I was sorry that Alec had dismissed Merideth's overture, but I was also relieved. I did not want to have to see him at my grandchildren's graduations or weddings. My disinclination to share Merideth with Alec helps me understand how difficult it must be for adoptive parents to see birth parents come into their children's lives. It is good that I know the fear of being usurped. Had Alec chosen to develop a relationship with Merideth, it would have been easy to see him as an intruder and Merideth's interest in him as a betrayal.

Maybe someday, he'll change his mind and contact her. If so, I know I must be understanding. She is, after all, Alec's child too. But then again, she is neither his nor mine, nor was she Anne's. Finally, we have little claim on our adult children. Their love and devotion is theirs to grant or withhold. Merideth's love for me is her gift, not her obligation. I would have it no other way.

34 Coming Home

Wilmington, Easter 2001

MAUNDY THURSDAY, the day for the reconciliation of all penitents and the consecration of the holy oils, the day of Merideth and Michael's arrival in Wilmington. It was unusually warm and humid even by Southern standards, but far from enervated, I was primed with energy and, as is my nature, more than prepared for the visit. In the weeks before, John and I had put a bright, fresh coat of periwinkle paint on the walls of the room where Merideth would sleep, polished the pine floorboards, assiduously cleaned the rest of the house, raked the yard, filled the flower beds with new annuals, and packed the refrigerator to the brim. Kezia was driving home from Charlotte; both she and Helen were eager to meet their half-sister.

The days that followed did not produce any gauzy, Hollywood moments of discovery and redemption; Merideth and I didn't stop to search each other's eyes for profundity. Instead, we just had fun. We spent our time at the beach and at our local tourist attractions. They were sunny days, the only real tension occurring when two-year-old Emma became inconsolable when we were climbing up and down ladders and through hatches, deep in the belly of the battleship U.S.S. North Carolina, which sits directly across the Cape Fear River from downtown Wilmington. Although Helen and Kezia were nervous about meeting Merideth, they were immediately charmed by her as she was by them. I had meticulously planned each day's activities and meals, and rather than finding

my ultra-organization over the top, Merideth appreciated my preparations. We have learned that we are both fairly obsessive planners and
like to leave little to chance.

We decided to have a small, informal evening gathering for Merideth and Michael and their children so that our friends could meet
them too. By now we had shared the story with many, and they came
with flowers and gifts—not to gawk at Merideth but to share in our
joy. There was no precedent for this fete—at least none that I knew
of. There was one person that I invited who called to decline, adding
pointedly that she thought Merideth's visit should just be a time for
Merideth to get to know us, not to be put on display. That response
gave me pause, but Merideth assured me she and Michael would enjoy
the party, and when I saw how much fun they did have, I knew my
friend had been mistaken.

The party had the air of a "welcome home" celebration: welcome
to this family and to this circle of friends. Children were in abundance,
dashing through the house from backyard to front, only stopping to
grab handfuls of M&Ms as they passed the dining room table. Merideth
was completely relaxed, glad to have the chance to meet our friends,
and by doing so, she remarked, she came to know us even better.

Miraculously, everything we planned for the visit went well. Slowly,
my nervousness dissipated. Merideth took a picture of me that sums up
the holiday. There I am, casual as ever in shorts and a T-shirt, standing on the sidewalk in front of our house with my coffee mug in hand,
Michaela, Drew, and Emma posing sweetly on either side of me. I look
natural, relaxed, and happily content. I'm a young grandmother, but
the picture makes clear how pleased I am with my new role, and my
grandchildren seem equally elated.

I didn't sleep much during the visit. I found myself lying awake,
alert and amazed that Merideth, Michael, and my grandchildren slept
in the next rooms. I mused on the restorative power of disclosure. It was
only two years ago that I had begun to tell with much trepidation the
secret of Sorrow. Now on these warm April nights, I sighed with a sense
of wholeness that I had never imagined for myself. Finally and forever,
my daughter had come home.

*Janet, Michaela, Drew,
and Emma at Easter,
2001. Photograph by
John Clifford. Courtesy
of the author.*

Martha's Vineyard, 2004

Several years have passed since that first Easter homecoming. Merideth and I have become fast friends, close sisters, beloved aunt and niece, a kind of mother to an already-grown daughter—all of those describe our relationship, but not precisely. We are, of course, biologically mother and daughter, but because we were separated for thirty-five years, we have had to build a relationship with no ready models to follow, no established parameters to conform to. We have explored new territory for the heart.

I have come to know Merideth in the most stable time of my life. I have finally and forever left off my pursuit of the tambourine man; gone is the desire to go under his dizzy, dancing spell. I love my husband; I have a marriage that will last; I live in my own home and work at my own fulfilling career. I have raised my children and still support them emotionally when I can. They know they can turn to me whenever their own security is shaky. Merideth is caught in the sometimes frantic but secure web of raising her own children and pursuing her career as well. I'm not Merideth's mother in the way that I am for my other three children, but then, each of them asks different things of me. And as in my relationship with Todd, Helen, and Kezia, I feel I have achieved a sense of secure constancy with Merideth.

Because Merideth's life is so stable, grounded as it is in a tight community, an active church and family life, a secure work environment among not just coworkers but among friends, it seemed to me at first that she had no need for me. I was a part of her family structure because I was her birthmother, but her life was complete and safe; I was a welcome but unnecessary addition. She had been returned to me with an already intact support system, one that lonely people would envy greatly. This was fine. I know that relationships based on want rather than need are much more likely to be successful, and although I needed Merideth in my life to feel complete, I did not want to be an additional burden to her already overly committed life.

Spring 2003

When Merideth called to tell me she was pregnant with her fourth child, I was glad for her and for Michael. Four children make for a big family these days. In my circle of friends, I am the only one with four children. Most of my friends and coworkers are either childless or they have one child upon whom they shower carefully selected educational toys and to whom they give uninterrupted quality time when the child is not attending his or her expensive preschool. Friends raised their eyebrows when I told them Merideth was pregnant with her fourth.

But I understood Merideth and Michael's desire for another child. Like me, Merideth's children furnish her with the major part of the happiness she gets from life. Our careers are fulfilling and necessary to our sense of worth, but we both agree it's our children for which we feel that fiercest pride, it's our family that gives us our sense of well-being. For years after Kezia's birth, I had wanted a fourth child. Perhaps my desire for one more baby was not healthy; I know I was still hoping to fill the emptiness that was Sorrow. My children did bring me a healing happiness. Why not more?

Then, one afternoon as John and I drove home from Raleigh, our cell phone rang. John answered. It was Merideth. He quickly passed the phone to me, mouthing silently, "Something's wrong." Following my eager "Hello," I heard a small, shaky voice, a voice I had never heard before: "I lost the baby." And then, Merideth began to cry. This was a heartbreaking experience for her, something, for which she was emotionally unprepared. She had never miscarried. Pregnancy to her meant a baby, but this time, the embryo that had just begun to form flickered out quickly. As I offered murmurs of condolence and understanding, her voice began to steady.

She told me the details, how she and Michael had been together when the doctor gently told them he could not find a heartbeat, how they had held each other and cried together. She told me about her physical condition, that she would be fine after a weekend of rest. And I told her again and again that I was so sorry this baby had slipped away, that I knew how painful this day was, that I didn't underestimate her sense of loss, that I knew this passing would always hurt, that her grieving was justified and right. I called her "sweetheart" for the first time, an endearment I have always used for Todd, Helen, and Kezia. I told her that I loved her, that she could weather this, that her tears were valid and vital. I used all the words I could find that would offer comfort and soothe her loss. I said to her what my parents could not say to me: "Turn to me; turn to me; let me help you; I am here with you always, without fail." In saying those words that a mother can give her daughter, I did help her. I helped her through that day and then the next and then through the weeks that followed. I knew intimately that her grief was not small.

Out of this loss came the knowledge that Merideth and I will be connected as mother and daughter for the rest of our lives. The link between us is mutual and strong. We can turn to each other in times of need and sorrow. Our commitment is secure.

Merideth needed me twice in the first thirty-eight years of her life. Once, in the very first minutes of her life, when I was not allowed to help her. I was not permitted to offer her the love and care I wanted so badly to give and that she, a helpless newborn, urgently cried out for. But years upon years later, she reached out to me to ease her pain. And now I could.

San Diego, Thanksgiving 2003

Merideth has been afraid to fly since her son Drew was born. Returning from long business trips, feeling desperate to get home to her baby, she had had to endure some torturous bad weather landings. Still, despite her fear, she has decided to make the trip to Southern California to meet her grandparents (Mase and Pop), her aunts, uncles, cousins, and their children. Merideth, Michael, and the children had met Mase when she had traveled to the East Coast to attend a Mason family reunion, but Pop was already unable to travel. Now Pop is ninety-one and frail; Mase is ninety and sometimes befuddled by details; my sister Anne is living with pancreatic cancer, a precarious journey of its own. It's time, Merideth decides, to make this trip before the infirmities of age and illness make this reunion impractical. And so we make plans to meet in San Diego for Thanksgiving. It will be a big gathering: the two great-grandparents, the three sisters—Katie, Anne, and me—our spouses, six of our children, four of their spouses, and seven of the great-grandchildren. And there is even more cause for joyful anticipation because Merideth is pregnant again and well into her second trimester. There will be no miscarriage this time.

Planes arrive, pickups are handled, and we all gradually assemble. Merideth weathers the flight well, her composure holding steady even through the unsettling landing that everyone who flies into San Diego must face. Most of us stay at the inn close by Mase and Pop's condominium. It's a warm, sun-drenched California afternoon, and Michaela is standing on the balcony of her family's room, eager to get down to the pool below her. She sees a familiar-looking man playing with two children in the pool and calls out in her chirpy voice, "Hi Uncle Mark!" She's never seen Mark, my sister's son, in person before, but Michaela is a bright girl with a good eye and she has recognized him from pictures I've showed her.

Mark is confused for a moment. He thinks to himself, "Who is this little girl who clearly knows me? After all, she's calling me 'Uncle Mark.'"

Merideth walks out on the balcony to see who Michaela is talking to. Catching sight of Merideth, Mark calls out, "Hi Janet!"

Merideth pauses and looks around for me.

"Wait," Mark thinks. "That's not Janet! Wait a second . . . that's . . . that's Janet's daughter. That's Merideth!"

"Sorry!" he calls; "Hi Merideth! I'm Mark. I thought you were my Aunt Janet."

Again our uncanny resemblance is both surprising and confirming.

Michaela charges down to the pool to play with her new cousins, Samantha and Jake. Drew and Emma join them and soon two more cousins arrive, Matt and Andy. There are now seven children romping in the pool, ages ranging from ten to two. Without any attention given to formalities, the children begin to play. They are all already excellent swimmers except for the two-year-old, but even he can dog paddle. These seven children are not identical, certainly, but they share the same lithe, athletic bodies that my sisters and I inherited from our parents.

Michaela, Drew, and Emma have never hesitated in establishing the ties that now bind our family. They have a host of aunts, uncles, and cousins in southern New Jersey, and now they have a host of aunts, uncles, and cousins in Southern California. That their mother, Merideth, had for decades been an unacknowledged shadow in this sunlit landscape is irrelevant to them. They are unabashedly here in the present, enfolded into a family that greets them as if they had always been here. No one hesitates. These children rightfully feel the warmth that all children should feel when surrounded by their large and rowdy extended family.

Later that day up at my sister's home, they join their screeching, rambunctious cousins and tear across their Aunt Katie's temporarily white carpet, out the sliding doors, and around her pool. Neither the children, nor Merideth, nor Michael needs me to make them feel at home. My family embraces them all naturally, as if they were never gone.

The days in California pass smoothly. We enjoy each other's company, especially on Thanksgiving Day as we gather together to feast on turkey, give thanks for our homecoming, and laugh heartily with the kids as they conduct mad-dash balloon races around the swimming pool. With dismay, I notice my sister's white carpet has now turned to a shade of gray, victim of the ash from recent forest fires that we have tramped into the house. My trepidation about being the guilty one, the black sheep no matter what, comes rushing back. Am I going to get in trouble for this ruined carpet? Am I the one who will be held accountable? Some roles in a family are apparently impossible to relinquish.

Nonetheless, I can see how much my mother and father love Merideth—there's no question about that. She is home for the holidays. Though I may never be able to completely escape feeling guilty for disrupting their lives, today, we celebrate.

Martha's Vineyard, 2004

And so, it seems we have a happy ending. Our Thanksgiving feast was akin to those held in millions of homes all over America. We will live on in accordance with Tolstoy's famous axiom of *Anna Karenina* that all happy families are happy in the same way—complete, undivided, loyal, entwined. The lost child, whose absence had kindled our unhappiness and kept us unique for so long, had been returned. The cast-out granddaughter, sacrificed to obsolete appearances, had come home.

Why do I want to paint such a perfect picture? Nothing is ever as unproblematic as that. Whatever secret, painful thoughts my parents, my sisters, or my children harbored on that holiday, I will never know. If there were diverse agendas or self-serving motivations, they were set aside. We seemed to have an intuitive sense of the performance that was necessary—a sort of mutual ritual of grateful acceptance. We did not slay a fatted calf, but we celebrated Merideth's homecoming in no less a ceremonial manner.

We were restored, and yet . . .

 *And Yet*

Martha's Vineyard, 2004

HOW TO ACCOUNT for Merideth's successful homecoming? What changed in our family and in our particular (though not unique) version of American culture from 1965 to 2000? We could not speak of her for so long, yet now we could welcome her home.

Perhaps the reasons are to be found in evolving social attitudes toward sex, parenthood, and marriage, as well as in the shifting social practices that determine how we will respond to unwanted or unplanned pregnancies. Today, less than 3 percent of unmarried white women choose adoption when coping with an unplanned pregnancy. In 1965, when I became pregnant with Merideth, almost 20 percent of unmarried white women (half of whom were teenagers) placed their babies for adoption. It is no wonder that when I was at the Florence Crittenton Home, most of the girls were a lot like me. Although we felt like social outcasts, singular in our exile, we were, in fact, part of the social strata of that time that fed the adoption industry with healthy white babies.

"Unwed mother" and "illegitimate child" were demeaning labels that we wanted to escape, and the shame of such labels was immediately transformed as soon as adoptive parents stepped in. Our humiliation became their blessing. They wanted our babies, and they were judged by those with authority to be much more qualified for parenthood. Therefore, a socially sanctioned system was in put place that resulted in a steady output of healthy newborns produced by young girls made to feel incapable and unworthy.

But cultures change. Mothers who make adoption plans today may still be judged as ill prepared for parenthood, but they are also commended for making a noble choice. Often they are coddled and congratulated by pro-life advocates. If they are white, they are aggressively courted by couples willing to pay up to $30,000 for a private adoption. If I were carrying Sorrow today, I would be a precious commodity with a valuable product to offer. A couple looking to adopt would gladly pay for my room, board, and medical care throughout my pregnancy and delivery. It would be against the law for them to actually pay me for my baby, but they could indulge me with travel, clothes, and other "perks."

Clearly, attitudes about adoption have shifted, but for my family, accepting Merideth after decades of concealment probably had more to do with the near-eradication of fifties sexual mores than anything else. Today, more than one-third of all births are to unmarried women who are neither secreted away in "maternity homes" nor judged as sexually ruined. The stigmas of "unwed mother" and "illegitimate child" have been almost entirely erased. If statistics remain stable, this year over a million children will be born outside of marriage and will be embraced by their mothers, fathers, and extended families. The premium that was put on virginity forty years ago has disappeared. If a young woman decides not to have intercourse until her wedding night, her friends will most likely look upon her as foolishly misguided because of the practical possibility of sexual incompatibility. Conservative politicians and religious leaders may still preach abstinence, but in fact, sex is usually not put off until marriage.

The sexual revolution has been so widespread and thorough that even my thoroughly traditional parents, now in their nineties, have been fundamentally changed. In 1969, when I was twenty-one, my parents still expected me to be celibate even if I could no longer be virginal. When they discovered that I had spent time alone with my boyfriend in his apartment, they refused to let me live unchaperoned for my last year of college. Now, even for them, premarital sex is expected. They did not hesitate to reserve only one room at their neighborhood inn for their granddaughter and her boyfriend to share when they came to California for our Thanksgiving family reunion.

What else made it possible to bring Merideth out of exile? In 1965 we were a culture obsessed with discretion and concealment. The media never pried into JFK's flagrant affairs, yet whether we wanted it or not, Kenneth Starr insisted we learn the most intimate sexual peccadilloes of Bill Clinton and Monica Lewinsky.

The culture of disclosure has even reached my parents—up to a point. My mother well understands that secrets can be unhealthy and will often talk about the past, unless my father is around, that is. If he is there, he consistently shushes her with a "Now, now" and a dismissing hand gesture that signifies the end of this particular conversation. My mother always complies, although I can feel her frustration. My parents will never be able to casually speak of my father's brother. His excision from family lore was for them permanent. Only in future generations will we be able to talk of Richard, struggle with his inconceivable actions, and work through the enormity of his desperation. Nonetheless, although my father deeply resists personal disclosure and would never turn the channel to *Oprah* on a quiet afternoon, he understands the benefits of facing some demons from the past. He readily admits that he has found a greater peace of mind now that Merideth has been found and taken her place in our family.

Like my father, I am not fond of talk shows, yet indubitably, Oprah, Geraldo, and Montel have influenced me, my family, and our culture. We have become a nation of witnesses to confessions. Pop psychology encourages us to plumb our pasts and tell all. Harboring secrets, we are told, can be poisonous to our mental and physical health. The confessional memoir has become the genre du jour.

Having confessed my own secret in my first book and reaped tremendous psychological benefits, I could understandably promote public confessions without qualification. But there are hidden dangers lurking in the seemingly benign seas of honesty. My revelations proved successful because I had a tight-knit, dependable safety net that included my husband, my children, my extended family, and my friends. I could take the risk and tell all because I had a net to catch me if the results turned negative and left me in an emotional free fall. Although my telling gave me a happy outcome, the net still had to work for me. When I sat down to that

Thanksgiving dinner and watched my family interact, I felt the strong secure chords of that net.

Almost forty years have passed since Merideth and I were separated.
In 1965, I had no options and perhaps my parents didn't either. Now, there
are several options for dealing with an unplanned pregnancy, and young
women are choosing adoption less and less. Yet when they do, some things
haven't changed. Birthmothers are still expected to fade into the shadows
after giving birth while the spotlight focuses almost exclusively on the
adoptive parents. The new parents' happiness is celebrated and honored
by our culture. We so love happy endings that almost all adoption narratives are still cast in this positive light. But they remain oblivious to the
suffering girl left alone in a bleak, gray room.

Maybe this will change. Maybe. On the day I first met Meredith, Drew,
only six years old, accepted without question that Merideth had two mommies. His ready acceptance may be a key to this conundrum. The heart is
expansive. It can grow to make room for the newcomers in our lives. It
can expand to encompass new family configurations. Merideth captured
my feeling exactly when she remarked on how it felt to become part of my
family as well as the family who had adopted her: "The human heart is
relatively boundless, I believe. There's no cap on how many people you
can love or to what degree. So there's plenty of room for all of us to have
this wonderful extended family."

Mother and daughter. We look alike, sound alike, we have many of
the same gestures, the same habits, the same values. We were always connected, always linked by blood, by the heart's longing. Our separation
was heartbreaking and did not have to happen. A culture can change and
still maintain one of its most essential fundamentals: family is essential—
all of the family.

The River

> You cannot step into the same
> river twice; for new waters
> are always flowing on to you.
> —Heraclitus

Southern New Jersey, March 2004

CORRECTING THE MISTAKES of our past is the stuff of fantasy, of wistful daydreams. Occasionally we can make small amends through apology or renewed effort, but those opportunities are rare. More often we resign ourselves to pensive regret. We live for years with disabling memories, we try to overcome our losses by giving thanks for what we do have, we enter therapy to work through lingering symptoms, we write narratives, hoping they will finally put to rest the nagging pain. And then there are moments of grace and insight that seldom come through conscious will or preparation. They surprise and grant us new understandings, new ways to be in the world. Merideth granted me such a moment and, with it, the opportunity to relive and repair the trauma of her birth.

Merideth and Michael were deeply saddened when Merideth had miscarried last spring, but they were hopeful that another try would bring them their fourth child. And it did. Before our Thanksgiving family reunion, Merideth had announced joyfully that she was pregnant and that the baby would be born around her birthday in March. This time her pregnancy had proceeded smoothly, and by Thanksgiving, we all knew she was carrying a boy.

Merideth and Janet, 2004.
Photograph by Peter Reynolds. Courtesy of the author.

At about the same time, John and I were both granted sabbaticals for our winter/spring semester, a concurrence we had dared not hope for. Then, even more remarkably, a kind and generous woman, Christine, offered us her home on Martha's Vineyard for sixth months where we could write uninterrupted. We packed up boxes, loaded the car, coaxed our dog into the back seat, and drove north, arriving on the Vineyard on a dark, windy night in December.

Freed from our teaching responsibilities and only a day's drive from Merideth's home, I was grateful when Merideth asked me to come for the birth of her baby. Mid-March arrived, and full of anticipation, John and I drove to Merideth's coastal town for an amazing confabulation of events. Just as unmanageable circumstances had conspired on the night of Merideth's birth to leave me alone and desperate, now, thirty-nine years later almost to the day, random events had again coalesced. Once again a baby was to be born, but this time my stars were arranged propitiously in the universe.

Merideth's doctor knew the baby's birth would be quick, and had urged Merideth to allow her to induce her labor. Merideth had hesitated at first, but I had urged her to consider that approach. I didn't want her to have to endure a panicky drive to the hospital if her labor pains intensified too quickly. The designated morning arrived and Merideth and Michael headed for the hospital, while I took over packing school lunches, pouring orange juice, and hustling Drew and Michaela out to the school bus. While Emma and I colored Easter eggs, my mind was on Merideth. I knew she had to be in pain, surely, but I also knew she was as safe as could be with her husband and her doctor at the hospital. Michael called to assure me all was well. So different from Merideth's own birth; everything was going as planned. The day passed; the children arrived home from school, bubbling with excitement. Was their baby brother here yet?

The phone rang. It was Merideth, ebullient and talking fast. "He's here! Dale Mason is here!" An easy labor, a flawless delivery, a perfect baby. She wanted us to come to the hospital—now!

When we walk into the hospital room, Dale Mason (who is called "Mase" after his great-grandmother, my mother) is one hour old. Merideth, radiant, is nursing him peacefully. The children are fascinated and adoring, craning their necks to peek at Mase, begging to hold him. But Merideth shushes them and instead, beckons to me. Slowly she rewraps Mase in his tiny, soft blanket and then, she hands him to me. I reach and take this baby from my daughter, the daughter I had reached out for so desperately years and years ago.

Silently, I walk with him to the window and am immediately swept back to that frigid, bare morning in Akron with Sorrow wailing just out of my arms' reach. This time I have been given the baby to hold. I bend and kiss his forehead. Finally my arms can cradle the baby. Tears come quickly and my chest tightens in the old familiar way. I glance outside into the thickening twilight. Tiny snowflakes are beginning to fall, and I feel myself falling, falling back into that black pool of sorrow. My Sorrow.

But this baby, this baby with Sorrow's funny-shaped head, with her damp crown of dark hair, with her red skin and old-man hands, this baby stops my fall. Mase looks up into my eyes, quizzically with a deep, penetrating gaze. "Why so sad, grandmother? I am here. You have me tight against you. You do not have to let go. No one will take me until you are ready."

I turn back to the warm room to find it aglow with rosy, enraptured faces. Six loving people, my family, whole and restored, encircle Mase and me. My chest loosens, I breathe again, my tears subside. When I am ready, I hand my grandson back to his mother, my daughter, knowing she will lovingly hand him back to me whenever I ask, whenever I need.

I walk back to the window. The snowflakes are gentle, tiny. This will not be the massive blizzard of thirty-nine years ago. Nor is there an evil nurse to slap away my tears. There is a nurse, but she's much more like Mary Poppins than Nurse Ratched. Gently, she gives Mase his first bath, instructing Michaela, Drew, and Emma on how to help her. Her calm, angelic patience penetrates and comforts us all. Rather than cold and bleakly gray, the room is ablaze with light and warmth. When the baby cries, we all murmur to him softly and his whimpers subside as he moves from one set of arms to the next.

Later, I lie awake long into the night, marveling at the exquisite design my life has become. It is as if I was forced to live through the flawed and misbegotten side of an ill-tossed coin, and then it was flipped, and I was given the opportunity to live the other gleaming side—the side so harshly denied me long ago. The pain of the journey that began on that frigid Ohio night in March fades: Sorrow's birth and loss have been overlaid with joy. Mase's birth brings me close to my conclusion. My narrative ends as the circle comes round.

Martha's Vineyard, April 2004

I am repeatedly moved and healed by the splendor of the natural world: I linger through a field of lupine, marvel at snowflakes falling on bare quiet woods, cleanse my soul as I submerge my body in glacial lakes and frigid mountain streams, yet I am not an overtly spiritual person. I do not belong to an organized religion. I do not seek an enlightened consciousness; I rarely pray. I am skeptical of fundamentalism. I do not believe that there is a god who hears my particular prayers and decides whether to intervene or not. But I do believe in the sacredness of people and am deeply aware of intricate and holy mysteries, patterns in which I have played a small part. How else to explain the extraordinary chain of events of this year?

Now as I write, Mase is one month old and April is passing all too quickly for us on the Vineyard. My book can conclude with an ending so full of poetic justice that it seems implausible: the lost daughter who loves me places her baby in my arms.

I pause to gaze through Christine's huge picture window overlooking Crystal Lake, where the two elegant mute swans have recently finished constructing their nest and a group of manic red-breasted mergansers perform their zany mating dance, preening, bowing, and scooting about. I try to shake off the uneasiness that has followed on the heels of last night's dream.

Dream Three:

I am alone in a disheveled beach house with my grandchildren. Outside, a ferocious hurricane is furiously blowing the palm trees that border the yard. They lean far to the left, and the waves, usually hundreds of feet away, have almost reached the line of trees. The house has been built on stilts for weather just like this, but I know we should have evacuated hours ago. I awaken the children, and they follow me cautiously down the stairs to the carport, but my car has vanished. We step nervously into the gray seawater that is quickly rising. We all hold hands and begin to make our way up to a small hill. I can see Merideth in the distance. I wave to reassure her that we are fine, we'll be fine. She's shouting to me through the roar of the wind: "Where's Emma? Where's Emma?" And I realize I have left Emma behind. I look back at the beach house. She's there, still asleep in her crib. Or has she awakened? Is she calling, crying, "Mama? Grandma?" The seawater has taken over the carport, surrounded the house, and is moving quickly up the stairs. I push myself back toward the house, but the water swirls around my thighs. I can't move forward. I dive and try swimming but the current is too strong, I'm making no progress. I surface, gulping for air. I'm alone in the black water. In the distance I can just make out the house, deluged now by high, angry gray waves.

I had dragged myself out of my dream, my nightgown clammy, my damp hair clinging to my neck and walked from room to room through the cold house. Our puzzled dog followed me patiently as I wandered, his sleepy steadfastness helping to calm my beating heart, loosen my aching chest.

Now, as I watch the morning sunlight ebb across the lake as rain-laden clouds move in over the sound, I ask myself, "How is this possible?"

"Must I still endure this guilt?"

"Must I again and again betray, forsake, and abandon the baby?"

I sit back, sigh, and let the dancing Mergansers, the shimmering pond, the gliding swans do their work. I know I will relax, but I also know that it will be difficult to find sleep tonight and that it will take days to shake the dark, dismaying mood such dreams cast over me. Now I realize that my "lost baby dreams" will continue to haunt me. Despite all I have been given to erase her specter, that empty, forlorn girl, who was forced to leave her baby behind, lives on in me. Endlessly she paces the dim, gray room.

When she intrudes, as she inevitably will, I will try to calm her by replaying the day of Mase's birth; I will take pleasure in my daughter returned, in my family restored; I will take heart in the surety that I will not fail my children, my grandchildren, my parents, my husband. The baby will not be left behind in the darkening meadow, in the closed up room, in the imperiled beach house, in the frigid delivery room.

Heraclitus tells us we cannot step in the same river twice, yet I have tried and tried to do so—with the births of Todd, of Helen, of Kezia, and now again of Mase—re-creating the river, letting it flow through me, desperate for its healing waters. Surely a new baby to hold should take away the harm done so long ago. I have attempted this many times now, taken this step into the deep water, even as I know we cannot repeat the past. There is the birth and the new baby brings us joy, but both are forever new, never a copy. The circle of my journey closes, but not completely. It will fall open again and Sorrow will rush in.

And so, the dream returns, the memory endures. A baby cries and I cry for her. We live on together even as we are forever denied each other. With empty arms, I will carry her on through the years ahead, never forsaking her, never letting go of Sorrow.